Climbs of the Cordillera Blanca of Peru

David Sharman

Published by Whizzo Climbs
PO Box 412, Aberdeen, AB9 6JA,
SCOTLAND

ISBN 0 952358 0 4

Distributed in South America by:
Nuevas Imagenes SA
Antunez de Mayolo 879
Lima 33, PERU

Distributed in North America by:
Alpenbooks
3616 South Road, C-1
Mukilteo, WA 98275, USA

Distributed in Great Britain by:
Cordee
3A DeMontfort Street
Leicester, LE1 7HD, GREAT BRITAIN

Bill Beynon
570 Gower Road
Upper Killay
Swansea
SA2 7DR
Tel/Fax: 01792 296769

DISCLAIMER

This guide is compiled from information from a variety of sources. The inclusion of any route does not imply that it remains in the condition described. Mountains can change unpredictably: rock can deteriorate and snow and ice features alter considerably and rapidly. All mountaineers must rely on their own ability and experience to gauge the difficulty and seriousness of any climb. Mountaineering is an inherently dangerous activity.

The author of this guidebook accepts no liability whatsoever for any injury or damage caused to mountaineers, third parties, or property arising from the use of it. Whilst the content of this guide is believed to be accurate, no responsibility is accepted for any error, omission, or mis-statement. Users must rely on their own judgement and are recommended to insure against injury to person and property and third party risk.

Contents

Illustrations

Introduction

In Peru is a mountain range known as the Cordillera Blanca. The range offers the best equatorial climbing in the world on over two hundred 5000m and 6000m summits, as if the European Alps had been raised up 1500m and cable cars and overcrowding banished overnight. It is a place where reliable weather and half a century of intensive exploration combine to create a wealth of fine super-alpine mountaineering set deep in the heart of exotic Peru.

The highest villages are only a few hours drive from the regional town of Huaraz. Beyond, beautiful valleys penetrate far into the heart of the long narrow range. After about a day of walking, never more than two, you arrive at one of a myriad of base camp sites, above which soar the magnificent icy summits themselves. The whole area is inside a national park, thus the environment and local culture remain largely unscathed by the ravages of modern development. This all combines to create an unrivalled sense of adventure for such an accessible region.

There is no need to organise a massive expedition to visit this wonderland, indeed such an approach is inappropriate. Small, informal groups are better, and simple pairs perfectly suitable. This guidebook is written to help you extract the maximum enjoyment from this approach.

How To Use This Guide

In this guide the Cordillera Blanca is divided into massifs which are discussed from North to South. Peaks in each massif are treated in arbitary ridgeline chains; the most convenient first and then subsidiary groupings.

Routes on peaks usually are described in a clockwise direction from an appropriate natural feature in the North-West quadrant. Details are recorded of the first ascentionists of the principal feature of the route as described. This may not be identical to the original line as easier or safer alternatives have evolved, or the mountain altered in character. The routes are described in the fullest reasonable detail available and important variants are noted. On certain peaks routes are not normally completed to the true summit due to extremely hazardous ridges, however they too have been included.

Grades, times, and distances are given, where known, for the elusive average reasonably fit and competent mountaineer who makes no route finding errors. At all times the mountaineer must exercise judgement in making a personal assessment of these factors under the prevailing conditions and circumstances. Additional information of relevance to a route - such as approach details from base camp areas - is often contained within descriptions of adjacent routes. Directions are consistently given in the sense of movement of the climber in ascent and often cardinal directions are used for clarification. UIAA and French adjectival grades are used as these are felt to be the most appropriate systems.

A cursory description of a route on an outlying or low peak is normally indicative of many variations being possible at a similar standard.

Fees

To date there are no peak fees charged in Peru. An attempt by the Federation of Peruvian Climbing Clubs to have a peak fee imposed was rejected in 1994 (the Federation lacked the authority to do so). A nominal charge is made for visiting the park - see below. The Parque Nacional Huascaran is contemplating modest fees for the five or six most crowded peaks, as much to spread climbers through the range as to collect funds for the park.

General Information

Very little general information on how to travel to and in Peru is included as plenty of other books provide this information in a far more comprehensive manner than this climbing guide can hope to. Two guidebooks are especially recommended; *The South American Handbook* and *South America On A Shoestring*, details in the back of this book.

Most mountaineers will choose to fly first to Lima. In Lima two useful hostels which are friendly, cheap, clean, and near the centre of the old city and bus stations are; *Hostal San Sebastian, Jironde Ica 712, tel. 232740* and *Resedencial Roma, Jironde Ica 326, tel. 277576*. Whilst there is an internal flight from Lima to Huaraz (actually to near Carhuaz) baggage weights are very limited on this. A far cheaper alternative is to take a coach to Huaraz. There are half a dozen coach services of which the following seem to be reliable and security conscious, and which are gathered in the same area of Lima; *Rodriguez Transportes, Jironde Roosevelt 354, tel. 280506, Expreso Ancash, Jironde Carlos Zavala 177, Empresa 14, Jironde Leticia 604, tel. 286621*. You must be alert for organised gangs of thieves and pickpockets in all areas of Lima, but especially around the bus stations.

Once in Huaraz you can choose from a variety of hostels and private houses to suit your budget and taste. Some are marked on the map: *Hostal Andino (Chalet Suisse)* is the best and most expensive, *Hostal Copa, Edwards Inn, Alojamiento Galaxia, Hotel Barcelona, Pension Maguina* are all reasonable compromises frequented by climbers. A bunkhouse is above the Casa de Guias but it is no cheaper than the hostels where cheaper dormitory rooms are available. Hot water is always a hit or miss affair in Peru so the public showers on Avenida Raymondi / Av. Gamarra are useful, or a trip to the thermal baths at Monterrey (10 minutes by bus) where there is also a small crag There are couple of dozen good restaurants around the centre of town - just follow your nose. A similar approach to wine, women, and song generally serves, otherwise try the *Tasco Bar* (a legendary hangout of bullshitting climbers) or go dancing in the *Tambo*.

Plenty of small stores and market stalls sell a range of tinned food, mashed potato, pasta, rice, and soups. The chocolate tastes awful. If you are stuck for foodstuffs try the shop on the corner of Raymondi and Luzuriaga. Bus services along the valley road to all the small towns and villages leave frequently from the many bus offices on Av. Fitzcarrald. If you are going all the way to Yungay and Caraz try to get one of the express services.

A short description of the common approach walks (treks) is included. In conjunction with the maps and a sense of adventure this should be enough for most mountaineers.Additionally most mountaineers will choose to hire arrieros (donkey drivers) and so will have a local guide. It is possible to find out more about most of the approach walks by asking in Huaraz or the villages.

Maps are included with this guide. If you want to obtain others then go to the Ingemmet / Electroperu offices in Huaraz for USGS-style maps. These are topographically accurate but names, trails, and heights do not correspond to the ones quoted in this guide.

Environment

The climbing community is becoming more aware of its capacity to wreck the fragile high mountain environment for future generations and so these notes are intended to help you minimise your impact on the area.

Past ascents in the Cordillera Blanca have been both expedition style, with fixed ropes linking a string of camps, or in the more lightweight alpine style. Occasionally a rapid solo ascent of a route has been incongruously followed by twenty sieging the same line in blissful ignorance.

Nowadays it is generally thought that climbing in the Cordillera Blanca does not necessitate fixed rope tactics, although the move away from this has resulted in some of the ridges being avoided in order to maintain an adequate safety margin. Ultimately safety must be the deciding factor when choosing whether to siege a line, but if you are tempted to siege why not consider climbing an easier line more elegantly. Further considerations are that climbing alpine style also allows each mountaineer more of the 'fun' of leading, and allows for smaller groups which are inherently more flexible.

It is accepted practice to leave some climbs equipped for abseil with ice stakes or pitons, but not to leave fixed ropes strewn all over the mountain. All litter should be carried off the mountain and then either burnt in base camp or carried back to Huaraz. The practice of burying cans and bottles is unacceptable - the environment cannot absorb it and if you can carry it up then you can carry it down as well. Failure to do this results in some base camps becoming rubbish dumps which require good-natured people to clean up for you.

Groups of more than four in total should dig a toilet pit. Wild shitting can quickly turn base camps into unpleasant and unhygienic minefields. When going to the toilet on moraines and glaciers try not to foul water supplies. Remember that your freeze dried shit will crumble to a powder and blow around for years so use a crevasse if possible to prevent this dust contaminating fresh snow. Alternatively put your shit in a plastic bag and carry it down the mountain for disposal below the snow line.

A large expedition can be beyond the capacity of some base camps to absorb. especially if you remember that other smaller groups might be visiting the same area at the same time. The optimum size for a group seems to be between four and six mountaineers. This allows some of the fixed costs to be shared, gives a choice of climbing partners, and allows for a decent card game on rest days.

Parque Nacional Huascaran

The highland areas surrounding the Cordillera Blanca lie within the confines of a national park, the Parque Nacional Huascaran, which has been declared as a zone where no further development is permitted (in theory). At some park entrances tolls are collected from tourists and the money used to support local conservation programmes. The tolls are about $1 a day and are usually collected only at theLlanganuco and Pachacoto entrances, although more control posts are planned for the near future. (The park is developing a new tourism management plan which may alter some regulations and fees.) It easy to be cynical about the effectiveness of the park system and the use to which this money will be put, but there are many deeply committed people working hard with slender resources who do value all aid that is offered.

Geology

The Cordillera Blanca is one of the youngest mountain ranges of the world. It was created when an ancient plain was thrust upwards between five and eight million years ago to form the continental divide. This had the effect of deepening the two pre-existing adjacent river systems; that of the Santa which empties to the Pacific, and the Maranon which eventually flows to the Amazon and the Atlantic. The uplifting occurred in two distinct stages which relate to the forming of the quebradas and the more incised gorges. Later glaciation scoured the granite sides of the quebradas which were exposed in retreat to leave fine rock walls.

The granite batholiths which underly the central and northern parts of the range are flanked by highly folded and faulted sedimentary formations; the Jurassics of the Maranon valley and the Cretaceous of the Santa valley. Along the interface between the granite and sedimentary formations are various metamorphic rocks and mineral deposits. Rather than being well defined this zone can extend right across the range and old mine workings are found high in many valleys. The more common were for silver and lead, some of which are still in operation, and for coal which outcrops frequently. So although the area is conceptually a simple structure, in practice rocks other than . granite will be encountered almost anywhere and individual massifs contain a more detailed description of what to expect in each location.

Glaciation

The Cordillera Blanca is strewn with hundreds of short valley glaciers, and a few ice caps, which are all that remain of the greater Pleistocene glaciers which once advanced as much as 15km further, down as far as ca.1400m. The retreat has occurred in stages, each temporary halt piling up successive moraines which can be easily observed as you walk through the valleys.

This retreat continues and many lesser peaks are known to have lost their snow cover since colonial times. The glaciers are currently receding at an average annual rate of 2.1m of altitude, which is quite fast in glacial terms. The lakes in the Cordillera Blanca were formed quite recently as the result of this rapid recession. In only the last fifty years many new lakes have been formed and small lakes greatly enlarged, a process which has had dramatic consequences.

The water in these lakes is held in behind weak moraine dams of dirt, gravel, and boulders. As the water seeps through this porous mass so it steadily erodes the structure of the moraine. Glaciers hang above, constantly calving seracs which plunge downwards into the water, generating enormous forces which thrust against the dams. Eventually the weakened moraines collapse, sending great walls of water and mud hurtling into the valleys below. The trigger for these alluvions is often an earthquake, because even a relatively small tremor can catastrophically disturb the delicate balance of the moraine dams.

Earthquakes and Alluvions

The temple ruins at Chavin have been repeatedly covered by alluvions such as these, caused by avalanches falling from Huantsan into a lake. It is possible this is a cause of the culture's decline: perhaps they simply decided the gods were against them and gave up.

A similar alluvion ripped through Huaraz in 1941 when Laguna Palcacocha surged down the Cojup valley, emptying a lower lake as it went. Huaraz lay directly in its path and 5000 people were killed as huge boulders were left stranded where houses had once stood. Other alluvions devastated the Quebrada de los Cedros in 1950 (from Laguna Jancarurish) and the Quebrada Carhuascancha in 1965 (from Laguna Tumarina). The 1941 disaster led to the formation of an Office Of Lake Control which has undertaken the task of locating and monitoring lakes throughout the range. Dangerous lakes have then been stabilised by complete or partial drainage, and the construction of spillways through the moraine dams. This organisation has since evolved into the modern day Office of Glaciology and Water Resources of Electroperu, the company responsible for hydroelectric power generation.

Not all alluvions can be protected against. In 1962 huge seracs were pushed off the side of Huascaran Norte by the movement of the summit ice cap. This huge mass spilled down to completely destroy the town of Ranrahirca and several smaller settlements, killing 4000 people in the process. The only solution was to rebuild the town in a safer site and fortunately this was out of the path of the 1970 alluvion which again fell from Huascaran Norte.

The most recent disaster was caused by a massive earthquake in 1970 which was centered near Chimbote on the coast, and which measured 7.8 on the Richter scale. The tremors practically wiped out the Callejon de Huaylas and caused extensive damage to the Callejon de Conchucos. It is thought that about 80,000 people were killed and over one million left homeless. Ninety percent of Huaraz was destroyed and at least half of its population of 30,000 killed.

The earthquake shook enormous sheets of granite from the side of Huascaran Norte. Great slabs of rock, 10-15 million cubic metres in all, fell off the West face. Combining with three million cubic metres of ice and ploughing up earth as it went, this great muddy mass travelled at 300 km per hour to the Rio Santa. It blocked the river and flowed downstream to the hydroelectric plant in the Canon del Pato, a total distance of 65km.

A small portion of this torrent jumped a 200m-high ridge and buried the beautiful town of Yungay and all the 18,000 inhabitants. The only survivors were 240 people who ran up a knoll to the cemetery, and a crowd of children who were watching a circus outside the town. All that remains today as evidence of the old Yungay is the cemetery, and four palm trees, amongst barren fields.

International aid poured into the area as the extent of the devastation became apparent. The aid was distributed from Huaraz and so many mountain-dwellers moved down to claim their share. People from other parts of Peru also moved to Huaraz to take advantage of the opportunities left in the disaster's wake. Huaraz has since grown to a city of over 100,000, perhaps not as picturesque but certainly better prepared for the next quake. Yungay is struggling bravely to establish a new identity in a new location, and all over the region the task of reconstruction has brought with it a parallel modernisation.

Climbing Conditions

Rock is not the mainstay of climbing in the Cordillera Blanca and where encountered presents only the normal problems. High outcrops of sedimentary and metamorphic rocks are very frost shattered and loose although a concrete-like mixture of ice and shards does occur. The granite is generally more solid but the best of it must be the quebrada walls which are rarely climbed and barely exploited.

In contrast the peculiar Andean snow conditions are a major feature of the Cordillera Blanca, with beautifully delicate feathery flutings and serried ranks of neve penitentes.

The neve penitentes are spikes of snow which incline towards the midday sun in orderly rows supposedly reminiscent of monks at prayer. They range in size from a few centimetres to a metre or more, and form in hot windless conditions which allow very high temperatures to exist at the snow surface. They grow during the dry season, often emerging from beneath the wet season's snow cover, and can turn to ice penitentes if they become waterlogged.

North-facing slopes receive plenty of sunlight and hence rapidly form good neve and ice. In consequence crusts can quickly consolidate between successive snowfalls in the rainy season to create the possibility of large slab avalanches at the beginning of the dry (climbing) season. Digging a snow pit is recommended to discover whether this is likely to be a problem on your route. As the climbing season progresses the neve turns to wonderful chewy ice, and at a later stage penitentes can become large enough to be bothersome on ca.50° slopes, needing smashing down to clear a route. I think that these penitentes subsequently act as anchors for rainy season snowfall which would explain the relative rarity of avalanches. The afternoon sun will normally turn North slopes from these wonderful conditions to deep slush so an early start is worthwhile. Higher up you will begin to find honeycomb ice structures (cheese ice). Whilst sometimes capable of supporting your weight they won't accept it via an ice axe pick: you will need to climb using snow stakes to spread the load.

South-facing slopes normally remain in the shade and so rarely consolidate to any great extent. Instead runnels or flutings form, of seemingly bottomless fluffy snow, separated by fragile-looking fins which are actually quite substantial and often support large mushroom formations. The runnels begin to form at about 40° and somehow continue to exist until near vertical. When the runnels become steep it is often easier to put away your ice tools and dagger using long snow stakes. The snow stake is the most convenient belay but another possibility is to look into the wind-scooped hollow beneath a mushroom where solid ice may be exposed. This often makes an excellent bivouac site as well, and it is usefully out of the main bed of the runnel which channels debris in a storm. Generally one side of the runnel will recieve more sun and so provide firmer climbing on ice, this is normally the West-facing side.

East and West slopes exhibit intermediate characteristics. As a rough guide East-facing slopes are more akin to South facing slopes, this is possibly because the warming effect of the sun is less in the morning. The demarcation line is very distinct on ridges, where pillars of cheese ice to the North support huge mushrooms which drop off into bottomless powder a metre to the South. The cornices normally hang out to the West or South but will occasionally reverse to create what most people consider unjustifiable climbing. If this is the case then try traversing the face well below, or simply content yourself with gaining the ridge (as many do), or wait until the next major earthquake shakes the cornices off.

Because of the intense dry season sun the ice can burn off on the steeper snow and ice routes. This is especially true of some crux icicle pitches which may simply disappear. The best conditions for the harder routes seem to occur from late May to mid July; after the ice has formed bu before it has melted away. Conversely the best rock climbing conditions are likely to be after mid July. Thus the optimum time for the difficult British mixed route on the West face of Cayesh would probably be mid June, whilst the adjacent technical rock climbs of the German, American, and Czech routes are undoubtedly more popular in early August. Fortunately the majority of routes are not so difficult as to require perfect conditions and attempts are feasible throughout the whole of the dry season.

Climate & Weather

The climate and weather of the Cordillera Blanca are determined by the relationship between the moist air coming from the Amazon basin to the East and the drier desert air to the West. Except when disrupted by events such as the El Nino ocean current reversal the year divides into a dry season and a wetter season. The main climbing and walking season is the dry season, which runs from early May until the beginning of September. During this period the weather cycle is very stable with several days of good weather followed by one or two of bad. In October, November, and April this pattern is reversed although occasional periods of settled good weather do occur.

A typical dry season day begins with a cloudless dawn at 6:00 a.m. and soon becomes warm. On a windless day the noon temperature will frequently be over 20° C at 4000m in the valleys, and I have often watched water dribbling over ice at near 6000m despite the 0° C shade isotherm being at about 4800m. The temperature will plummet during the brief twilight, before the sun sets at 6:30 p.m. and there will normally be an overnight frost above about 4500m.

Bad weather invariably approaches from the East. Strong easterly high altitude winds rake summits and lentil-shaped caps of pressure cloud develop. Moisture laden clouds move up the eastern valleys and begin to pour through the passes after dawn, retreating again at night. They shed their load of moisture as a light afternoon snowfall or drizzle. This is not normally a major obstacle to climbing but route finding in these circumstances can be awkward.

If the clouds do not dissipate overnight then you may be in for one or two days of heavier rain and snow, with consequential avalanche danger, before the clouds roll back over the passes and fine weather resumes. The exception to this general system is when North-South winds occur. These cause the Amazonian and desert air masses to rub together and generate spectacularly intense electrical storms. I have never seen bad weather develop from the West.

This pattern stabilises in May and only begins to break down in late August when the cloudy days become more frequent and strong winds more of a problem. Despite this climbing is possible well into September in many years.

Equipment

Daytime temperatures are quite warm, sometimes excessively so when in direct sunlight, and nightime temperatures warmer than in alpine winters. Thus slightly amplified summer alpine equipment will be found to suffice. A light-coloured long-sleeved bottom layer, floppy sun hat, and a total block sun cream will be useful to guard against sunburn on sweltering glaciers. Those intending to do a lot of climbing in the deep cold snow of south faces should take insulated over-gaiters. A good quality sleeping bag is essential and it is a matter of personal choice whether a lightweight high-mountain tent or a bivouac bag is preferred - however the former can often double as a two-man bivouac bag. When bad weather does occur wind is likely to be the biggest problem so good windproofs are important.

In the past mountaineers have preferred to use longer axes because of the deep snow, but nowadays snow stakes can fulfill this function equally well and short 'technical' tools are more in vogue. A broad icecream-scoop adze often provides better purchase than the pick. Any type of decent crampon and plastic boot combination should be sufficient. Carry a range of snow stakes from 50-100cm, dead men, and broad tubular ice screws for belaying. The longer stakes are most easily used if they can be slung like a rifle when actually climbing. Friends and small pitons are more useful rock kit than wires and nuts. Some people save weight by the potentially dangerous practice of climbing on one 50m half-rope (9mm) and carrying 50m of 7mm static cord to use as a pull-through on abseils. Telescopic ski poles are invaluable. Apart from being a blessing when walking on moraines, they also make good tent stakes in deep snow and provide an effective means of deterring vicious dogs, or of encouraging burros.

Cooking at base camp for large parties is best done with local paraffin/kerosene Primus stoves. Higher up it is possible to run petrol stoves on benzina blanca to provide a cheap, if temperamental, heat source. Plastic jerry cans are readily available in Huaraz but need careful inspection for holes and a decent seal at the cap. The Camping-Gaz type of disposable butane cartridges can be purchased in Huaraz in limited quantities and at very expensive prices. The Epigas type of self sealing propane/butane cartridges currently cannot be bought in Peru. It is preferable to import these in your baggage as a hazardous cargo requiring special packing for the flight to Peru; you will need to consult the airline for details of their requirements.

Peruvian batteries are of dubious quality and the 4.5v flat cells used in most head torches are extremely rare. All batteries need to be brought into Peru as a matter of course, the same is true for most freeze-dried mountain food. However it is possible to buy enough varieties of soups, pasta, potato powder, and tinned fish to serve as the basis for a cheaper but monotonous bivouac diet.

All equipment to be brought into Peru must be carried as personal baggage even if this means paying a lot for any excess weight. It is foolish in the extreme to attempt to import in any other fashion as customs officials have much to gain by obstructing the clearance of cargo. By writing to airlines in advance you can often negotiate a special deal for an extra 20kg allowance, but in fact the normal allowance is adequate if you plan carefully.

Everything necessary for base camps can be bought in Huaraz: cookers, fuel, pans, bowls, lanterns, plastic sheeting, etc., and a wide variety of foodstuffs and alcohol in shops and the market. Fresh beef can be kept for up to seven days at base camp and eggs and vegetables for up to twelve days, dependent on the storage conditions. Live chickens can be carried for pets, until the beef runs out, but should not be relied upon to produce eggs. Trout can be fished for or bought from the high mountain families along with guinea pigs, potatoes, and other tubers. If all else fails you can even use tinned foods.

Local Employees

There are a number of different types of local employees who can assist your trip; arrieros, guardians, cooks, porters and guides. All can be encountered in and around Huaraz, or to a lesser extent other towns. The wages are set by the porters and guides' associations but are normally negotiable and should be regarded as being guidelines only. If you decide to make all your arrangements through a trekking agency then expect to pay a considerable premium. Often locals will exagerate times and difficulties to try and make more money from you. Remember that you are paying and so have every right to make most decisions.

Arrieros

The donkey (burro) is the ubiqitous pack animal of the Cordillera Blanca. In the villages which are the departure points for base camps and trails are a number of men who are experienced at managing burros for the special needs of the foreigner: these men are arrieros. If you cannot find an adult who needs work then practically any campesino child above the age of ten is perfectly competent.

Once you have located an arriero you have to haggle over his wages, the cost of the animals and how many will be needed, and whether the arriero will need a helper. An arriero should earn about $8-10 per day and a donkey should cost $3 - 4 per day. A donkey can carry 30-40kg and a horse can carry 60-80kg. An arriero can manage five animals. You will have to share your food and shelter with the arriero but he should provide his own blankets or sleeping bag.

Having settled all this the arriero will have to locate some animals because he is unlikely to own enough himself. This may take some time and if you need more than about five be prepared to wait half a day. Alternatively send a message to the arriero a day in advance with the collectivo driver, or, in the case of villages near Pomabamba (on the East of the range), pay one of the Huaraz local radio stations to broadcast a message during the daily message programme.

Guardians and Cooks

Theft can be a problem around base camps so groups should hire a guardian for $10 per day. The guardian will provide his own equipment and will only require a tent space. He will expect to perform simple tasks such as water carrying, wood collecting, or washing-up. He can be sent ahead to find an arriero for either the outward or return journey, and will often help with cooking.

If you want a proper cook then be prepared to pay extra, $10-20 per day, and in return receive vastly better meals. A cook normally provides his own utensils and may have one or two Primus stoves. He can be sent to buy provisions in the market before leaving for the mountain and in short can be an excellent investment for a group.

If you are only one or two climbers but still wish to operate from a base camp then there are only two cheap solutions (aside from good luck). One is to hide your surplus equipment amongst moraine boulders when going up to a route. As you do this you must be paranoid about who might be observing you. An alternative is to pay a tip to the guardian of an adjacent group's base camp.

Porters

The porters' assocation recognises three classes of porters. Class III porters are the arrieros, cooks, and guardians. Class II porters only carry loads on paths and so are of limited value to mountaineers. Class I porters have a little experience in ice techniques and can operate on glaciers. They carry 25kg loads and cost $15-30 per day for which price they should provide all their own equipment. You are responsible for the safety of your porters and should not leave them to their own devices in potentially dangerous situations. Consider whether you have adequate insurance to cover any porters you employ.

Guides

As the only guides' association yet recognized by the Ministry of Tourism, the Peruvian Mountain Guides Association (AGMP) can look for work in Peru. The AGMP has its headquarters in an attractive chalet-style building near the Plaza de Armas in Huaraz. The AGMP has been developed since 1978 as part of a Swiss aid programme and has recently become fully affiliated to the International Union of Mountain Guides' Associations (UIAGM). A number of competent climbers with guiding experience have not joined the association, and therefore cannot work as guides legally.

As in other mountain areas, there are variations in skill and experience among the guides, so it is worth enquiring of your guide's previous experience. AGMP guides carry a blue logbook (Libreta de Diploma de Guia) which has space for you to write a recommendation; aspirantes (apprentices) carry a black logbook. Try to find a guide who shows respect for the mountains rather than an overconfident attitude. Prices range from $40 to $60 a day according to the difficulty of the route. When negotiating be sure to establish exactly how much is included (food, transport, arrieros etc.). Unfortunately few of the guides can speak a foreign language. Those who do generally speak either English or German. The graded list has been annotated with a plus symbol (+) to denote some of the routes which are popular with guides and clients. (Note: The new park tourism plan may change some of the regulations relating to guides.)

Mountain Rescue

Mountain rescue in Peru is a do-it-yourself affair. For years plans to establish a rescue team have been thwarted by a lack of funds and jurisdictional disputes. In any case by the time a rescue party can be sought from Huaraz most serious emergencies are usually resolved. Thus all climbers in the immediate vicinity must aid as far as is possible.

The biggest problem is evacuating the injured to base camp level, onwards evacuation is then relatively easy. Generally the only solution is to lower the casualty to the glacier and then to sledge and stretcher them down. This is exhausting and will normally require at least six people, preferably more. All guides must take a rescue course and so can provide additional semi-skilled labour for this task. After base camp use local transport (horses and pick-up truck) to one of the better hospitals; Yungay, Caraz, Huaraz, and Lima. It saves money to pay each part of the rescue separately (including personnel) rather than agreeing to a lump sum for the entire job.

Peru does possess helicopters capable of flying above base camp level but the pilots are understandably unwilling to land above ca.4500m. The helicopter must be requested from the air force, via your embassy, and a deposit of at least $10,000 will be needed in advance. The embassy will also ask for a guarantee of eventual payment in full from an insurance company.

In the unfortunate event of a death transport the body (when possible) direct to the morgue in one of the main hospitals. Later seek the permission of the judge and police (PNP) for having done this (if you mount a specific rescue mission to collect a body later on you should seek the judges permission beforehand as, technically, the judge must be present when you recover the body). All the morgues are unrefrigerated so the autopsy must be arranged quickly. You will need the presence of the judge and the PNP at this, as well as two doctors. Afterwards collect a copy of the autopsy report from the judge, the death certificate from the hospital director, and a copy of the statement (denuncia) that you will have to make to the PNP. These papers will be needed to transport, bury, or cremate the body. As soon as possible inform your embassy and the next of kin and try to comply with their wishes - this will also be a concern of the Peruvian authorities. If someone dies and the body cannot be shown to a policeman then you should ask the PNP for a certificate of disappearance as this will help you handle the legalities when you return home. It is important to follow these legal procedures carefully to avoid misunderstandings and delays at a difficult time.

Medical Notes

This guide cannot attempt to provide comprehensive medical advice and so you should be familiar with the contents of one of the medical handbooks listed in the bibliography. Just reading the advice in one of these handbooks is not enough - you must be able to practice it in an emergency.

At least three months before leaving for Peru find out from your local family doctor what vaccinations you will need and arrange to take them. Consult with your doctor about the contents of your first aid kit, bearing in mind that your most likely ailment will be travellers diarrhoea. Before packing lots of expensive medical equipment and powerful drugs consider whether you know enough to use them successfully, and whether you would actually take them on a climb - the things you leave at base camp probably won't do you much good.

If you do pack any strong drugs then, as a minimum, make sure you seal them well and carry a letter from your doctor detailing what they are and why you have them. The only way to make absolutely sure that the police will not cause you any problems is to submit a detailed list to your local Peruvian embassy at least one month before departure. A copy will be stamped and endorsed and returned to you as being proof that you are indeed carrying medical equipment. In my expereience this often requires a trip to the embassy in person. You will undoubtedly be asked to provide medicine at some point, normally by arrieros or whilst passing through villages. Think carefully before obliging as you probably cannot do any long-term good and certainly cannot control how the medicine will actually be used. Perhaps the best approach is to keep a large stock of vile tasting vitamin tablets as at least you can't do much harm by handing these out.

Finally, before returning home, donate any spare medical supplies to one of the local hospitals. Again, whilst you cannot control how they will be distributed, many of them will be put to good use by genuinely caring staff.

Map of Huaraz

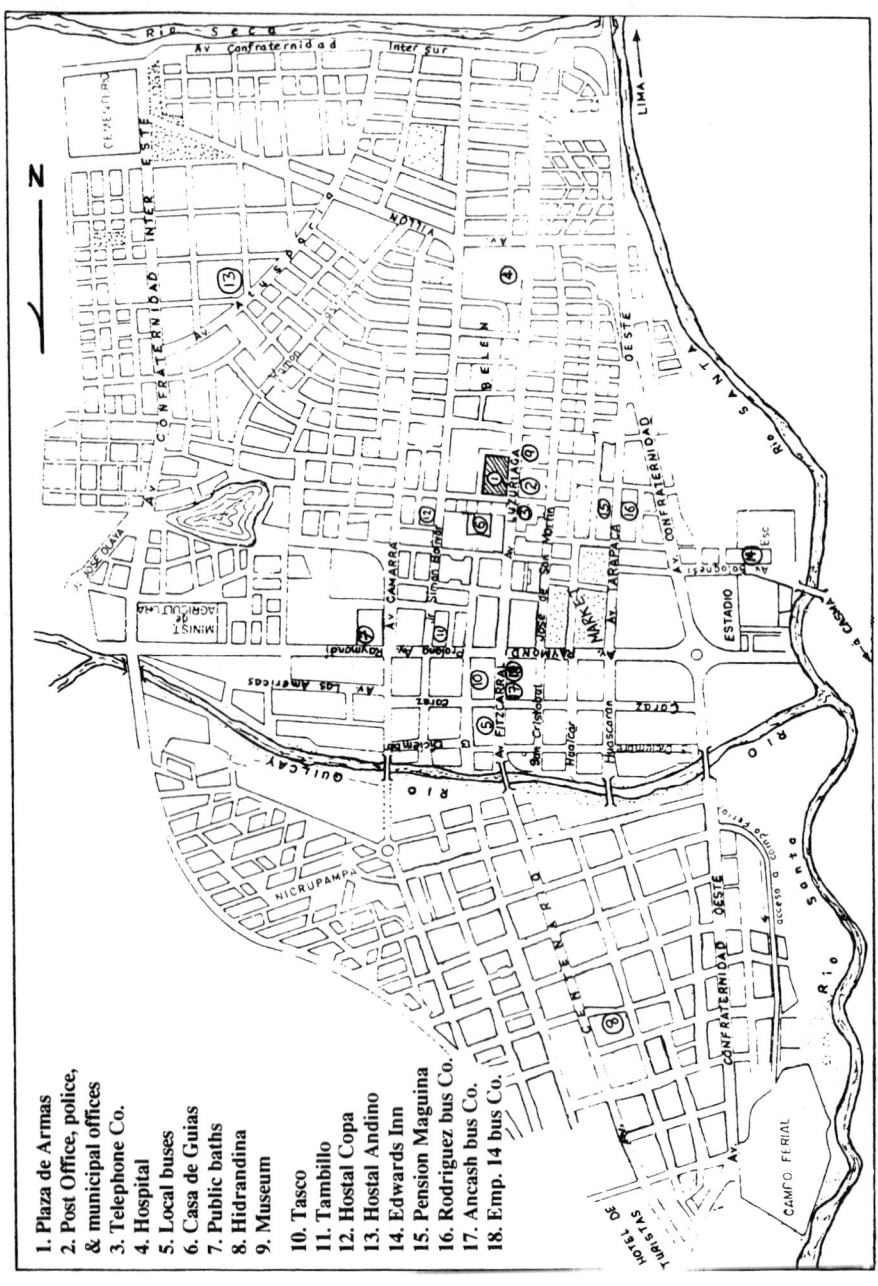

1. Plaza de Armas
2. Post Office, police, & municipal offices
3. Telephone Co.
4. Hospital
5. Local buses
6. Casa de Guias
7. Public baths
8. Hidrandina
9. Museum

10. Tasco
11. Tambillo
12. Hostal Copa
13. Hostal Andino
14. Edwards Inn
15. Pension Maguina
16. Rodriguez bus Co.
17. Ancash bus Co.
18. Emp. 14 bus Co.

CHAMPARA MASSIF

This small massif is quite isolated at the far North of the range and the name Champara simply translates as the very appropriate 'ultimate' in reference to this. It has been included here for historical purposes although it is seldom visited by mountaineers. The best approach was from the road to the North at Tarica and then the trail to Punta Carbon, but it is advisable to ask for the current situation in Yungay.

P5050:

An unnamed peak to the W of P5326. H.Bernard,P.Borchers,E.Hein, H.Hoerlin; 4 June 1932.

San Julian, 5326:

N. side; E.Hein,H.Hoerlin; 5 June 1932.

Champara, 5749:

W. side; A.Awerzger,E.Schneider; 2 June 1936.
Approach from Hda. Santa Rosa up Q. Coringuillo to Qoyllorcocha.
From the lakes ascend to a col ca.4900m on the W ridge of Champara.
From col traverse on steep N cliff of very steep weak snow ribs to summit plateau. 1 1/2 days return from lakes.

Champara Este, 5450:

NE. side from Q. Racuay; E.Hein,H.Hoerlin,E.Schneider; 29 May 1932.

P5273 (Champara Chico or Co. San Miguel):

NE. slopes from Qoyllorcocha; R.von Ascherraden,H.Kinzl; 2 June 1936.

MILLWAQOCHA MASSIF

A comparatively insignificant group of mountains which nevertheless offer opportunities for day routes to those climbing from the Q. de los Cedros. It is reported that all the routes are similar in nature and difficulty. The name Milluacocha is a literal translation of 'wool lake' although no one is quite sure of the significance of this. Pilanco translates as 'place of small ponds in the wet season' which is rather apposite.

Milluacocha Central (Millwaqocha), 5480:

SE. ridge; V.Angeles,M.Inokuchi,Y.Hamano,N.Kaburaki; 21 August 1962. F.
From Q. Alpamayo go up a long moraine and short glacier to minor summit S of main peak and traverse snow to main peak via SE ridge, one day return.
SE. slopes; D.Marmillod, F.Marmillod; 1945.

Pilanco (Pilanco Central), 5300:

N. ridge; D.Atherton, R.Goody, D.Morton, R.Wylie; 7 July 1966.
From L. Pilanco ascend to saddle with Pilanco Norte and climb N ridge in one day return.

Pilanco Sur, 5150:

NE. ridge; D.Atherton, R.Goody, D.Morton, R.Wylie; 22 June 1966.
From col ca.4830m climb granitic ridge in one day return.

Pilanco Norte, 5286:

S. ridge; D.Atherton, R.Goody, D.Morton, R.Wylie; 8 July 1966.
From L. Pilanco ascend to saddle and climb S ridge, avoid cornices by detouring onto W side near summit, one day return.

SANTA CRUZ MASSIF

The Santa Cruz massif is one of the most important for mountaineers, containing a spread of quality routes. It marks the effective northern end of the range and is composed of ridgeline chains anchored by the major peaks of Santa Cruz, Quitaraju, Alpamayo, the Pucahircas, and Taulliraju. Because of its sprawling tentacled form many different approaches are possible. Most visitors enter at Cashapampa and use the Q. Santa Cruz trail to Arhuaycocha or Taullipampa, or prefer to set up a base in the Q. de los Cedros to the N. The main alternatives are to approach to Ls. Safuna from Pomabamba, or to Jancapampa.

Peaks W of Pucahirca are underpinned by the granite batholith except for Abasraju, which derives its ruddy colour from loose Jurassics as do Pucahirca, Pucarashta, and Pucaraju. The 'puca' in their names refers to this red colour. Taulliraju and Rinrihirca are grey peaks of more solid granodiorite.

Santa Cruz-Quitaraju-Alpamayo-Tayapampa Chain

This chain contains some of the most popular routes of the Cordillera Blanca on the easily accessed Quitaraju and Alpamayo. The huge bulk of Santa Cruz has longer, more serious, face routes for experienced parties whilst Tayapampa and Jancarurish offer fine climbing at easier grades. The two most important base camp sites are the one in Q. Arhuaycocha, a side valley of Q. Santa Cruz, or the upper end of Q. de los Cedros. Both are beautiful settings to relax in.

Viscacha (Colicancha Oeste), 5320:

Double rock summits on ridge N of Norte. A viscacha looks like a very furry long-tailed rabbit and lives amongst boulder jumbles where it feeds on lichens and herbs. Colicancha is a corruption of 'gorikancha' which can be translated as the meeting place of the sun, as for the famous temple in Cuzco.

W. ridge; K.Hamada, A.Yamada, Y.Komatsu; 26 July 1967.
From Kullicocha outlet stream climb W rock ridge, one day.

Santa Cruz Norte I, 5829:

W. ridge; A.Miyashita, M.Nishigori, T.Hayashi, K.Kobayashi; 24 July 1967.
Use Q. Los Cedros approach as far as Kullicocha and traverse around N side.
From S side of Rajucocha ascend NW glacier and NW ice face to W ridge at ca.5400m. Ascend snow and ice of W ridge to summit. First ascent two days from glacier.

Yuracraju, 5180:

S. ridge; A.Ames, P.Baltazar; 20 July 1965. F.
From Yuraccocha climb W moraines and rocks of S ridge to the top in 3h from lake. The name means the 'white mountain' and it is on W ridge Santa Cruz Norte)

Santa Cruz Chico (Atuncocha), 5800:

NE. face; D.Michael, I.Ortenburger, L.Ortenburger; 2 July 1958.
From Q. Alpamayo (Q. Los Cedros) climb NE glacier and steep ice gully of NE face gaining N ridge near summit, 12h from camp ca.5200m.

SANTA CRUZ MASSIF
Map of Santa Cruz Massif

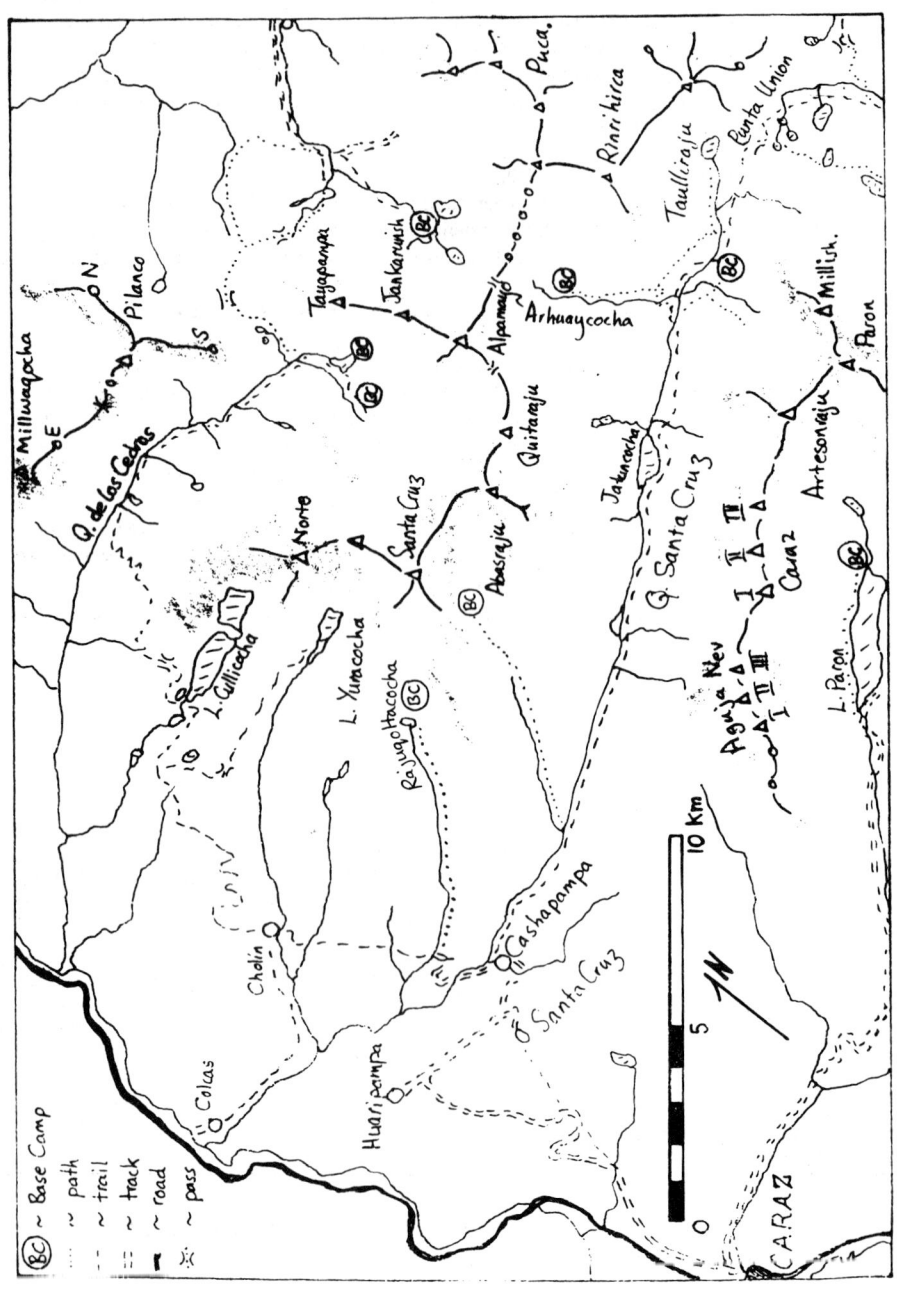

18

SANTA CRUZ MASSIF

Santa Cruz (Pukaraju or Pico de Huaylas), 6259:

This mountain is undoubtedly one of the supreme peaks of the Cordillera Blanca and contains a good selection of upper-middle grade routes to delight the experienced mountaineer. A massive granite and ice pyramid the name may come from the cross which can be seen by imaginative locals viewing the mountain from the village of Santa Cruz, another explanation is that it is named for a general who fought the Chileans nearby. The most accessible route is the W ridge but whichever you select you are unlikely to encounter other mountaineers.

N. ridge; N.Jaeger; 31 May 1977. TD.
From the foot of the NE face traverse steep slopes diagonally right in the direction of the col with Santa Cruz Chico. At a rocky bench climb delicately up steep ice to reach the ridge at a step. Turn two large gendarmes on the left and continue up a number of rock and ice steps to reach the wider, but often steep, upper ridge, 51/2 h by Jaeger on the first ascent.

NE. face variant; D.Dingman, J.Gancy, L.Ortenburger; 14 August 1959.
Right of the Swiss route climb moderately steep rocks to gain the lower snowfield.

NE. face (Swiss route); F.Marmillod, A.Szepessy; 20 July 1948. D+.
From the L. Jankarurish base camp area follow a faint track, initially along the E bank, then crossing to the N/W bank of the river flowing out of the Santa Cruz cirque. At the end follow a moraine crest up to the NE icefall. There is a good campsite by a small lake, or camp by the glacier. Go up the glacier towards the right side of the face, left of rocky slabs, 3-4h. Cross the bergschrund high up, ca.5600m, and ascend right- wards linking two snowfields by a mixed section, 50-55° , to join the N ridge ca.6100m. Ascend the ridge passing another bergschrund below the summit pyramid. The face is exposed to stonefall, 10-12h, 900m, often used in descent.

Santa Cruz - NE faces

1. N. ridge	3. Swiss	5. Santa Cruz Chico
2. NE Face variant	4. French	

SANTA CRUZ MASSIF

NE. face (French route); R.Ghilini, B.Prud'homme; 31 May 1977. TD.

Approach as for Swiss route and cross the bergschrund left of the summit to gain a rightwards slanting snow ramp. Follow this, and its continuation after a mixed section, to reach two icy defiles. These guard the upper ramp which is longer, icier, and leads to the summit pyramid, 750m, 10h. This elegant route appears exposed to stonefall.

S. face direct; N.Jaeger; 15 June 1978. TD-.

A direct route which climbs straight through the lower ice to meet the 1977 line. Cross the bergschrund, ca.5300m, directly below the summit and a little to the left of a tongue of rocks which reach downwards.

Climb reasonable ground to gain a couloir running up between two rocky spurs, which leads to the summit pyramid, 6h, 900m.

S. face; H.Gloggner, W.Janner, A.Muller; 14 August 1977. TD-.

From the foot of the face, ca.5400m, climb 50° slopes on the lower part of the wall at the left side, Traverse right during the middle snowfield to climb direct to the summit up the rocky upper part of the wall. This gives the hardest climbing with the crux being a 5m section of vertical ice ca.5800m after which a bivouac can be made. Continue on 60° slopes directly towards the summit, 900m, 18h. In dry years this becomes a harder mixed route, V+/VI-.

S. face; M.Suarez, R.Navarrete; 4 August 1984. TD+.

From the left end of the S face climb 800m 65° ice and mixed ground to gain the SW ridge above 5900m. In dry years extremely difficult climbing has been encountered on rocks just below the ridge (eg. Yugoslavs in 1987 overcame a 150m 90° VI section); 1200m, 18h, 60-80°, V/VI.

Santa Cruz - S face

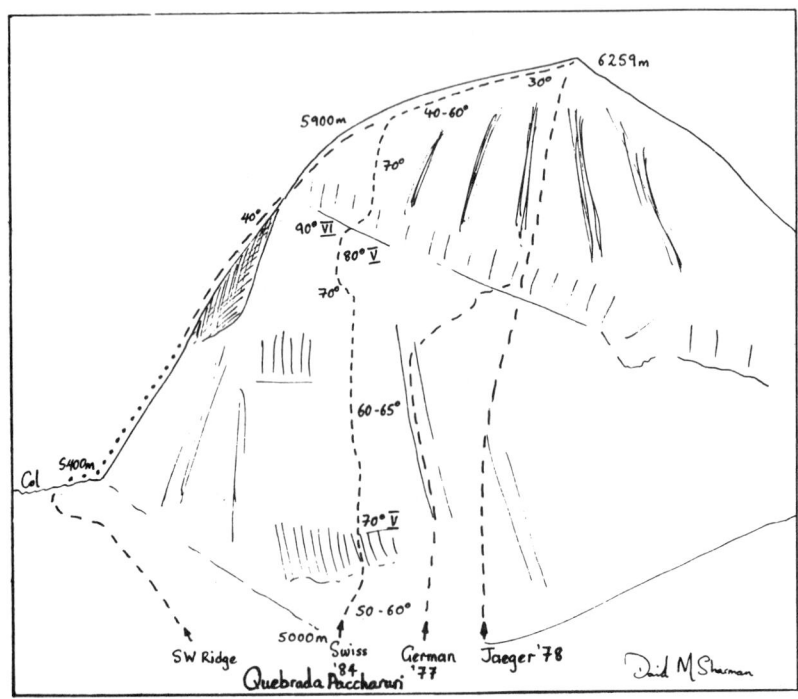

20

SANTA CRUZ MASSIF

SW. ridge; S.Gloggner, P.Gloggner, F.Niedermaier; 12 August 1977. D+.

Approach from Cashapampa through the Q. Santa Cruz to the Q. Paqtsaruri (Paccharuri) to a base camp in meadows at ca. 4400m, 1 1/2 days. Cross the crevassed glacier and traverse around the ridge at a small col near P4580, on easy rocks, to gain a bivouac at the foot of the SW face, ca. 5400m. Alternatively approach as for SW ridge, up Q. Rajucolta.

Climb the SW face for 330m, on 55-60° ice with one rotten rock band, to reach the shoulder of the SW ridge at 5600m. Follow this 40° ridge to the summit past a bivouac site, ca.6100m. This route has been used to descend the mountain in one day.

SW. face; J-M.Lang, B.Douillet, P.Sombardier; 5 August 1980. TD.

This is a cold route, always shadowed and frequently with very hard ice.

From the village of Cashapampa follow the Q. de los Cedros trail to the hot springs of Huancarhuaz, 3km. Follow a faint trail up the S side of the river in Q. Rajucolta to swampy meadows. Cross these and bivouac near a small lake by the moraine, 8km, one day. Cross the crevassed glacier, initially towards the centre of the face and then the left side, 5-8h. Cross two bergschrunds and start up the left side of the face, 70°. Avoid a rock wall capped by seracs by turning it on the left.

Santa Cruz - SW face

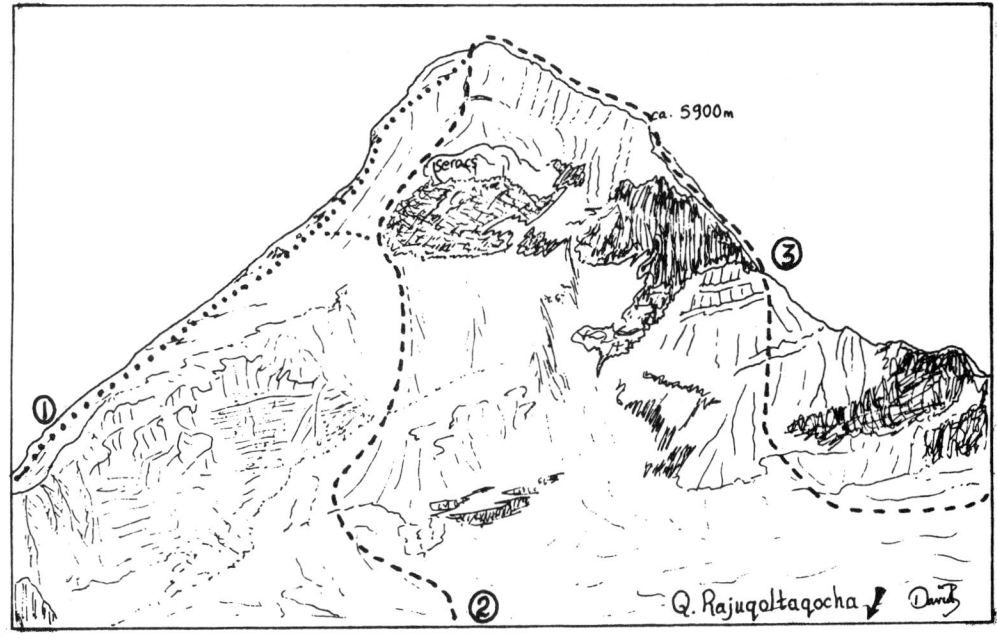

1. W. ridge   2. SW face   3. SW ridge

Climb rightwards up 50-60° flutings (this section R.Gocking, A.Berliner; 13 August 1987) to a difficult bergschrund (bivouac site) ca.5900m and climb more flutings to the top, two days return to glacier. An alternative is to continue the traverse leftwards to the W ridge, or to begin from the W ridge after approaching via the Q. Yuraqqocha (Yuraccocha).

W. ridge; K.Hadley, R.Matous, M.Wells; 18 June 1980. D+.

From Yuraccocha skirt the icefall and lower glacier to reach a camp on the col ca.5350m with Q. Rajucolta. Ascend snow slopes through scattered seracs to a bivouac site under a prominent sickle-shaped ice wall ca.5800m. Pass this on the right and climb 55-60° ice runnels for 350m to regain the snow slopes of the ridge crest.

Climb this to the summit.

Carhuallum (Qarwallum,), 5290:

Unknown route on highest point W ridge Santa Cruz; H.Hein, E.Schneider; 25 August 1932.

Abasraju, 5550:

Strangely this peak has only had two ascents despite being centrally sited, it deserves more. 'Abas' means broad (lima) bean.

E. face; N.Jaeger; 13 June 1978. TD.

This route is reportedly objectively very serious. Jaeger descended by the S ridge to a small col, ca.5450m, and then the tricky ground of the crevassed W face. An alternative would be to continue down the S ridge (AD in ascent, D.Sharman 1991). At the NE corner of L. Jatuncocha is an enormous boulder. Behind this follow a well-defined path which zig-zags steeply up the left side of the waterfall to enter Q. Quitacocha and a large lake, 2h, not suitable for burros. Continue along the path to an upper (dry) lake bed. Go up the small valley between Abasraju's footslopes and the huge moraine which curls up to the Abasraju-Quitaraju col to arrive at a prominent snow cone ca.5000m.

Climb this and slopes above to the base of a mixed couloir. Trend right to gain a spur of red rocks and climb the crest to a steep snow couloir which leads to the summit, 700m, 61/2 h.

Quitaraju (Kitaraju), 6040:

Ascents by the W ridge and N face are common, and rightly so because these are excellent routes on this broad mountain. It is named for the large amount of snow it collects, or traps.

WNW. face; R.Gilbert, P.Kellerman; 7 July 1976. TD ?.

From Q. de los Cedros go towards Santa Cruz and climb glacier towards Quitaraju-Abasraju col. Climb the 650m ice face on 60-70° ice, with 90° ice in places, through two small rocky sections. Follow W ridge to summit, 2 days for ascent.

W. ridge; A.Awerzger, E.Schneider; 17 June 1936. AD.

Normally approached from Alpamayo-Quitaraju col, otherwise ascend chaotic N icefall from Q. de los Cedros. Cross the glacier basin towards towards Quitaraju-Loyacjirca col, 11/2 -2h, where there is an area of large seracs. Pick the easiest line through the centre of this steep N flank, occasionally 60°, to join flat W ridge with large cornices hanging S.

Climb to summit at E end, 4-6h from bottom of seracs.This ridge is often used in descent.

N. face; E.Cotter, D.McKay, M.Nelson; 11 July 1964. D-.

From Alpamayo-Quitaraju col cross basin to bergschrund, ca.5400m, just to the right of an obvious rock rib in the centre of the N face, 11/2 h.

Climb directly to the top of the rib and thence to the summit ridge 100m W of the summit, 4h, 45-50°, often in-situ abseil anchors. It is possible to climb an equivalent line slightly to the right where there is abundant evidence of large slab avalanches. To the left of the rib is raked by stonefall but has also been climbed.

E. face; D.Tic, M.Romih; 11 May 1986. An 800m rise climbed in only 3h.
SE. ridge; H.Saler, H.Schmidt, B.Schreckenbach, K.Schreckenbach, K.Sussmilch, W.Weinzierl; 6 July 1969.
A remarkable first ascent which continued down the W ridge and W icefall before reascending the Abasraju-Kitaraju col in circling back to base camp.
From Q. Arhuaycocha ascend moraine to SE glacier edge, ca.5250m, and then climb steep SE wall, on ice flutings and rock. Then follow the sharply corniced SE ridge to summit, 3-4 days in ascent.
S. face; S.Sveticic, Z.Trusnovec; 4 July 1986. TD.
A short steep glacier tumbles out of the bay of the S face and is flanked by two spurs. Start on the right side of the tongue, cross to the left and traverse along the side until under the face, 2h. Cross the bergschrund directly under the summit and climb the 50-55° ice slope past another bergschrund halfway up. At the top climb 60-80°ice then overhanging mushroom-edged flutings, 14h, 800m.

Loyacjirca (Loyaqjirka), 5600:
A fairly unimportant training peak which has a large unclimbed W face. The name is a common corruption of 'white mountain'.

N. arete; N.Jaeger, R.Ghilini, B.Prud'homme; 1977.
Pleasant rock climbing lower down on solid granite cracks.
NE. face; J.Colomer, M.Martin, F.Sabat, M.Velasco, P.Xaus; 21 June 1972.
Climb NE face from N glacier.
SE. slopes; B.Huhn, F.Knauss; 22 June 1957. F.
Best approached from Q. Arweiqocha via col ca.5300.
Climb easy 40-50° ice to airy summit in 4h from col campsite.

P5650:
NW. face; M.Martin, M.Velasco; 5 July 1972.
This is the prominent point on the NE ridge of Quitaraju close to Quitaraju.
Climb from basin W of Alpamayo-Quitaraju col.

P5600 :
N. ridge; M.Martin, M.Velasco, A.Yanac; 6 July 1972.
This is the point on the NE ridge of Quitaraju closest to the Alpamayo-Quitaraju col.
Climb N ridge from col campsite.

Quisuarraju (Arhuaycaca), 5380:
E. slopes; E.Angeles, B.Boller, E.Steiger, G.Steiger, R.Schatz; 26 July 1965. F.
From Q. Arhuaycocha easy rock climbing on E slopes which would be a worthwhile acclimatisation route. Direct it is 200m, II/III. Various other points between this and Quitaraju have been climbed at a similar standard.

Alpamayo, 5947:
An ascent to any point between the N and S summits is generally thought satisfactory, however the first complete ascent was by the 1957 party. The southern end of the ridge normally carries the true summit. All the SW face flutings to the W of the French direct have been ascended, generally as a result of route finding errors, and in fact Ferrari actually climbed the runnel immediately left of the French direct. Any of the SW face runnels would be a pleasant excursion, well worth the effort and highly recommended. The name means 'muddy river' which hardly reflects the stunning beauty of this soaring ice pyramid.

SANTA CRUZ MASSIF
Alpamayo - SE face and approach

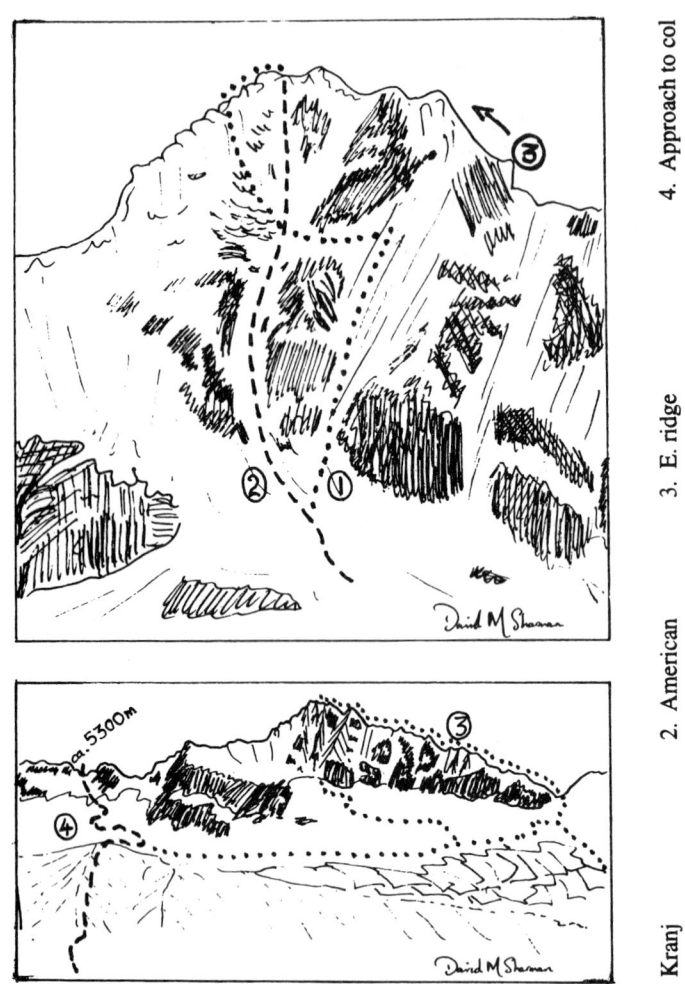

4. Approach to col

3. E. ridge

2. American

1. Kranj

N. ridge; J.Jongen, G.Kogan, R.Leininger, M.Lenoir; 1951. D.
From the L. Jancarurish campsite cross the Rio Alpamayo and follow a cairned path up the side of the moraine on the E bank of the lake. After a few zigzags cross a meadow and climb a steep slope on the left. Cross a small plateau to the E and camp by the glacier, 2h, 2½km.
Climb the complex and everchanging icefall towards the col, 5670m, with Jancarurish, 4-6h.
Cross a small bergschrund and go up the N ridge, 45-50° at the bottom. Avoid large cornices by climbing mixed ground and turn the summit serac on the left (60-80°), 6-8h from col. Abseil and downclimb route or traverse easily to Ferrari. Parties based in Q. Arhuaycocha can reach this climb by traversing the upper reaches of Q. Tayapampa. Follow the stream above base camp and climb a scree cone to gain the right extremity of the Alpamayo E glacier, 3h. Cross easily to the

col ca.5200m between Alpamayo and Pucarashta. Abseil 40m over rocks (easy in ascent) and traverse under NE face to Jancarurish col, 4h, some stonefall danger.

Climb 200m of 45° snow and loose rock, II, before continuing up route.

NE. face; J.Joll, J.Stanton; 6 July 1970. D.

Use either approach as for N ridge, or climb NE glacier icefall from Q. Tayapampa.

Climb the face by linking icefields from lower left to upper right through sections of rock. Best descent is Ferrari route. 1-2 days return.

E. ridge; H.Schmidt, W.Weinzerl; 26 June 1969. TD.

Approach via Q. Santa Cruz and Q. Arhuaycocha. Gain col ca.5200m on E ridge and climb the ridge to summit; frequent double-sided cornices, and 100m ice wall at top. Original abseil descent of SE face, or gain Ferrari route. 3-4 days.

SE. face (American route); R.Wyatt, D.Jenkins; early July 1979. TD.

This route is left of the Yugoslav line in the lower half of the face, but continues directly to the top crossing over the Yugoslav line.

Climb the gully system in the left-centre of the face, mainly ice with an occasional rock step. At 5800m is an ice cave leading into a small bivouac ledge. Above continue up a gully in the centre of the face, passing several rock steps and tunneling through and climbing over successive cornices to break onto the E ridge 30m below the summit. Two days in ascent.

SE. face (Kranj route); T.Cesen, M.Dolenc, P.Markic, Z.Trusnovec; 5 June 1979. TD.

From Q. Arhuaycocha go up glacier as if to col ca.5300 and bear rightwards to under the 750m high face.

Climb mixed ice and rotten rock, generally 65° with 80° sections. The route starts up the right-hand of the two main gullies and follows this for 500m until it hits the prominent rock buttress. It then traverses left and follows steeper flutes to the top of the S ridge, 15h.

S. ridge; G.Hauser, B. Huhn, F.Knauss, H.Wiedmann; 20 June 1957. TD.

Climb steep cornices, and adjacent flutings and gullies of SW face. Two days from campsite at Alpamayo-Quitaraju col, ca.5300

SW. face; S.Connolly, W.Barker; 30 June 1980. D+.

This climb is commonly called the French direct. A summit ice tower collapsed, killing a French pair attempting the third ascent. Previously descended by Yugoslavs, 5 June 1979.

From Alpamayo-Quitaraju col ca.5300m cross easy slopes of deep snow to the base of the main fluting which leads directly to the right (S) summit.

Climb the bergschrund, often difficult, and then the 50-65° ice fluting, 4-7h from col to top, descending Ferrari or abseiling this route, 350m.

SW. face; C.Ferrari and others; 20 June 1975. AD+.

From Q. Arweiqocha (Arhuaycocha) base camp follow a cairned path NW past a distinctive skeletal qenwa tree. Ascend a moraine crest and rock slabs to the glacier edge, 1 1/2 -2 1/2 h, some bivouac platforms. Continue following cairns N for 200m over ice and moraine before circling E up the glacier towards the Alpamayo-Kitaraju col. The 300m ramp to the col ca.5300m varies each year but can include short sections of steep ice with stakes in situ, 3h. The best camp site is 30m down on the W side. Cross easy slopes to the bergschrund and follow the line of the bergschrund up left to snow bridges just before its high point, 1-2h. Follow flutings and abseil anchors diagonally rightwards to gain mid-point of summit ridge. Seven pitches, 45-50°, 3-6 hours from col to ridge. Guided parties often leave fixed ropes on this very popular climb which is commonly used for descents.

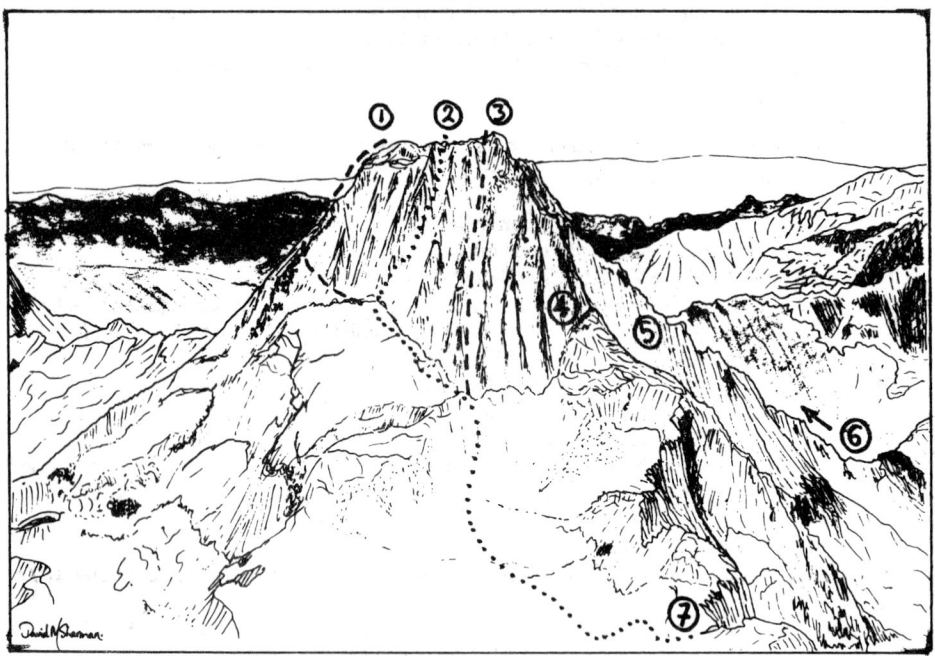

1. W ridge
2. Ferrari
3. French direct
4. S ridge
5. SE face
6. E ridge
7. Col camp ca. 5300 m

W. ridge; M.Steinbis, P.Gessner; 20 July 1966. D-.
From N col traverse NW face to reach W ridge and ascend this, avoiding cornices by climbing flanking faces. Alternatively gain ridge from a campsite at the ca.5300m col, either by traversing below the bergschrund, or by climbing several pitches of 50-65° ice in one of the flutings at the left side of the SW face, to exit onto the W ridge higher up.

Jancarurish, 5601:
The name means 'the icy place at the end' which is what this mountain is; being at the upper end of both Q. de los Cedros and Safuna.

From either valley it offers pleasant open routes at amenable grades.

N. ridge; A.Ames, F.Mautino; 15 August 1965. PD.
From the ruins of the Electroperu huts at L. Pucacocha go S, down to the sandy plain, then W along a path to reach L. Lullacocha. Go over rocks on the right to the glacier, and up this to the Jancarurish-Tayapampa col, 3h.
Climb a snow slope left of a rocky cliff and then the easy N ridge, 3-4h, 8h from huts.
E. ridge; H.Gregoritsch, H.Barnthaler; 14 August 1980. PD ?.
Follow N ridge route to glacier edge and traverse to ridge.
Climb two rock steps and a final 50° snow slope to the top of a minor summit on the E ridge, Kaikuraju, ca.5350m. A col seperates this from the true summit. One day return.

SE. face; W.Fiut.P.Malinowski; 18 June 1973. AD ?.
Ascend from Pucacocha to climb the snow and ice face just left of E rock buttress. One day return.
S.ridge; J.Glasgow, P.Gough, D.White; 12 June 1970. F.
From Pucacocha ascend to col at base of S ridge, then climb ridge. One day return.

Tayapampa, 5675:

Similar in character to Jancarurish and providing a similar wealth of short routes. Named for the abundant taya lupine growing nearby.

N. ridge; R.Gilbert, B.Gilbert, M.Blatter, P.Kelemen;a July 1976. PD?.
As for W slopes but continue directly up N ridge.
N. face; M.Andrews, W.Katra, J.Milne, 18 June 1974. PD?.
From Pucacocha in Q. Tayapampa ascend E glacier, crossing E ridge into NE glacier basin. Cross the bergschrund and go up left under some rocks, then climb the snow face to emerge on the W ridge by the summit, 300m, 55° +, 6h from base of face.
E. ridge; J.Stanton, H.Wilson; 13 June 1970. PD?.
Climb this from Q. Tayapampa in one day return.
S. ridge; J.Ricker, N.von Tunzelmann; 26 July 1968. F ?.
From L. Pucacocha follow N ridge of Tayapampa towards the col area. Ascend SE spur of S ridge and W side of summit tower on Tayapampa. This is the normal descent route to Q. Tayapampa, one day return.
W. slopes; R.Goody, D.Morton; 11 July 1966. F ?.
From L. Jancarurish cross Rio Alpamayo and walk towards the Paso de Safuna, to the lake at the glacier edge.
From here go up to a glaciated col, 3km, 3h. Go up the N ridge, traverse around the W side of the summit and then climb the short S ridge to the summit tower, 2-3h from col.

Pucahirca Norte-Central-Sur-Pucarashta Chain

This chain sweeps down in a long jagged ridge from Pucahirca Norte III to the col with Alpamayo. It has not proved a popular place for repeat ascents, possibly this is because the journey to Pomabamba seems daunting to many.

From Pomabamba it is a pleasant walk to the two base camp sites at Jancapampa or Ls. Safuna. Recent additions to the Pucahirca-Pucarashta S wall are accessible from Arhuaycocha and deserve traffic.

Pucahirca Norte III, 5919:

NW. face; M.Andrews, W.Katra, J.Milne; 24 June 1974.
From the ruins of Electroperu huts by the Ls. Safuna in the Q. Tayapampa ascend crevassed NW glacier basin to a point left of a minor col ca.5400m on the NW ridge. Climb neve diagonally to the centre of the NW face, 55-60° , and directly up to the summit past a bergschrund ca.5900m, 9h from base of face ca.5400m. Continue along the ridge to Pucajirca Norte II if desired, 2-3h more.
SE. ridge; R.Hopponen, H.Walton; 12 July 1955.
From Pomabamba go up Q. Yanajanca to camp ca.4050m.
Climb steep crevassed eastern glacier to col between Pucahirca Norte III and II. Glacier steepens above ca.5400m. Ascend SE ridge.

SANTA CRUZ MASSIF

Pucahirca Norte II, 6030:
NW. ridge; N.Clinch, A.Kauffman; 14 July 1955.
As for SE ridge of Norte III to col and then up corniced snowy ridge.

Pucahirca Norte I, 6046:
The true Pucahirca Norte and the highest summit of the Pucahirca chain. The name literally means 'red mountain' because the underlying argillites and metamorphic rocks weather to a pronounced ruddy colour. **N. ridge; J. Nakagawa, J. Nakazima, T. Nakamura; 12 June 1961.**
From Q. Yanajanca begin ascent of NE glacier which descends between Pucahirca Norte II and III, but traverse S and cross over the base of the E ridge of Pucahirca Norte II.
Climb the NE/SE curving glacier which descends from ice falls between Pucahirca Norte I and II.
Ascend icefall (giant crevasses) to col between Pucahirca Norte I and II.
Climb N ridge. Final ascent from camp ca.5400 beneath SE wall Pucahirca Norte II in 8-9h and 7h for descent.
W. face; a number of attempts on this steep face have come to grief after large ice avalanches.

Pucahirca Central, 6014:
NE. face; M.Giacometti, G.Battista Scanabessi; 7 July 1982.
Approach from Pomabamba via Q. Jancapampa. Cross the very broken glacier to the base of the face, ca.5400m.
Climb a couloir to the right of a pillar of broken rock which is itself to the right of the summit, 70° at top. Gain the corniced summit ridge, 6-10h, abseil descent.
E. ridge; J.Glidden, R.Gocking, L.Ortenburger, B.Cox; 8 July 1977.
Approach fom Q. Santa Cruz as for E ridge Rinrihirca.
From the snowfield ca.5300m climb snow slopes under the SE face to camp ca.5800m.
Climb a narrow snow flute leading to the E ridge, right of a broad mixed flute leading direct to the summit.
Climb the difficult corniced and mushroomed E ridge, 60° , to a confused and unstable summit area. Two days return from 5800m.
SW. ridge; G.Dionisi, G.Marchese, L.Ghigo, M.Fechio; 13 June 1961. D ?.
From Q. Santa Cruz cross glacier above Taullicocha to the Taulliraju-Rinrihirca col ca.5300, see E ridge Rinrihirca. Cross SE snowfield.
Climb SE face to broad but crevassed SW ridge, climb this and 20m summit icewall. One day return from SE snowfield.
W. face; all but the final few metres of this difficult 1000m face ascended by Italians in 1980.

Pucahirca Sur, 6039:
This peak is the pivotal point from which the three ridges radiate to Alpamayo, Rinrihirca, and Pucahirca Norte. The SW face is a good route though somewhat exposed to seracs and the lower couloir would be lethal during snowfall.

S. ridge; E.Schneider; 1 July 1936. D+ ?.
Best approached from col ca.5300m to S as for E ridge of Rinrihirca, although originally reached by climbing from the gorge of Q. Jancapampa, ca.3800m, in one day (solo after glacier).
From snowfield ascend the S ridge, detouring onto W face around three ice balconies. At present this is severely corniced.

SANTA CRUZ MASSIF

SW. face; D.M.Sharman, D.A.Thomas; 20 June 1991. TD.

Approach as for S face Pucarashta Central but angle rightwards across the slabs to gain a glacier bench ca.5000m, 21/2 h from base camp. Traverse easily below the S faces, past good campsites, aiming for the large couloir which falls from by large seracs on Pucahirca Sur. Pick a way easily through bergschrunds to this couloir, 21/2 h, and climb it past a short rocky step at the bottom, 80°. Stay in the 65° main couloir until left of the seracs and then exit rightwards through ramplike crevasses to to the upper snowfields, 4-5h, 400m. (The couloir continues up before curving right and tunneling under mushrooms to become the upper bergschrund - not recommended!) Follow gentle slopes to cross the upper bergschrund on the right, and then continue up the summit pyramid, 5h. Abseil and downclimb descent.

Pucahirca Oeste, 5900:

W. ridge; J.Glasgow, P.Gough, D.White, J.Stanton, H.Wilson; 16 June 1970.

From Pucacocha in Q. Tayapampa ascend to Pucahirca- Pukarashta col.

Climb steep soft snow on W ridge. Three days return, bivouacs on W ridge in cave above col. At present there are two large seracs which stretch right across the ridge.

Pucarashta Este, 5700:

S. face; P.Moorey, M.Davie; 20 June 1991. ED1.

Approach as for S face Pucahirca Sur to an obvious ramp at the right end of the face, 31/2 h from Q. Arhuaycocha. Climb ramp rightwards to end, trend up and right across icy slabs, V+/VI-, 80°, to gain a snowfield. Traverse left across this and a rock rib, III/IV, to gain the obvious couloir descending from the sharp notch in the ridge, right of the summit. Follow this, turning a rock band and mushroom rampart on the left, III. Above traverse right to regain main couloir and follow this, exiting steeply leftwards at the ridge.

Climb N side of ridge to top, 10h, 550m high, abseil descent.

W. ridge; M.Andrews, W.Katra, J.Milne; 15 June 1974.

From Ls. Quitaracsa ascend N ice slopes to col between the Pucarashtas.

Climb in deep snow on corniced W ridge. Descent by N slopes, 45°, to ice shelf in traversing back to col on N ridge of Pucarashta. Two days round trip.

Pucarashta Central, 5650:

The Pucarashtas' ridgeline offers routes and further oportunities to those climbing from either Ls. Safuna or Arhuaycocha. Pucarashta means 'red snow falling', a type of name common in Quechua.

N. ridge; J.Ricker, N.von Tunzelmann; 28 July 1968.

From Ls. Quitaracsa in Q. Tayapampa climb N ridge and NE face. One day return.

S. face; P.Moorey, M.Davie, S.Di Ponio; 16 June 1991. TD-.

Above Q. Arhuaycocha base camp follow the crest of the lateral moraine leftwards around the lakes until below the col between Oeste and Central. Scramble up scree slopes and rock ribs to snowpatches directly above, 21/2 h.

SANTA CRUZ MASSIF
Pucahirca - Pucarashta - S faces

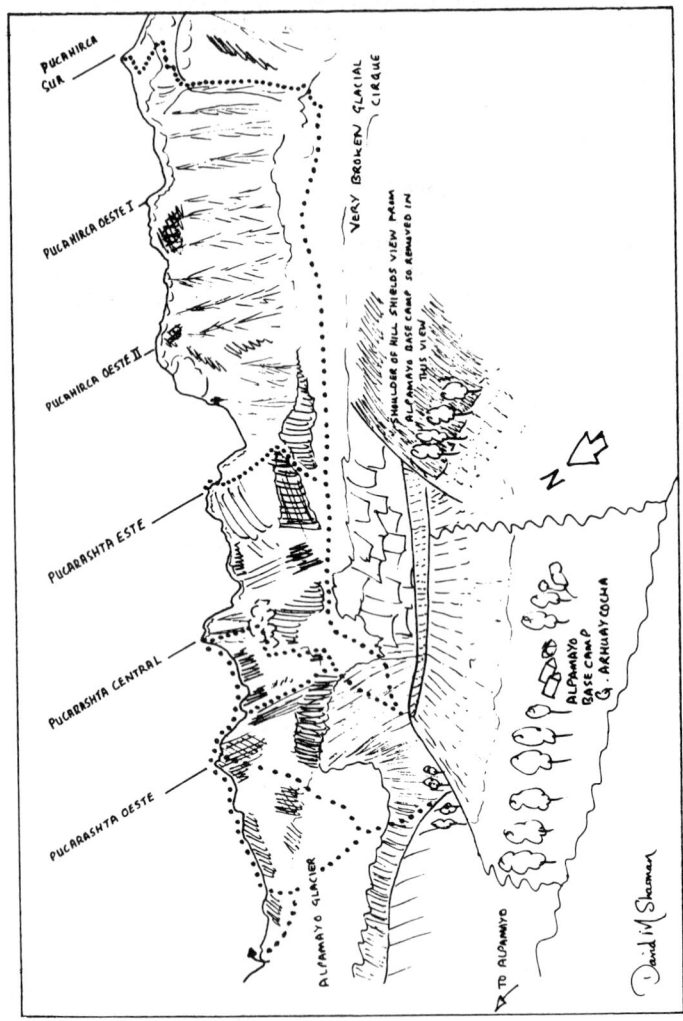

Climb a rock step via a short gully below and to the left of the first serac field, 70° /III. Traverse right across the top of the seracs and round a corner to a snow gully leading up the the left side of a second serac field. Traverse the top of this to a huge open bivouac site below the couloir descending from the summit, 2-3h. Climb the couloir past 80m of 75° /IV mixed ground. Continue past rock bands, III, to exit left onto ridge 5m below top, 5-6h, 250m from bivouac, abseil descent.

W. ridge; N.Kekus, D.Howard; mid July 1980. TD ?.

From col with Alpamayo climb this 1 1/2 km ridge over Pucarashta Oeste and minor summits. Difficult ice climbing, V rock, and dangerous ice mushrooms. Appears long and awkward.

30

SANTA CRUZ MASSIF

Pucarashta Oeste, 5450:

SE. face to col; N.J.Kemp, D.A.Thomas, D.M.Sharman; 15 June 1991. D-.
This line is marred by only climbing to a minor point in the Oeste-Central col but nevertheless is interesting and useful for acclimatising. It could be combined with the W ridge of Central for a more complete trip. Approach to snowpatch of S face Pucarashta Central, 2 1/2 h. Climb a leftwards trending gully line to the left of a narrow ice runnel. This exits at the col ca.5250m left of a minor point ca.5300m, 450m long, 4h, 40-60° . Continue up point on N side of easy rock and ice, good bivouac site at col.

SW. face; S.Lee, N.Kemp; 19 June 1991. D+.
A fine Scottish-style gullying trip. Follow the E bank of the stream above Q. Arhuaycocha base camp and climb a scree cone to gain the right extremity of the Alpamayo glacier, 3h, good bivouac sites at base of route. Start up the right of the pair of obvious gullies and follow this to a difficult mixed pitch at two-thirds height, IV. Immediately above turn a chockstone chimney on the left and continue to reach the ridge at the high point, 6-8h, 12 abseils in descent.

Safuna (to N of Pucahirca Oeste), 5410:

S. ridge; G.Knauseder, H.Claus, F.Surer; 22 July 1976.
From glacier N of Pucahirca Sur.

W. face; S.Holzmann, H.Barnthaler; 20 July 1980.
From Pucacocha climb to the base of the wall with difficulty. Ascend gentle slopes and then a steep serac zone to a plateau at ca.5000m, below the summit wall.
Climb this on a 50° ice hose to the col on the S ridge with Pucahirca Oeste.
Climb S ridge, 1-2 days.

Rinrihirca-Taulliraju Chain

The centrepiece is definitely Taulliraju, but easier climbing on the adjacent peaks should not be ignored - the views from high up are magnificent. The best approach is up Q. Santa Cruz to a base camp in Taullipampa.

Pucrapucraraju, 5790:

The name refers to saw-toothed ridge of the continental divide as seen from Arhuaycocha.

NE. wall; S.Calegari, A.Farina, N.Poloni, O.Rossetti; 9 July 1960.
From Taullicocha gain snowfield to E of peak as for E ridge Rinrihirca. Ascend glacier to steep NE couloir. Rock sections overhang at the base, less steep at the top.
Climb beneath cornices of N ridge on E side. Ice tower on summit. 8h ascent, 5h descent to snowfield. The NE face may have been climbed direct in 1972.

Rinrihirca (Rinrijirka), 5810:

For some reason this is the 'ear' mountain. Despite its curious name the E ridge is a good easy route, and the S face lines offer harder sport.

N. ridge; S.Calegari, A.Farina, O.Rossetti; 29 June 1960.
From Taullicocha cross Talliraju-Rinrihirca col to camp on snow field ca.5300m.
Climb NE glacier wall to N col, some ice-covered granite, then N ridge to summit; cornices overhang to W. Two days ascent, one in descent, to ca.5300.

E. ridge; unknown first ascentionist. AD+.

Follow path towards Taullicocha and then cairns up a gully left of a rock buttress, cross slabs and gain the glacier as high as possible, 3h. Easily cross glacier to col ca.5300m just right of the rocks of the E ridge, 2h. The ridge has three obvious steps in it. Avoid the rocks of the first step by using gentle snow slopes on the right. Follow the crest more closely for the second and third steps, avoiding ice towers as necessary, 2-3h.

S. face; R.Payne, M.Hair; 20 May 1986. D.

From a bivouac on the glacier edge at ca.4800m go to the bergschrund ca.5000m and ascend the right side of the face, and a couloir, to reach the E ridge ca.5500m. Follow this to summit, 750m, 8h.

S. face; A.Paleari; 28 May 1982. TD ?.

Climb the mixed ground left of seracs and then 80° ice and snow flutings direct to the top, 7-9h ascent.

Curicashajana, 5510:

A small peak, aptly named for its spiny crest, which boasts a couple of good acclimatisation routes.

SE. face; M.Davie; 13 July 1991. AD.

From Taullipampa ascend grass and scree of slopes below S ridge. Circle right to gain the foot of the left to right diagonalling snow ramp which underpins the rock buttress of the SE face, and which has a rock gap in the centre, 2h. Follow the ramp rightwards to 100m of rock, III, before exiting up through 65° seracs. Meet the ridge left of the right summit and follow it easily to the higher left summit, 4h.

W. face; F.Comtesse, G.Hartmann, H.Reiss, H.Spoerry, L.Spoerry; 5 August 1965. F.

From bottom of Q. Arhuaycocha climb SW glacier and W face, easy slopes but with crevasses to be avoided. Alternatively gain S ridge above rock pyramid, climbing from either Arhuaycocha or Taullipampa, 6-7h from valley. Often used for acclimatisation and gives good views of surrounding summits.

Taulliraju, 5830:

A great soaring cathedral of a mountain which has inspired many difficult routes. It is named for the taulli, a purple-flowering lupine abundant in the pampa below. Selecting a route is almost as difficult as climbing it, but the easiest is either the SSE ridge or the N face.

N. face; P.Busch, J.Bajan; 29 July 1979.

As with other climbs in the area this can be approached from Q. Santa Cruz as for E ridge Rinrihirca, or by climbing steep cliffs out of the Q. Jancapampa.

From the snowfield ca.5300m ascend the prominent rib in the centre of the N face. Straightforward 55-60° ice leads to good hard mixed ground, and finally to granite. Surmount overhanging summit mushroom and descend, two days return from snowfield. An abseil line E of the ascent line is dangerously raked by falling stone and ice.

N. face; M.Davaille, C.Gaudin, R.Sennelier, P.Souriac, L.Terray; 18 August 1956.

Cross col above Taullicocha to camp on snowfield ca.5300m.

Climb N face on steep ice slope to NE ridge ca.5600m. Obstacles above include 30m granite slab (bivouac site at base) and summit ice tower. Three days return to ca.5300m.SSE. ridge (Tuctubamba Este variant); S.Richardson, M.Miller; 9 June 1983. TD ?.

From Q. Santa Cruz cross Punta Union to the Q. Waripampa. The glacial cirque is split by four spurs which rise to the pyramid of Tuctubamba, 5240m. Further E is a prominent spur rising to P5030.

Climb four difficult pitches up the W side of the spur to reach a bivouac on the crest, two pendulums, V/A2, and hard climbing on vegetated but sound rock. Above avoid the crest on the icy N side with some sustained mixed climbing to gain the broad plateau to the SE of the main summit, 12h. Traverse behind Tuctubamba and the S buttress to reach the col of the SSE ridge, ca.5300m. Follow this to the summit.

SSE. ridge (French guides' route); J-P.Balmat, D.Monaci, H.Thivierge, J.Fabre; 31 May 1978. TD- ?.

From Punta Union head up the rock slabs towards the S buttress and gain the SSE ridge through the first notch in the ridge. Cross a glacier plateau behind the S buttress to reach the col ca.5300m between the buttress and the SSE ridge.

Climb the ridge to steep and difficult icy mixed ground at the top, 17h. The SSE ridge is often used in descent.

S. buttress (French army route); B.Prom, M.Gryska, D.Gleizes; 4 July 13988 (to buttress top only: completed to summit by C.Fowler, J.Arnow; late July 1988). TD.

This line takes the obvious couloir in the buttress which is on the right of the SW face, to the left of Tuctubamba. Traverse rock slabs and glacier from Punta Union and climb two pitches of 80° ice to gain the 70°, 400m couloir. Exit left onto mixed ground (possibly aid needed on granite headwall) and thence buttress summit. Descend 100m and climb SSE ridge from col ca.5300m to gain main summit.

SW. face (Jaeger route); N.Jaeger; 9 June 1978. ED1.

This route only seems feasible when good ice conditions exist otherwise two short rock sections will need negotiating.

Climb ice runnels in the back of the large diedre to the right of the E buttress. These narrow tongues of snow, and immense ice-coated smooth slabs lead from the bergschrund at ca5100m to gain the SSE ridge at a prominent shoulder ca.5550m., which is followed to the summit, 750m, 8h. The lower half is the crux, containing two vertical bulges and uncertain belays.

S. face; S.Mizobuchi, T.Nagashino, M.Yoda; 18 August 1976.

Route details unknown except for line on diagram. Appears at least as hard as adjacent lines.

SW. face: E. buttress, (Fowler-Watts route); M.Fowler, C.Watts; 26 may 1982. ED+.

This route is an absolutely classic test-piece which has defeated many competent parties. A serious undertaking which climbs directly up the crest of the prominent E buttress. By the right toe of the buttress climb a pitch of rock cracks, V, to gain prominent snowy gangways on the S side. Follow these for two pitches, over several steep sections, until it is possible to trend leftwards to gain the snowy crest of the buttress.

Climb this, mainly on the left, W, side and traverse 20m left to gain an icy couloir leading to the top of the ridge. Above this the angle increases and very steep rock grooves trend slightly right for two pitches to an ice patch. Continue just right of the crest up very steep mixed ground for 4-5 pitches to blank granite walls. Aid a thin crack horizontally leftwards for 10m to the very crest of the buttress. More aid up chockstones in large flake cracks gains the snow band at two thirds height (right of this are narrow, Friend 1, cracks which may be an alternative).

Climb one mixed pitch and then an aid section (from a bad bolt follow sky hook holes and edges, small Clog 2 hooks and one larger one useful) to gain a 30m icicle crux which must be climbed to reach the final snow slopes, of more difficult climbing on vertical rotten ice to pass to the left of a rocky cliff and then exit onto the SSE ridge a few pitches below the summit, 4-6 days, A3+/V/90° . Abseil or SSE ridge descent.

SANTA CRUZ MASSIF
Taulliraju - S face

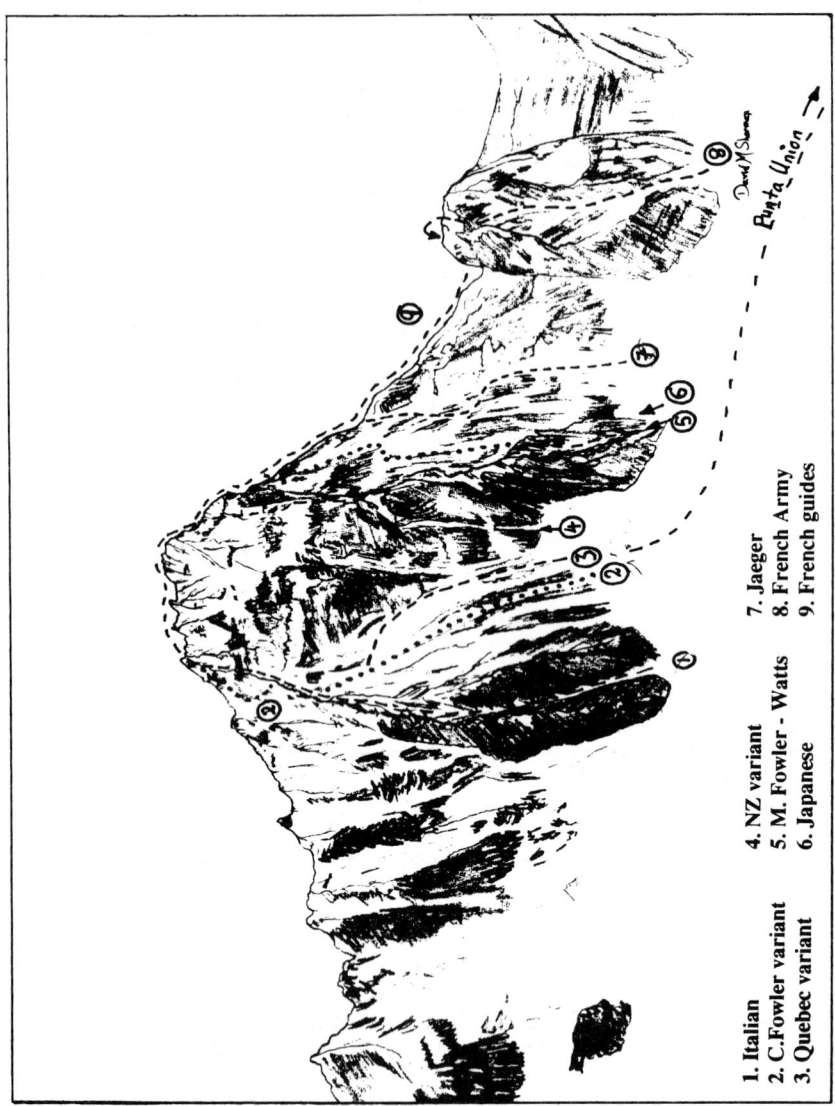

Legend (within figure):

1. Italian
2. C.Fowler variant
3. Quebec variant
4. NZ variant
5. M. Fowler - Watts
6. Japanese
7. Jaeger
8. French Army
9. French guides

David M Sumner   Punta Union

SW. face: E. buttress (NZ variation); P.Sykes, L.Clay; 10 July 1989. ED 2/3 ?.
Frequently the SW face is too thinly iced to climb the lower pitches of the Fowler-Watts route.
This cunning variation takes superb ice pitches in the centre of the SW face to the left of the E
buttress. It then crosses rightwards via a slabby diedre to meet the icy couloir leading to the top of
the ridge, 65-85°, IV/V. Continue up the E buttress with difficulty.

SANTA CRUZ MASSIF

SW. face: W. buttress (Quebec variation); G.Bourbonnais, Y.Laforest; 11 June 1983. TD+.
In the centre of the SW face climb any of the obvious ice runnels to meet the rock headwall.
Traverse up and left below this to continue up the Fowler variation, 75-80°. All the runnels go at a
similar standard.

SW. face: W. buttress (C.Fowler variation); C.Fowler; 5 June 1988. TD+.
Climb the ice runnel which leads to directly below the rocky step of the Italian route, 75-80°.
Safer and faster than the Italian start especially when combined with the leftwards traverse around
the rock step of the ridge, see below.

**SW. face: W. buttress, (Italian route); G.Calcagno, P.Perona, U.Vialardi, C.Piazzo, T.Vidoni,
S.de Bendetti; August 1980. ED1.**
From Punta Union (4750m) traverse smooth rock slabs N to the glacier. Contour leftwards in 21/2
-3h to the base of the W buttress: two compact granite walls seamed by a 400m high narrow ice
couloir which is occasionally raked by falling mushrooms.
Climb this steep ice to the ridge crest past peg belays every 50m, take the left exit and follow the
crest to the junction with the SW face.
Climb a short but difficult section of steep granite, V+/A1, and reach the summit ridge 150m later.
Unstable snow towers can be traversed to reach the summit and descend the SSE ridge, otherwise
abseil. 2-3 days. The difficult rock section can be avoided by traversing far to the left on ice, and
then ascending to the ridge; C.Fowler; 5 June 1988.

P5470:
NW. face; P.Fornelli, A.Garimoldi; 11 June 1961.
From camp ca.5300m on snowfield climb face of this, the second highest peak on the NE ridge of
Taulliraju.

Tuctubamba (Janapampa), 5240:
Another mountain named after a flower, it may offer an interesting solution to Taulliraju.

NE. side; A.Farina, S.Poloni; 12 July 1960.
Cross the Alto de Pucaraju, and ascend the E side of the main watershed, then the S glacier to col.
Climb steep, 50-60° ice on E ridge.
Climb couloir partly on NE face to reach N ridge. Cornices difficult near summit.
From col also traverse NW ridge of Tuqtabamba Este, 5030m. Tuctubamba Este was traversed
from the S by Miller and Richardson in 1983, whilst climbing Taulliraju, so the NE side route may
offer an easier way to the SSE ridge route's col ca.5300m.

Pucaraju, 5090:
NW. ridge; M.Conway, G.Mosely; August 1973.
Climb NW ridge from Alto de Pucaraju.
S. ridge; H.Huber, A.Koch, H.Schmid; 21 August 1955.
From Q. Waripampa climb steep W slopes to S peak, ca.4950m. Traverse 2km of S summit ridge
on rock and snow to top.

HUANDOY MASSIF

The Huandoy massif forms a great horseshoe with the Paron lake nestling in the middle, bounded on the N side by Q. Santa Cruz and with the Llanganuco lakes to the S. One of the lesser peaks, Pisco Oeste, is probabl the most climbed peak in the Cordillera Blanca. The major peaks include the four Huandoy tops, the double-headed Chacraraju whose S face contains such a concentration of elegant flutings, and symmetrical Pyramide which overlooks Paron with Artesonraju. All the peaks are granite with the exception of Yanapacca.

All but a mere handful of routes are available from just two base camps; Yurac Coral in Llanganuco, or by th shores of L. Paron. Both base camps are adjacent to roads giving this splendid massif unrivalled ease of access There is a regular tourist bus running to L Paron from Caraz, and one to Llanganuco from Huaraz. There is als a trans-range truck and bus service between Yungay and Yanama.

P5203:
Unknown route on point at head of Q. Wanqotepampa above Caraz; A.Szpessy.V.Ramirez; 27 Januar 1950.

Torre de Paron, (Collca, or Sphinx/Esfinge), 5325:
The peaks NW of L. Paron give a series of liitle visited routes. The rock climbs on Torre de Paron are all unrepeated but apparently could stand comparison with big wall routes anywhere.

NE. side; H.Gradl, H.Huber, A.Koch, H.Schmidt; 26 June 1955.
Climb from W end of L. Paron.
E. face; A.Bohorquez, Garcia; 1985. ED1.
The topo of the 1987 route shows where the start of the 1985 route is but I am afraid I don't know enough t draw them both on the same topo. VI+, A1, 10 days, 600m.
E. face; M.Olivera, A.Madrid, E.de la Cal, C.Polanco; 20 August 1987. ED1.
The route ascends left of the 1985 route. The crux is on the second quarter of the route, VI+, A3, 8 days, 900m.
SSE. face; J.S.Vicente, A.G.Bohorquez; 14 August 1988. VI, A3, 700m, ED, 12 days.

P5585:
L. Paron approach; G.Arcari, C.Casati, G.Frigieri, F.Nusdeo, V.Taldo, A.Pizzoccolo; 30 June 1965.

Aguja Nevada Chico, 5560:
N. ridge; H.Frommweiler, E.Haltiner; 16 July 1959.
From L. Paron climb N ridge and slopes from col with Aguja Nevado I.
S. ridge; A.Olszewski. R.Warecki; 22 August 1978.

Aguja Nevada I (Sur), 5840:
SE. ridge; M.Kulig, R.Pawlowski, A.Zyzak; 28 August 1978.
Climb from L. Paron and go up the summit pyramid directly.
S. face; A.Tuthill, J.Lieberman; July 1979. Loose rock.
From L. Paron ascend to col with P5560, then SW ridge.

HUANDOY MASSIF
Torre del Paron

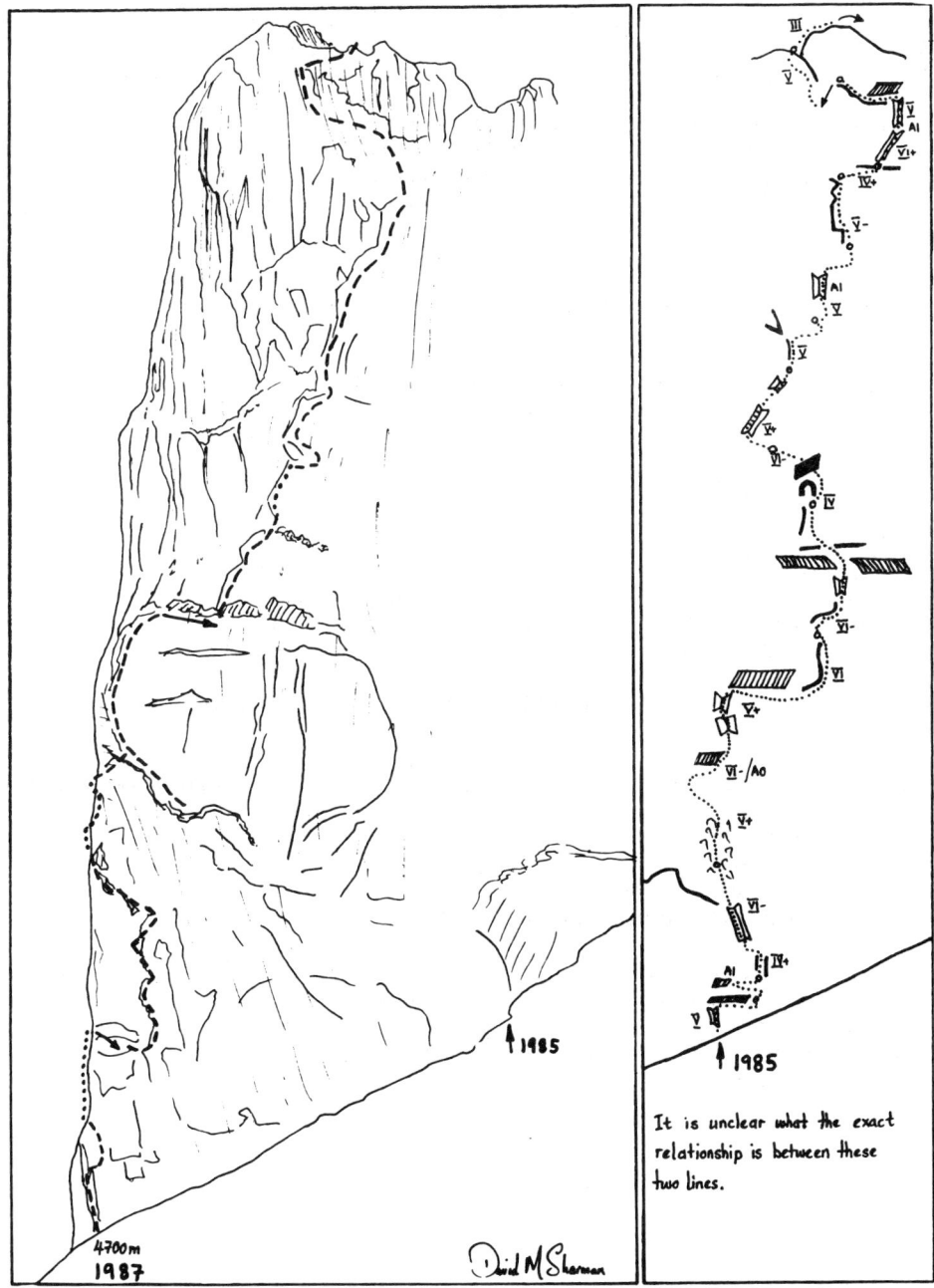

1985

4700m
1987

David M Sherman

III

1985

It is unclear what the exact
relationship is between these
two lines.

Aguja Nevadas & Caraz's

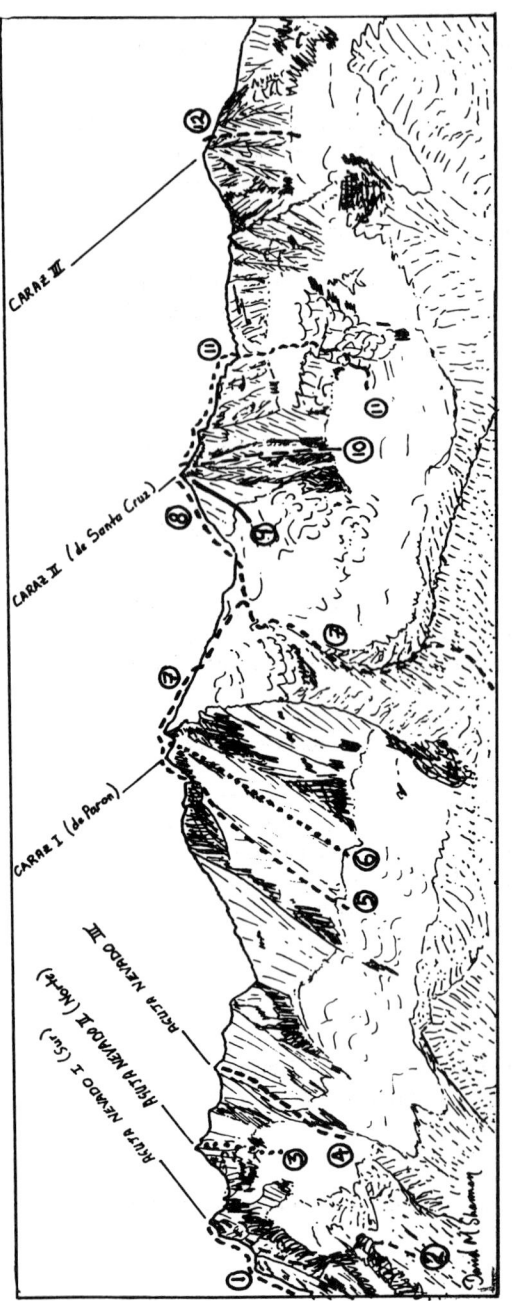

Aguja Nevada II (Norte), 5886:

N. face; J.Ackerly, S.Ackerly; 15 July 1977.

Approach over horrible moraine. Final mixed pitch up the needle-like summit most difficult. One day for face.

S. side; G.Arcari, A.Pizzoccolo, V.Taldo; 25 June 1965.

Climb from L. Paron. A number of lines have been climbed.

Aguja Nevada III, 5775:

SW. face; J.Porter, A.MacIntyre; 8 July 1979.

Climb loose, difficult, snow flutes and bypass tilting mushroom formations on steep rock. One bivouac, descend SW side of S face. Reportedly difficult.

Caraz I (de Paron), 6025:

The Caraz group offers a fine series of routes from L. Paron but nobody has anything good to say about approaching from Q. Santa Cruz, apart from the fact that it is possible.

E. slopes; H.Huber, A.Koch, H.Schmidt; 14 June 1955. F.

From the campsite at L. Artesoncocha turn N and follow a cairned path up a small valley leading to the Caraz peaks. When Caraz II comes into sight take a narrow steep stony path leading to a moraine basin surrounded by scree slopes, 2-3h, just below glacier (tent platforms). Ascend the less crevassed W side of the SE glacier and then pick a route rightwards through bad icefall to the plateau between Caraz I and II, ca.5700m.

Climb the easy E slopes to 50m of 60° snow before the highest (W) summit. This is an airy needle with a good view, 4-6h

1. S face
2. SE ridge
3. S side
4. SW face
5. 1980
6. 1979
7. E slopes
8. SW ridge
9. SW face
10. S face
11. E ridge
12. S face

from glacier edge. The other summit is only a short traverse away. It is also possible to gain this col from the N via Q.Santa Cruz. At L.Ichiccocha ascend the valley to the S.

Climb the steep N glacier, and steep treacherous rock face to col. Thence NE ridge to summit. The first ascentionists of this unrepeated variation died descending the rock face.

S. face; N.Hellewell, A.Sole; 20 July 1979.

From the hut at the L. Paron roadhead climb a steep gorge on the N side of the valley. Continue to the base of a rocky spur on the E side of the glacier, 3h. Ascend the crevassed E side of the glacier towards the S face. Cross the bergschrund directly beneath the small col between the twin summits (de Paron, and de Santa Cruz).

Climb 45-50° ice and then 250m mixed ground, 60-70°, V beneath col, 12h.

S. face; Y-C.Sonnenwyl, P.Morand, E.Loretan; 7 July 1980.

From the bergschrund climb directly to the left (W) summit: 700m of 55-70° ice leads to a nearly vertical 300m step; 80° ice flutes, then mixed ground, and finally A3 rock, 17h to summit. Either descend E slopes or SW ridge.

Caraz II (de Santa Cruz), 6020:

N. face; J.Ackerly, S.Ackerly; 19 July 1977. TD.

Climb dangerous gullies, boulder fields, and scree for 10h in the valley S of L. Jatuncocha, crossing over the toe of the NW spur of the E ridge low down. Ascend the icefall, 3h, and pass the bergschrund to climb a direct route up the middle of the face, avoiding a rock island. Steep neve penitentes lead to a rock buttress (bivouac ledges at top) two thirds of the way up. Above is steep snow, two days return to glacier.

E. ridge; H.Huber, A.Koch; 16 June 1955.

Approach up moraines above L. Paron to gain thin, narrow, doubly corniced SE ridge of 65° snow and ice. Descend SW face, 60° at top, allow for one bivouac above snowline. It is possible to climb this central ice runnel of the SW face after approaching as for E slopes Caraz I; PD, 200m.

S. face; J.Fisher, A.Warfield, M.Sheldrake; 10 July 1986.

Go up moraines above valley leading to L. Artesoncocha, and make a complicated, awkward approach through the icefall.

Climb the rightmost of three obvious couloirs running the height of the face, emerge on the E ridge 300m from the summit. Mostly 45-75° snow and ice, the crux is 30m steep rock at half height. (The first ascentionists did not finish the dangerous ridge to the summit.)

SW. ridge; V.Degasperi, R.Nicolini, B.Tabarelli, M.Pilati; 5 July 1971.

Ascend as for E slopes of Caraz I and then the short SW ridge. Alternatively climb valley S of Ichiccocha in Q. Santa Cruz then NW glacier and SW ridge from camp at 4800m.

Caraz III, 5720:

S. face; G.Bell Jr, H.Khesghi; 28 June 1987.

Approach over the S icefall.

Climb the feathery couloir which runs up just to the right of the summit. Eight pitches of 55° snow and ice then two pitches of 90° ice to the ridge. The lethal one pitch along the ridge to the top is still unclimbed.

Artesonraju, 6025:

One of the few mountains in the Huandoy massif with worthwhile routes available from Q. Santa Cruz, indeed all the routes are good value.

HUANDOY MASSIF
N. ridge: NE. spur; E.Hein, E.Schneider; 19 August 1932. AD+.
Artesonraju - S face

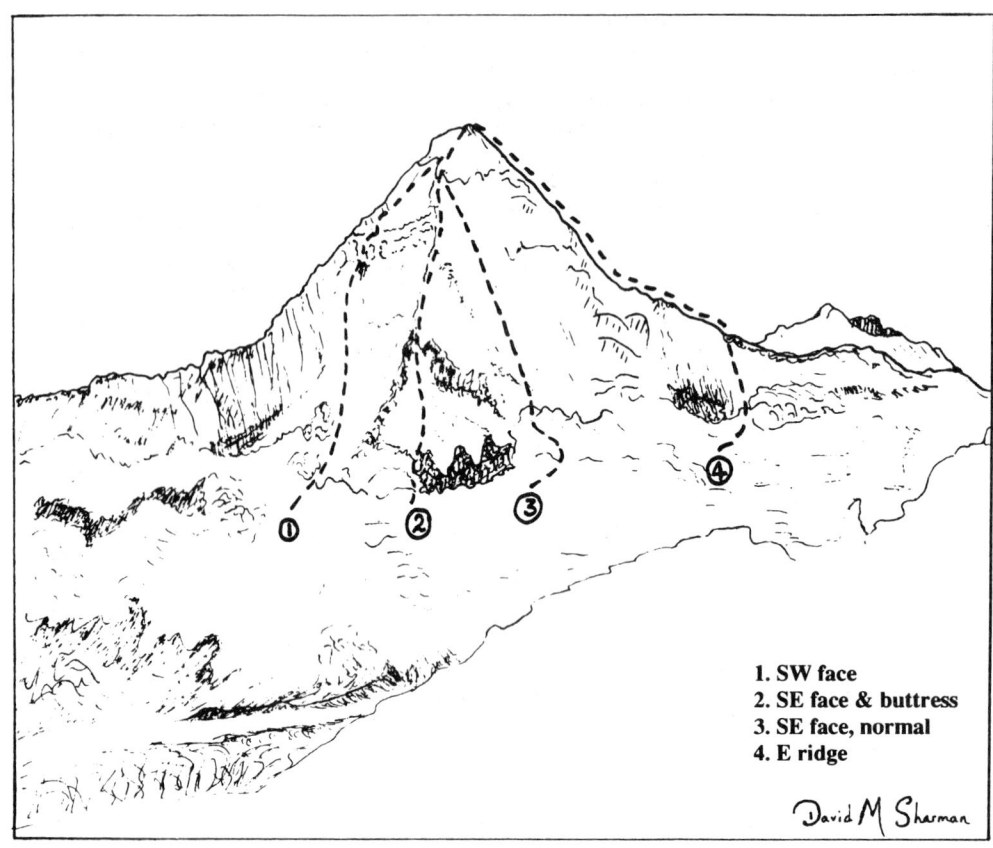

1. SW face
2. SE face & buttress
3. SE face, normal
4. E ridge

David M Sharman

From Taullipampa walk up the well defined path on the crest of the obvious moraine to an enormous cairn. Turn right up the slope, past more cairns, to another moraine crest. Follow this and then slabs to the right side of the glacier, 4h. Ascend the right side of the glacier to good bivouac sites below a prominent overhanging rock buttress, 2h.The camp sites are some 100m above the glacier and do not have water unless there is snow around. Continue up the glacier to the ridge, passing various serac obstacles, and then follow ridge crest to an obvious step.
Climb to the left on the adjacent 55° face to broad summit slopes, 5h. Abseil and/or downclimb descent. A disproportionate number of accidents have occurred on this route. Alternatively gain the N ridge by the NW spur, longer and harder.
NE. face; G.Hartmann, E.Reiss, R.Schatz, E.Steiger; 1 August 1965. D.
From Q. Santa Cruz follow the stream flowing down from the E glacier, and climb the moraine crest to a campsite. Continue along the moraine crest, first S then E.

Climb steep grassy slopes, and skirt left of some smooth slabs before going up a couloir and scree terraces to the NE glacier, 3h. Cross the glacier in the direction of a rocky slope at 5500m. Climb the central couloir of the face 45° , and traverse to the left under a rock band - one pitch of loose rock, IV+. Continue up rightwards on mixed ground to a final loose rock band which can be climbed directly III/IV. Emerge on the E ridge by the summit, 8-12h from the glacier, descend N ridge.

E. ridge; B.Janis, G.Lowe, M.Lowe, L.Ortenburger; 9 July 1971. D ?.
Gain col from N or S side and climb ridge of reportedly straightforward 40-50° snow and ice slopes, 1-2 days from glacier.
SE. face; K. Schreckenbach, H.Saler, K.Sussmilch; 24 June 1969. D.
The first ascentionists reached the base of the face by descending from the E col, after approaching from Q. Santa Cruz. Nowadays follow a path around the N shore of L. Paron to a small pampa, 2h. Walk up-valley and ascend the obvious moraine crest to the glacier edge, 11/2 h, campsites. Easily cross the Paron glacier, past a possible high camp ca.5200m, and approach the bergschrund between seracs on the right, and a triangular section of mixed ground on the left of the face, 3h.
Climb directly towards the summit, 45° -55° , often following a line of abseil anchors, 5-7h. Some avalanche danger early in the season, and a fragile summit cornice to pass. The whole face is accessible at about the same level of difficulty but easier snow can often be found on the left side of the face or on the S arete itself. Normally make three abseils and then downclimb.

SE. face & buttress; T.Sbrizaj, S.Semrajc, B.Naglic; 9 & 18 July 1993. TD+.
Approach as for normal route on SE face and climb 50° snow to the base of the triangular buttress flanking the SW face.
Climb this buttress, generally on the left, and continue up the face to link with the normal SE face route at the top. One day, IV and 85°.
SW. face; A.Sole, G.Spohr; 1979. TD.
Approach as for SE face and climb this facet of the mountain on similar ground, passing through seracs at ca.5600m using their weakest point on the left side of the face, 50-80°, 700m, 10h. This route has seen half a dozen ascents in recent years and is proving safer than at first thought. Descent by normal on SE face.

Millishraju I, 5510:

There are a number of disputed place names in the Huandoy massif and this is one of the many mountains sometimes called 'Paria'. The name Millishraju is suitable though, as it means identical twins in reference to the twin snow pyramid capping I and II. The traverse is a very worthwhile training climb.

Traverse by 'NE' and N ridges; H.Huber, A.Koch, H.Schmidt; 16 August 1955 and 1961 Torino party. F-.
From Taullipampa walk up trail to near zig-zags and follow a stream S to a bog. Circle left around a lake and go up scree and slabs, cairns, to an obvious col in the 'NE' ridge, 3h. Follow the snow ridge easily S over two very minor summits to Millishraju II and then I, 1 1/2 h. Return to II and descend N ridge past P5390. Turn P5100 and another small peak on easy snow slopes to the right before gaining cairns which lead leftwards towards the ridge crest and the trail, 21/2 h.
S. ridge; E.Angeles, B.Boller, F.Comtesse, G.Spoerry, L.Spoerry; 30 July 1965. PD ?.
From Q. Santa Cruz climb NW glacier and S ridge.

HUANDOY MASSIF

Millishraju II, 5500:

W. face; G.Hartman, R.Schatz; 29 July 1965. PD/AD?.
From Taullipampa in Q. Santa Cruz climb NW glacier and W face on moderate to steep ice in one day return, or climb the W side of P5390 (H.Saler, K.Schreckenbach, K.Sussmilch; 17 June 1969).

Paron (Grande), 5600:

S. ridge; G.Hauser, B.Huhn, H.Wiedmann; 25 May 1957. PD.
From a base camp at the E end of L. Paron walk up towards Artesoncocha and climb the glacier to the col between the Paron peaks.
Climb halfway up the S ridge on its E side. When the ridge steepens traverse out onto the W face until almost below the summit. Ascend 50° slopes directly, 7-8h from glacier edge. A good outing.

W. face; F.Langerholc, S.Stanovnik, F.Vicic; 30 May 1982. AD.
From the edge of the glacier reach the centre of the W face, 4-5h, and climb 200m of easy ground to the left end of the large central serac. Traverse right along the top of the serac for one pitch and then climb 80° crux before easing off again. Continue direct to the top, 400m, 4h.

W. ridge; R.Blatherwick, M.Richey; 10 July 1980. AD/D ?.
Climb this long ridge from a camp by the Artesonraju col in one day return.

Paron Sur, 5500:

N. ridge; E.Angeles, G.Hauser, B.Huhn, H.Wiedmann; 24 May 1957. PD.
Approach to col as for S ridge Paron Grande.
Climb the ridge avoiding seracs by traversing onto the W side, 2-3h from col. Likewise a good outing.

Piramide Norte, 5700:

N. ridge; G.Hauser, B.Kuhn, H.Wiedmann; 23 May 1957. PD.
From L. Paron gain col to N ca.5450m and climb N ridge.

Piramide (de Garcilaso), 5885:

A beautifully fluted pyramid whose faces once had a reputation for extreme difficulty but deserves reassessment with the advent of modern techniques.

SW. face; R.Renshaw, D.Wilkinson; 23 July 1979.
From a base camp at the E end of L. Paron climb E up a grassy slope leading to a moraine. Follow the crest of the moraine and go right over rocks to the glacier. Cross over the glacier until under the couloir running directly to the summit, 3-5h. Cross the bergschrund and climb 60° snow to steep mixed ground guarding the couloir one third of the way up the face, 80° . One pitch of this gives access to 55- 65° snow and ice leading to the summit cornices. Bypass these on the right, 10-12h from base of the face. Descend by abseiling the NW face.

W. ridge; M.Kulig, R.Pawlowski; 8 September 1978.
Approach as for SW face to a col at the base of the ridge.
Climb directly up the ridge, hazardous snow mushrooms at top. Three days.

NW. face; G.Hauser, B.Huhn, H.Wiedmann; 29 May 1957.
From a camp ca.4800m at the E end of L. Paron ascend broken NW glacier to camp at base of face, ca.5400m.
Climb 60° ice couloirs and snow of fluted NW face. One day return to glacier. Various combinations of flutings are possible at a similar standard on this 550m face like the Lowe variant:

HUANDOY MASSIF

NW. face variant; G.Lowe, M.Lowe; 5 July 1971.
Climb directly on a line to the left of the centre of the NW face, from the centre of the highest point of the crescent-shaped bergschrund (bivouac site) on 45-50° water ice and neve. Flutings of ice or powder snow near summit. One day return for face.

Chacraraju Oeste, 6112:

Although by no means worked out the S face of the Chacrarajus has a quite staggering number of steep and difficult lines; enough to bear comparison with areas such as the S face of Mont Blanc du Tacul for maturity. The N side bore the brunt of early development but still retains the greatest potential.

First ascents to the ridge linking the E and W summits are recorded. Not all parties were able to reach the true summits, this is best done by traversing well below the cornices, and obviously substantially increases the seriousness of the climbs.

The mountain owes its name to the resemblance of the S face to the furrows of a freshly plowed field, or chacra.

N. ridge; H.Abrons, D.Doody, T.Frost, L.Ortenburger; 23 August 1964.
From Q. Waripampa ascend NE glacier and gain access to N ridge via a small hanging glacier at the upper end of the NE glacier.
Climb along corniced N ridge, with short detours into deep snow on fluted NE face, to base of final summit tower.
Climb 250m of very steep ice-covered granite to final ice flutes leading onto summit snow cap, several days.
NE. face; B.Husicka, P.Hapala; June 1986.
A direct route emerging on the N ridge and continuing to the top. Their deaths occurred abseiling the Bouchard-MO Meunier line.
NE. face; M.Davaille, C.Gaudin, R.Jenny, M.Martin, R.Sennelier, P.Souriac, L.Terray; 31 July 1956 (first complete ascent).
Approach from Q. Waripampa to NE glacier and ascend this. Climb NE rock and ice face to col ca.5800m between E and W summits.
Climb heavily corniced E ridge of W peak, via some difficult rock and ice steps, several days.
S. face, (Yugoslav route); F.Knez, M.Freser; 8 June 1982. ED1.
From Laguna 69 cross the scree slopes on the left and climb diagonally across the main moraine. Traverse the moraine crest to a gully and then up to a small lake and tent platforms, cairned. This is just before the glacier, 2-3h from Laguna 69. This gives access to all the S face routes.
Climb 70° flutings to the right of the spur which falls from the E foresummit of the W peak, continue along ridge to top; 10h, from bivouac in the bergschrund on ascent and descent, 500m.

S. face, (Astier route); Y.Astier; 24 May 1979. ED1/2.
Makes a rising traverse across flutings in the broad bay right of the French direct to gain the ridge at the low point between the two W summits on steep and difficult ice.
S. face, (French direct); R.Desmaison, M.Arizzi, X.Chappaz, J.Fouque; 1983. ED1/2.
Climb the couloir which runs to the summit just to the right of the Bouchard-Meunier route, 2-3 days.

HUANDOY MASSIF

S. face, (Bouchard-Meunier route); J.Bouchard, M-O.Meunier; 1977. ED2.

This is considered the hardest route on the S face of the Chacrarajus. Weave through the initial rock bands to gain the steep couloir which runs directly to the summit, 65-90° snow and ice. Pass

Chacrarajus - S face

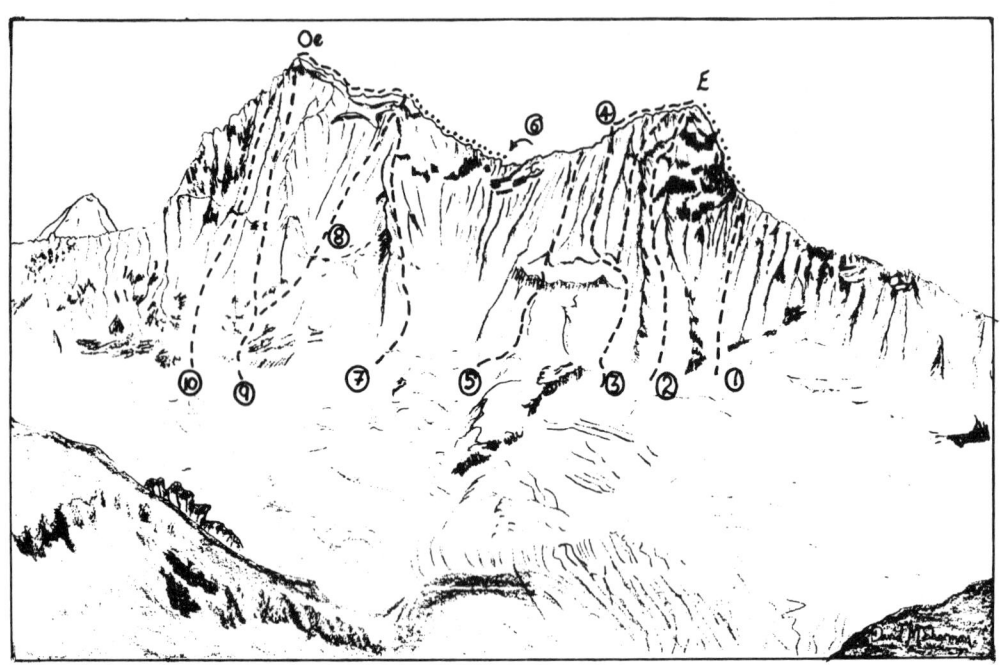

1. Japanese 76	4. Richey - Brewer	7. Yugoslav	10. Bouchard - Meunier
2. Jaeger	5. Japanese '72	8. Astier	
3. Spanish - Peruvian	6. NE face	9. French direct	

icy rock bands and traverse right near the top if ice towers bar the way, 850m, 2-3 days (28h).

Chacraraju Este, 6001:

NE. ridge; L.Dubost, P.Gendre, G.Magnone, J.Soubis, L.Terray; 5 August 1962 (first complete ascent).

From ca.5640m. traverse onto E face and back to SE ridge several times before reaching summit, several days. Fixed rope was used and is still clearly visible frozen into cornices and mushrooms.

E. face; P.Kozjek, G.Kresal; 19 July 1993. ED+.

Approach from the village of Yanama up a really beautiful valley off Huaripampa. On the right side of the E face a series of snowfields and ramps form a discernible line leading to a shoulder on the NE ridge at 5800m where a snowband stretches across the face.

Climb this line encountering progressively more and harder rock from 5550m onwards with the crux coming just under the snowband, VII, A2, 80°/V-VI, 60-70°, 21h.

S. face, (Japanese '76 route); K.Kondo, M.Yoshino; 19 July 1976. ED1?.
Climb 60° ice gully directly to rocks on the upper part of the SE ridge. Construct a campsite by levelling the ridge crest. Aid up a rock tower and climb four pitches in an ice-packed dihedral. *This must be out on the E face (author's note)*. Rotten snow slopes lead to the summit, 2-3 days, 600m.

S. face, (Jaeger route); N.Jaeger; 5 July 1978. ED1.
This popular route takes the broad couloir leading directly to the summit. From a bivouac in the bergschrund climb up the left side of the 50° couloir and turn a rock band on the left. The ice steepens and it is necessary to traverse rightwards across slabby rock to continue up the narrower upper fluting. A short, 5m, vertical rock band is passed on steep ice at the left end. The summit is one problematic pitch above, 900m, 9h from the bergschrund. Some variations are possible, such as traversing right into the rocks below the summit, descent by abseil.

S. face (Spanish-Peruvian); A.Garcia, F.J.Escolar, W.Silverio; 21 August 1984 (to ridge only). ED1?.
Climb between the Jaeger and Richey-Brewer routes. From the bergschrund ca.5400m climb 400m of 50° -65° snow and then 200m of 70-85° ice, beginning

Chacraraju Este - E face

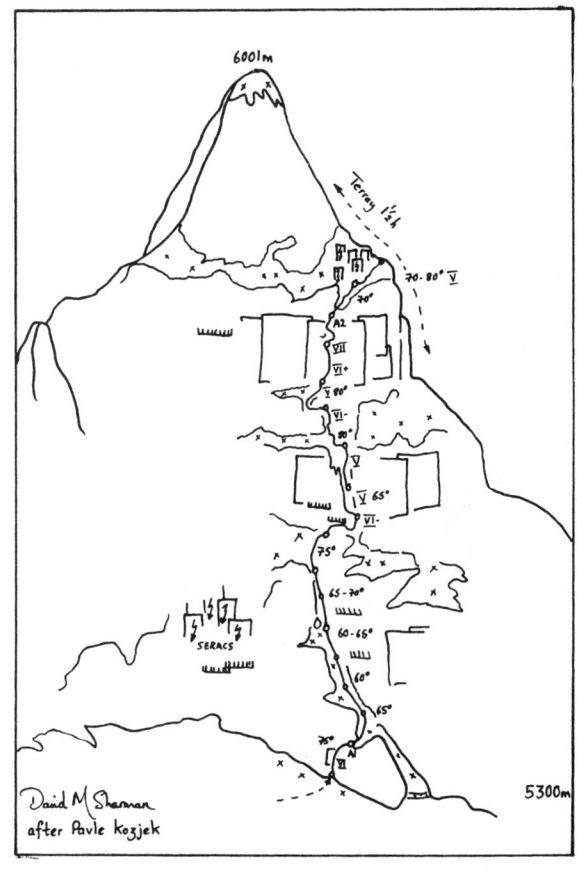

with a steep mixed pitch. Traverse the ridge to the top, 1-2 days from bergschrund.

S. face, (Richey-Brewer route); E.Richey, M.Brewer; late August 1978. ED1.
From Laguna 69 climb straight up the rocky slope behind the lowest of two huts. Cross over rocky ground to the glacier. Skirt a slight rock wall on the right to the start of the S face routes, 2-3h. Ascend the runnel system which gains the ridge 150m W of the summit, 1-2 days with bivouac possible in bergschrund of hanging glacier at half-height.
Climb 55-65° snow slopes to gain right extremity of hanging glacier. Move left and enter a 65° runnel which steepens to 85° at the top, sometimes with a band of V+ mixed ground exposed. Finish with a 1 1/2 h traverse to summit.

HUANDOY MASSIF

S. face, (Japanese'72); D.Kochi, Tanaka; 1972. TD/ED.
Climb through the central icefall and then to the ridge just to the right of the col. On the first ascent the cornices swept the Japanese back down the route. In July 1988 C.Fowler, J.Arnow, B.Mooz made a series of rising traverses in 21/2days return, starting as for this and finishing near to the summit after passing an overhanging serac en route. A similar line was repeated in 1993 by P.Kozjek and G.Kresal with the lower 800m going at 60-75° and the final 100m at 85°, ED, 13h.

Yanapaccha (Yanapaqtsa), 5460:
A slightly isolated southeastern outlier of sedimentary rocks. Most of the routes on the Llanganuco side have been climbed at some time. A good peak to acclimatise on for those based at Yurac Coral. The name means 'black waterfall'.

S. spur; N.Kekus, D.Howard; early July 1980. TD.
Climb the 1000m high S spur directly to the summit.
From Llanganuco cross the Portachuelo and traverse to the obvious spur descending dirctly from the summit. A large flat ledge provides a good bivouac before the lower rock buttress which provides the major difficulties. 150m of easy climbing leads to three pitches of tricky mixed ground after which four more easier pitches lead to the ridge crest which is followed to the summit. two days up.
W. face; D.Mackay, H.Tothill; 18 July 1959. PD ?.
From the snow plateau of the W ridge make for the NW wall. Cross the bergschrund on the left between two serac barriers and climb 50-55° slopes towards the summit, 6-8h from glacier edge.
NW. ridge; F.Ayres, A.Creswell, R.Irvin, W.Mathews, D.Michael, L.Ortenburger; 23 June 1954. PD.
From Yuraq Coral follow the path leading to Laguna 69. At a hairpin bend on the extreme right leave the main path by a cairn and walk up the small river flowing down from the Yanapaqtsa glacier, 4km, 2-3h to the glacier. Climb up the glacier, skirting a rocky spur, towards a snow plateau. Traverse towards a couloir right of the NW summit thus avoiding a crevassed zone. Climb another couloir between two seracs to the summit ridge, 5-7h, 40-45° .
NW. couloir; J-P.Balmat, D.Monaci, H.Thivierge, J.Fabre; 5 May 1978. PD.
Approach as for NW ridge to climb the couloir right of the NW summit.

Yanapaccha Norte (Yanapaqtsa Noroeste), 5380:
NW. glacier; V.Angeles and party; July 1958. F.
From Yurac Corral follow the excellent trail up to the hut just below the NW glacier, 4-5h. The hut is only 5mins. From the glacier and then easy slopes lead to the top in 4h, taking in the N ridge for interest. A fine route.
S. face; L.Blanco, J.Ortis, J.Gonzalez; August 1977.
A steep route requiring a bivouac, no further details.

Pisco Este, 5760:
NW. ridge; J.Glidden, F.Mohling, L.Ortenburger, R.Reese; 23 June 1971.
From L. Paron ascend NW glacier of Chacraraju and climb mixed snow, ice, and rock slopes to gain NW ridge near its N end. Traverse to summit, one day from glacier.
N. face; B.Janis, M.Lowe; 23 June 1971.
From NW glacier of Chacraraju climb the steep couloir exiting on the NW ridge closest to the summit. One day from glacier.
E. ridge; L.Dalla Palma, M.Dalla Palma; 12 June 1985.
From SE glacier and Chacraraju col climb the 750m high ridge with ice of up to 85° and rock up to VI in one day.
S. ridge; D.Howard, N.Kekus; 3 July 1980. TD.
After climbing broken and difficult SE glacier climb a direct line up this ridge.

HUANDOY MASSIF

SW. side; D.Bernays, F.Bernays, F.Knight; July 1961.

From Q. Yanapaqtsa climb broken SE glacier and icefalls to cirque headwall. Climb headwall to col with Pisco Oeste, ca.5550m, on steep flutings with rock bands. Climb SW snow slopes to peak.

W. slopes; D.MacKay, J.Nelson, M.Nelson, J.Tothill; 1959.

Follow the normal route for Pisco Oeste to the col with Huandoy Este and descend northwards for 100-120m of elevation. Traverse around the W slopes of the SW ridge of Pisco Oeste on a heavily crevassed glacier with some danger from falling ice. Climb W slopes of Pisco Este to join NW ridge about 100m below summit.

Pisco Oeste, 5752:

It seems probable that all the obvious lines on the S face of Pisco Oeste have been climbed given its proximity to a popular base camp area. Confusion exists however as to the first ascent details. As a consequence of its popularity campsites are invariably polluted, which is a great shame since it takes

Pisco Oeste - S face

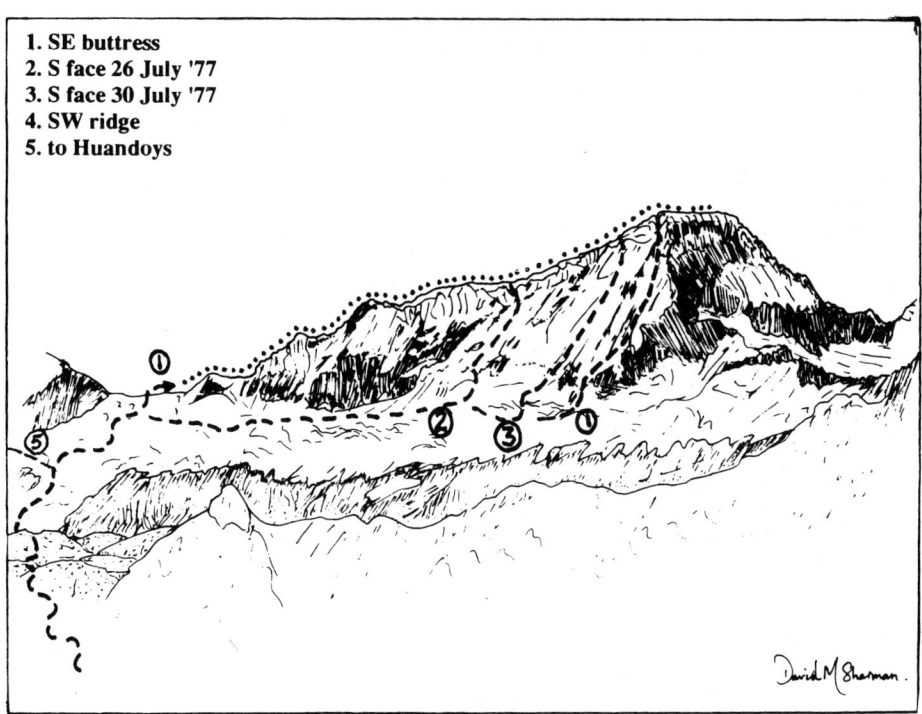

1. SE buttress
2. S face 26 July '77
3. S face 30 July '77
4. SW ridge
5. to Huandoys

so little effort to remove rubbish from here. After the first ascent of the SW ridge the porters drank vast quantities of Pisco, thus christening the mountain.

HUANDOY MASSIF
NE. ridge; L.Apollonio, D.Baldassi, R.Durin, A.Orlini; 20 June 1983.
Approach as for W slopes of Pisco Este and climb ridge crest to summit. Alternatively approach via NW ridge Pisco Este and traverse icefall to ridge. Either approach is somewhat threatened, 1-2 days return.

SE. buttress; R.Tuliszka, J.Marcinkowski; 11 August 1976. TD.
At the extreme right of the face, approach as for SW ridge and then traverse glacier under the face, 2h from lake. Cross the bergschrund at the highest point, almost directly below the summit. Climb straight up 45-60° snow and ice, passing a rock band of moderate difficulty in the upper third of the face (this is often covered in powder and provides poor belays). Exit through a cleft just left of a large cornice, 5-12h on face, 600m.

S. face; M.Barrard; 26 July 1977. D.
Start up an initial 55° neve slope directly beneath the left end of the summit seracs. Cross left 200m below these overhangs on a 90m, 75-80° rock band and exit onto the SW ridge via a Y-shaped system of vertical couloirs, 5-10h, 500m.

S. face; M.Barrard, C.Bougnaud, P.Vallencant; 30 July 1977. AD+.
A different and direct route, the easiest line on the face. After 1 1/2 h walk from the lake turn and climb the easiest line to the point at which there are no exit difficulties, 4h, 250m. There have been many ascents of combinations of all the gullies on the S face of Pisco Oeste of which these two are merely the first recorded

SW. ridge; C.Kogan, G.Kogan, R.Leininger, M.Lenoir; 12 July 1951. PD.
From the Yurac Corral base camp area in Q. Llanganuco cross the river and follow the path, past a signpost, up scrub on the hillside to the N. Cross a plain towards a moraine and walk up the crest of this until almost at the top. Descend slightly rightwards and climb a small gully. Still following the path go across flatter ground and climb the moraine to the left of a rock outcrop. Follow the path to a cairned boulder field, sand, then the massive boulders of the high camp; bivouac under boulder overhang, 3h. Take the cairned path which zig-zags up the S side of the large moraine by the high camp. From the crest follow more cairns down onto the very confused moraine-covered glacier. Judiciously follow cairns NW across this towards the Pisco-Huandoy col, skirting the SW side of a medium-sized lake to camp by a smaller, higher lake (foul water), 2-3h. Climb up a steep moraine on the left bank of the small lake and cross rocky slabs to the glacier. Make a wide detour to the left to gain the col, ca.5350m.
Climb the gentle slopes of the SW ridge, avoiding some large crevasses, 30-45° . At the top gain the short summit ridge on the right end by a 5m, 50° section, 3-6h. This is perhaps the most climbed route in the Blanca, certainly a lot of rubbish has been discarded by the thoughtless.
An alternative approach is possible from L. Paron. From Artesonpampa follow moraine to glacier, 2h, and then glacier on Huandoy side to short 50° slopes below col, 2h. Avoid E side which is exposed to serac fall.

Huandoy Este, 5900:
N. ridge; P.Hoessly, F.Hoyt; 1 August 1952.
Follow normal route for Pisco Oeste to reach col ca.5350m. Cross NE glacier to reach N ridge and climb this to the top. Rotten rock, IV and occasional V at bottom: beware of cornices overhanging to the W and steep snow on the E face at top, 1-2 days.

N. face; W.Siri, A.Steck; 1 August 1952.
Follow normal route for Pisco Oeste to reach col ca.5350m. Climb flat NE crevassed glacier of Huandoy Este and steep loose rock rib on N face, III. Climb 75° snow slopes at top of face where the route joins the N ridge. Ascend snowy N ridge a few hundred metres to summit, 10-15 hours return to col.

N. face (Croatian route); D.Butkovic, B.Ognancevic, B.Puzak; 13 June 1985.
From NE glacier ca.5500m begin climbing 100m to the right of a prominent central buttress. Go up a snow slope to a distinct chimney, climb this and traverse a snow slope left to the buttress.

HUANDOY MASSIF

Continue up mixed ground to a yellow band, ca.5850m, 7h, bivouac site. Traverse left and climb a chimney, then an ice corridor to the summit, 5h, IV-V+. Descend route by abseils.

N. face; L.Ortenburger and party; 1982.

Climb the central buttress direct to ca.5850m. Traverse right to the N ridge, 1-2 days.

NE. ridge; F.Piana, R.Casarotto, S.Martini; 4 August 1975. D+ ?.

A mixed ridge starting from col ca.5350m with loose rock, snow mushrooms, and cornices, one day to summit.

SE. face; F.Piana, R.Casarotto, S.Martini; 6 August 1975. TD ?.

Mixed line starting from right-hand (E) end of S face and continuing up NE ridge, two days.

SE. face; A.Lowe; July 1984. TD ?.

The obvious gully line which reaches the NE ridge at a sharp notch immediately right of the summit. Approach by traversing the glacier from the small lake camp on the normal Pisco route, 1-2h. Above the bergschrund climb occasional mixed sections to reach the pronounced ice flutings above, 60-70°, difficult at top. Emerge onto ridge 50m below summit, 10-14h, descend N side or NE ridge.

W. ridge; J.Hudson, R.Laba; early June 1969. D.

Climb couloir as for NE face Norte to col ca.5800m. Climb W ridge of gentle slopes with large crevasses and seracs.

Huandoy Norte, 6395:

This is the second highest peak in the cordillera and, together with the other three Huandoy summits, offers a good range of the more difficult climbs. The only problem is that there is no route

Huandoys - N faces

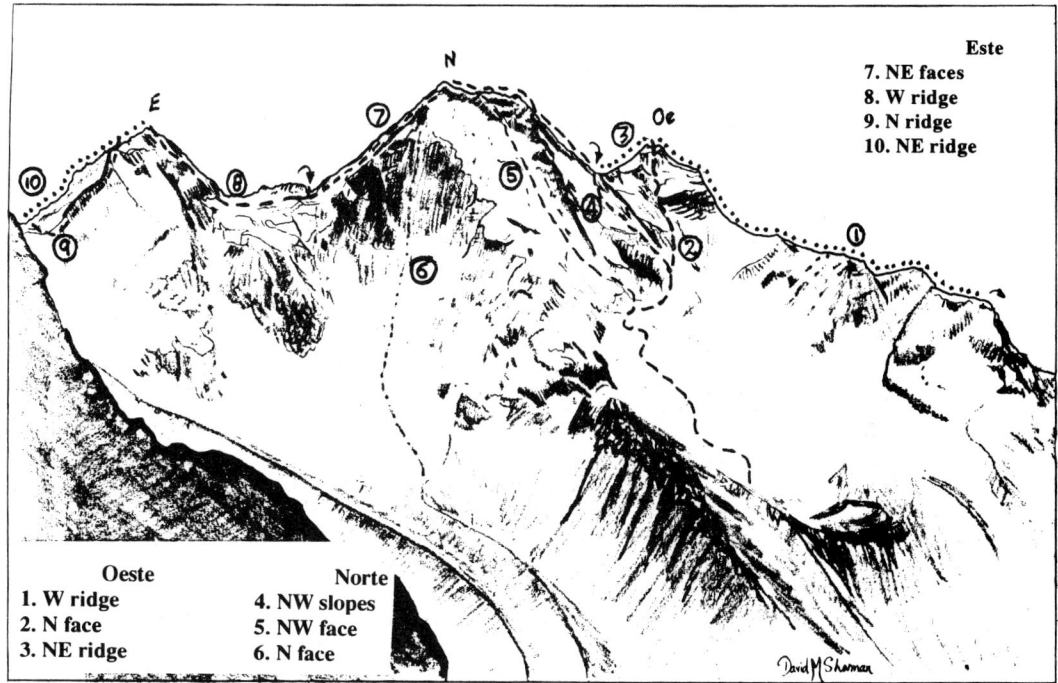

Este
7. NE faces
8. W ridge
9. N ridge
10. NE ridge

Oeste
1. W ridge
2. N face
3. NE ridge

Norte
4. NW slopes
5. NW face
6. N face

which is both easy and safe because the S slopes route is very exposed to stonefall in the couloir. The easiest safe line is probably the SW buttress of the South summit. If you climb a hard line and wish to traverse the summit plateau to an easier descent route you should not underestimate route finding difficulties if enveloped in cloud.

NW. slopes; R.Schatz, E.Reiss; 10 July 1959. D.
A remarkable first ascent in one day return from L.Paron. From Q.Paron follow NW face route to the glacier.
Climb up NW glacier to camp in the ampitheatre ca.5600m, 3-4h. Above cross the bergschrund (crux) and climb 600m of 50° ice to reach the saddle between W and main peak. Climb the broad SW ridge to main (Norte) peak. Normally 2-3 day return.

NW. face; J.Glidden, B.Janis, G.Lowe, M.Lowe, L.Ortenburger;18 July 1971. D+.
From the Electroperu huts at the W end of L. Paron follow the track towards L. Paron. After 10 minutes look out for some cairns on the right, directly under a rock cliff. Follow the path up to the right of the cliff. Follow the crest of a moraine up to the left side of the glacier, just on the right of a rocky spur. Camp at the edge of the NW glacier by a cliff overlooking the N glacier, 2-4h. Go up the left side of the glacier and then traverse right through a mass of jumbled seracs. Cross the bergschrund and climb the 50-55° snow and ice slopes on the right side of the NW face. Reach the summit ridge through a mixed couloir which splits a rock band at the top, 800m, 6-8h.

N. face; D.Tic, M.Freser, M.Romih; 2 July 1987. ED2.
An exceptionally difficult climb on this steep face.
From L. Paron go up the valley to the SW to reach the base of the N face on the left side where there is a steep rib. On its right climb 50-60° ice and V rock, to a bivouac half- way up the face. Climb five pitches on brittle vertical ice covered rock, VI/VII. A third day reaches the ridge which forms the right side of the NE face: climb a steep couloir to a bivouac site at a serac, VI+, 55-70° ice. Continue to the summit. Four days to summit, 1400m. Significant stonefall hazard.

NE. face; G.de Naurois, M.Parmentier; 28 July 1974. D+.
The safest route direct to the top of Huandoy Norte from the Llanganuco side.
From Pisco base camp area cross the moraine and traverse the glacier below the face of Huandoy Este (4h). Climb a steep snow and ice couloir which gains the lefthand of two small cols between the N and E summits, 400m, 45° and 70° at top (4h). Camp on the plateau below. Climb upwards, either on the NE ridge or the face, 500m, 50° , 6h. A 10m band of loose rock below the summit is passed at the narrowest point in the centre, III, some in situ pitons. One or two days to summit

E. face; J.Marcinkowski, J.Stryczynski, W.Waligora; 18 August 1976. D+/TD-.
Approach as for the NE face couloir but continue to traverse until it is possible to climb up rocks and mixed ground to the right of the buttress in the middle of the E face. At about half-height follow a ramp line leftwards through the buttress. Climb a system of couloirs and small ice spurs to exit almost onto the summit. The crux can be breaking onto the top, 50-55° , IV+, 14 hours climbing.

S. slopes; E.Hein, H.Schneider; 12 September 1932. AD+/D-.
From Pisco base camp area gain E glacier and ascend to ice cliff between Huandoy Norte and Sur. To do this either follow the crest of the medial moraine, 1h, and climb through the icefall, 3-9h, or (better) cross the moraine northwards as if climbing Pisco, 2-3h, and then circle eastwards under Huandoy Este, 3-7h, (beware of stonefall). Parties have wildly different opinions of the merits of either approach option. Then climb the short ice couloir on the N end of the ice cliff, 200m, 45° , to reach the snow platea, ca.5800 (severe stone-fall danger).
Climb S slopes or SW ridge from saddle to summit, 3-5h to saddle, 3-4h from saddle. A steep alternative route bypasses the ice cliff on the S side, using aid on rock sections (Americans, 1954). Various other routes have been taken up this ice cliff but the right-hand couloir is generally the best option.

HUANDOY MASSIF

Huandoy Oeste, 6356:

N. face; S.Untch, A.Hinkes; 18 July 1985. D+.
From L. Paron go up the glacier to below the N face. Climb 200m up the left edge of the obvious rock wall to a campsite in a bergschrund. Traverse up and right above the wall through numerous small rock faces, III and 75° ice. Climb awkward summit cornices. Either descend normal route to Llanganuco or descend diagonally down from the col with Norte.

NE. ridge; L.Ortenburger, R.Irvin, W.Mathews; 28+ July 1954. AD-.
From snow plateau ca.5800m climb 45° E slopes and then knife-edge NE ridge to summit, 4-5h.

S. buttress; E.Chrobak, T.Laukajtys, W.Szymanski, L.Wilczynski; 27 July 1972. TD+.
Approach as for the SW face and cross the glacier towards the right side of the face where a rock buttress forms the left wall containing the icefall. Climb up the left side of this rock buttress and reach the crest above. Climb this to the right side of the diamond-shaped rock buttress and turn this on the right to gain the top. Steep exposed ice and rock, V, three days.

SW. face; N.Jaeger; 29 June 1978. TD+.
Shortly before reaching the park checkpoint on the Llanganuco road, but after passing the last roadside huts, take a trail which leads N. Follow a network of paths by irrigation canals, past the salt pan of Qeshwacocha. At the entrance to the Q. Rajururi (Huaytapallana) follow a path which crosses to the N bank. At the end of this box canyon climb on the left up grass and steep slabs to the moraine and glacier, 7km, 4-6h.
Cross the glacier towards the centre of the SW face. This is quite crevassed below the bergschrund, ca.5400m, 4-8h. Climb the 55° snow slope towards the low point of the diamond-shaped rock buttress on the right side of the face. Climb difficult mixed ground, IV+, on the left edge of the buttress and find a line through the seracs above, 70-80°, 10-12h from glacier edge. The best descent route is as for the S slopes of Huandoy Norte. The W-flowing icefall to the S of Huandoy Oeste is exceedingly dangerous.

W. ridge; J.-L. Guyonneau, J.-L.Joubert, V.Lant, G.Lemoine, A.Zagdoun; 6 August 1974.
This unrepeated route was climbed with 1200m of fixed ropes over a period of one month. Approach as for SW face, but on climbing out of the canyon continue to follow the moraine crest which effectively forms the W side of the glacier. At the end of this are campsites where it abuts a rock rognon, 4760m. Above the rognon go right, up snow tongues which lead to a mixed arete. Climb this to the foot of a 100m rock step which is climbed by cracklines, III. Continue up snow to reach a plateau at 5250m and cross this eastwards towards a distinctive snowy high point which marks the W end of the ridge proper.
Climb steep snow slopes on the S side of this to reach its summit, 5760m. Then follow the very corniced ridge, cornices generally hanging over Paron, first descending to a distinct col. It is possible to find a campsite halfway along at 5860m. At 5940m the ridge ends in a steep steps. Pass an initial step by ice gullies on the N side, 3-4 pitches, IV.
Climb another immediately, mixed III/IV and then a vertical wall, V. A very steep 100m ice couloir leads to a rock arete which is climbed by cracks, IV, 3-4 pitches, to exit into a scoop on the W face. Leave this by a short steep ice couloir and make a rising traverse left to the summit icecap.

Huandoy Sur, 6160:

NW. face; A.Koch, H.Schmidt; 15 July 1955. AD.
From plateau ca.5800m climb NW ice face on fairly easy 30-45° slopes with wide sweeps to avoid large crevasses, 4-6h.

NE. face; Y.Astier; 1979. TD.
From Pisco high camp cross moraine and glacier to the S face, climb directly to the summit on ice and mixed ground.

HUANDOY MASSIF

E. ridge; P.Jongen, M.Massenat, G.Sterna, G.Theilou; 16 August 1972. TD?

Climb steep rock on E end of S face, and E ridge. 400m of rope fixed on face, four days to ascend ridge section.

Huandoys - S faces

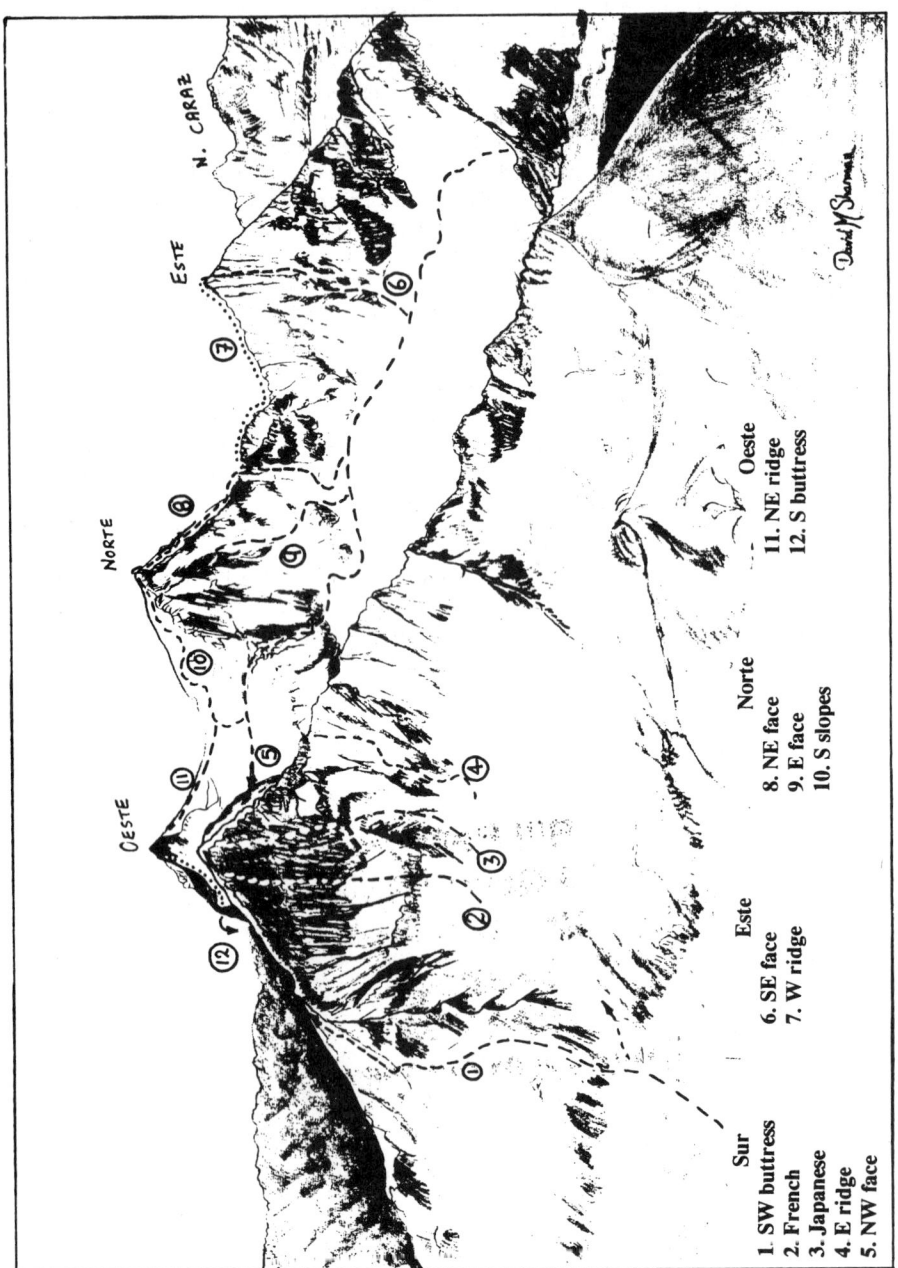

Sur
1. SW buttress
2. French
3. Japanese
4. E ridge
5. NW face

Este
6. SE face
7. W ridge

Norte
8. NE face
9. E face
10. S slopes

Oeste
11. NE ridge
12. S buttress

HUANDOY MASSIF

S. face, (Japanese route); K.Kondo, M.Yoshino, Y.Hayashi; 27 June 1976.

Nine climbers prepared this route over 24 days with extensive use of bolts and other aid paraphernalia.

From the Llanganuco lakes scramble up steep rocky slopes to the glacier at ca.4800m. Descend onto the glacier and follow the right, E, side to a begschrund ca.5100m at the base of a snowy spur falling from the E side of the face.

Climb this spur, 50-70°, to the rock wall at 5650m. Follow Japanese bolts directly up poor, overhanging rock to gain the summit plateau to the E of the summit.

S. face, (Italian route); A.DaPolenza, R.Casarotto; 6 July 1976. ED? .

Twelve climbers prepared this route over 28 days. Possibly the most logical route although still requiring direct aid eg. 350 pitons, and the use of hammocks etc. Climb as for the Japanese route to the top of the ice spur at 5650m, possible campsite. Descend 75m diagonally left on a 70° slope, and continue left on a rising traverse for 250m to the foot of a rock pillar. Ascend this diagonally left with difficult free and aid climbing. The crux is a vertical dihedral climbed with bongs and wedges, and there are sections of steep ice. There is a small bivouac site on the top of the pillar, ca.5900m. Continue straight up on large blocks seperated by rotten rock and ice. On reaching black stains below the summit avoid poor rock by climbing a narrow ice couloir on the left.

S. face, (French route); R.Desmaison, M.Faivre, P.Ottmann, J-C.Salomon; 22 July 1976. ED.

Similarly seiged by eleven climbers over a month. This route climbs directly up to the rock pillar of the Italian line, on exfoliated vertical and overhanging granite, '30 bolts, many pitons'.

SW. buttress; H.Abrons, T.Frost, H.Kendall, J.Kendall, I.Ortenburger L.Ortenburger; 28 July 1964.

Between the two Llanganuco lakes, above the road, is a monument to dead mountaineers. From this climb up slopes into the canyon and keep right to moraines which are ascended to tent platforms. Go up to the left of the rocky SW buttress to glacier at ca.5400m.

Climb snowy W face of buttress on the left of a large serac, and then along the crest to gain the easier SW ridge which is followed to the summit, 50°, 8-10 hours from high camp.

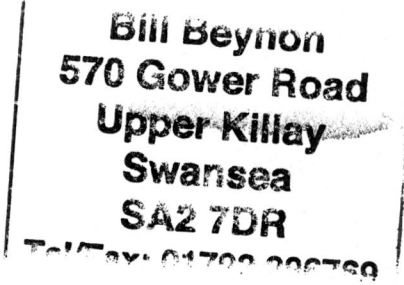

HUASCARAN MASSIF
Map of Huandoy & Huascaran Massifs

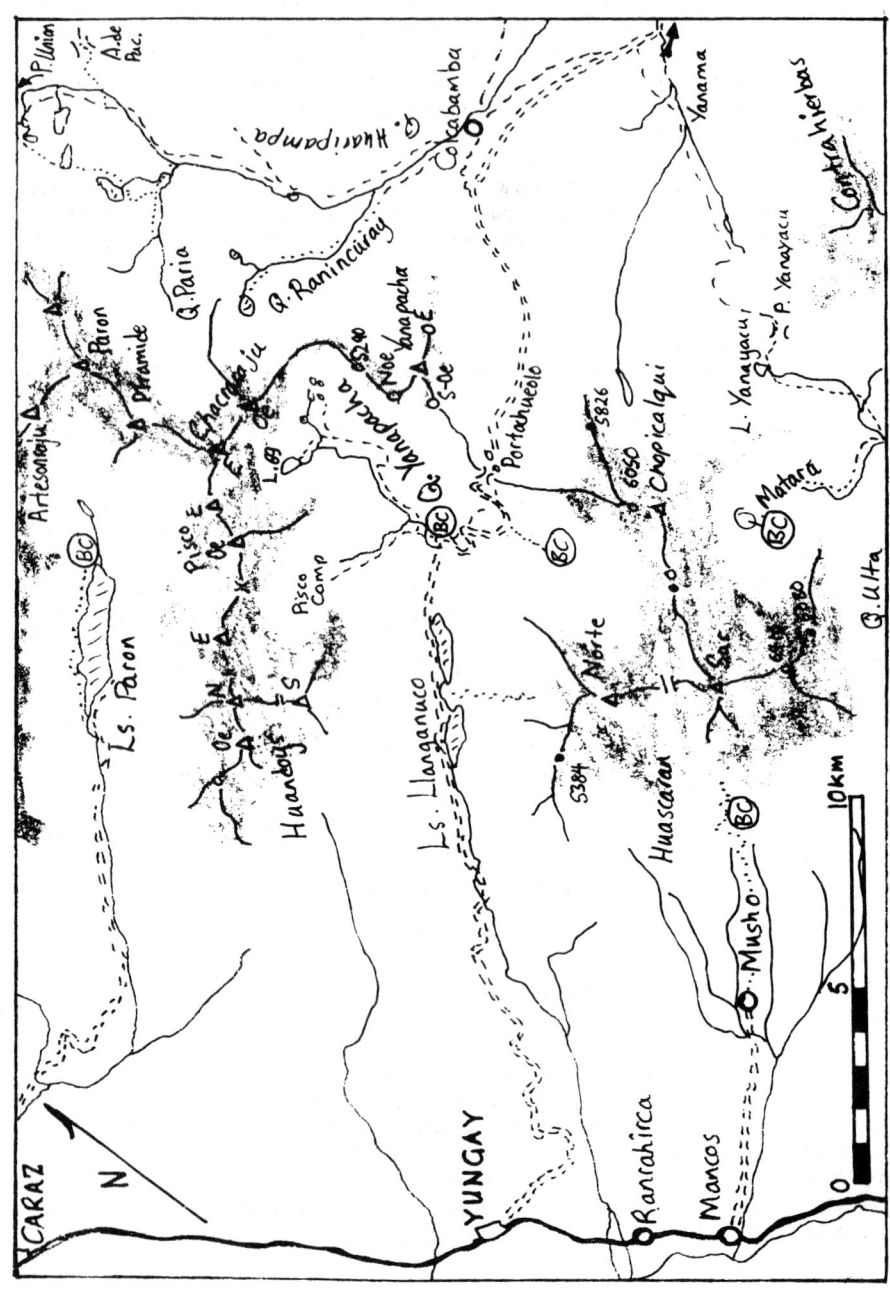

HUASCARAN MASSIF

Only three summits form this massif; the two Huascarans and that of Chopicalqui. However Huascaran Sur is the highest mountain in Peru and they are all bulky enough to support many good routes. The most popular is the Garganta route on Huascaran Sur. Whilst normally this is only a test of acclimatisation and endurance, problems can occur for the even very capable climbers. Relatively inexperienced 'trekkers' should think very carefully before attempting this route: falling into a crevasse is merely inconvenient at low altitudes, higher up even such a simple accident can rapidly become a serious epic.

Popular legend tells us that Huascaran was a woman spurned by her husband, who she castrated. She then fled from this tragedy with her children and when they halted they turned into the long chain of the Cordillera Blanca, their tears the source of the streams flowing to the Rio Santa and Maranon. A sad legend indeed.

Huascaran Norte, 6654:

NW. ridge: W. spur (Italian route); ED 1/2 ?. E.Detomasi, C.Piazzo, D.Saettone, T.Vidone; 25 July 1974.
From the base camp area of the normal approach to the Garganta cross the path of the 1970 avalanche track to the W glacier. To do this cross jumbled rocks, climb up a moraine and slabs to the W glacier of Huascaran Norte.
From 4800m climb the long and dangerously corniced W section of the NW ridge, 50°, with a mixed section at top, IV, bivouacs possible here at the junction with the Paragot route. Continue up mixed ground on the Llanganuco face, awkward ice penitentes, 50-60°. Go right, onto the W side, via a short gentle rock section, III. Bivouac here before the last very difficult rocks, a deep couloir, V. A1, IV at beginning. Join the summit ridge. Traces of fixed ropes are still evident, 2-4 days on ridge.

NW. face of NW. ridge (Polish-Czech variant); B.Danihelkova, Z.Hoffmanova, A.Kaploniak, E.Parnejko, E.Szezesniak; 14 July 1985. ED 1/2 ?.
From the visitor centre at the W end of the Llanganuco lakes climb up the narrow valley to the SE. Cross a short glacier to the base of the NW face of the NW ridge, 1 day.
Climb ice slopes to the right of a rock cliff on the left side. Above trend left under seracs and then go up to the crest of the NW ridge, 60-65° snow and ice. Follow the crest as for the Italian route to a junction with the Paragot route. This approach avoids the complex start to the Paragot and Italian routes. It is also possible to traverse directly from the seracs, across 55° slopes, to the top of the Pear; this and many other variations have been climbed between the Italian and the original Paragot lines.

N. face, (Paragot route); R.Jacob, C.Jacoux, D.Leprince-Ringuet, R.Paragot; 10 July 1966. ED 1/2 ?.
Cross between Llanganuco lakes to ascend gullies above Warmiqocha to top of moraines on W side of N glacier. Cross heavily crevassed glacier to base of an ice spur on W central part of the N face, 1-2 days.
Climb steep snow gullies, 80°, to reach a bastion of steep loose rock on the spur (the Pear), avoid this by climbing 60° ice on the right before traversing back left to regain the spur crest, then the crest to reach the junction of the spur with the ridge of the Italian route. Climb along the crenellated ridge to the junction with the N face ca.6250m. Traverse left for 250m into the middle of the final headwall. Climb up 200m of difficult, and steep, cracks and corners forming three tiers to reach the summit plateau, V and A1. 1600m, 4-7 days. Originally the Pear was taken more directly but access to the base of this line is difficult.

HUASCARAN MASSIF

N. face; R.Casarotto; 21 June 1977. ED ?.

This route begins left of the Paragot and slants up to the left side of the Pear. Then climb leftwards into the centre of the N face and continue directly up to the exit cracks of the Paragot,

Huascaran Norte - N face

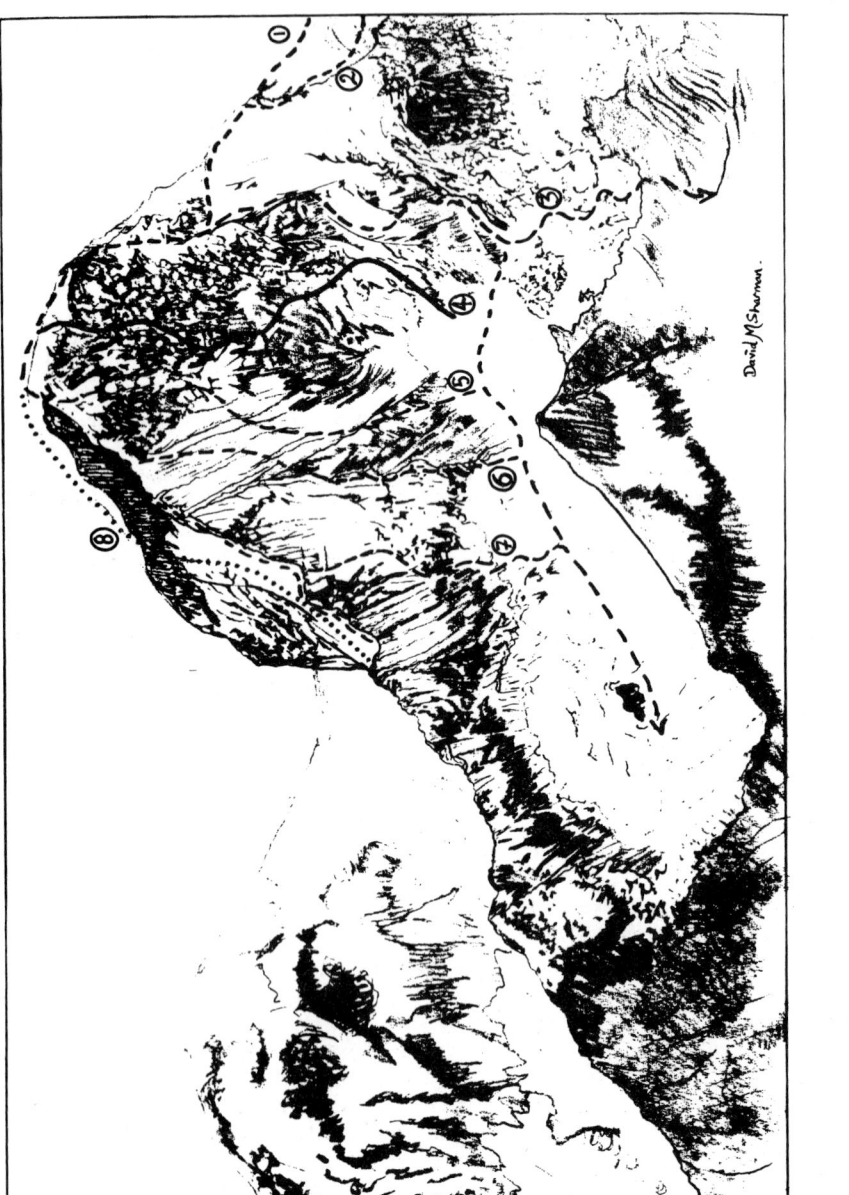

1. Italian
2. Polish-Czech

3. Paragot
4. Casarotto

5. Swiss
6. Spanish

7. NE ridge
8. NE face

1600m, VI+ and aid on both solid and rotten granite, snow and ice. Unrepeated, twenty days for first ascent, solo.

N. face (Swiss route); D.Anker, K.Saurer; 23 May 1986. ED 2+ ?.

This route begins right of the Spanish route and crosses it leftwards high up. Cross a difficult bergschrund and an icefield.

Climb two pitches of steep rock to the base of a big vertical icefall (bivouac site). Climb the vertical ice to the crest of the right toe. Continue up easier slopes, cross the Spanish route and climb up to the left of the base of the pillar. Three pitches of difficult rock on the left side of the pillar gain the NE ridge, follow this to the summit. Allow at least four days on face.

N. face (Spanish route); J.Moreno, C.Valles, J.Tomas; 20 July 1983. ED 2+ ?.

This unrepeated route climbs up the left side of the N face on extremely steep ground, VI, A3, 1300m. The first ascent was made in extremely dry conditions.

Climb the left toe of the spur falling from high on the NE ridge, VI, A1, 60° . At the junction with the right toe make an ascending traverse rightwards on 55-90° ice to the base of the rock pillar falling from the top of the NE ridge. Climb the rock pillar to its capping snowfield, VI, A3. Go left up the snowfield to join the NE ridge just below the summit. Allow several days for the ascent.

NE. ridge; R.Coene; M.Fevrier, J.Frehel, J.Porret; 18 August 1972. ED1.

From Q. Llanganuco ascend to N glacier. Either approach as for Paragot route or follow the path and road above Yuraq Coral. Leave the road at the right-most of the first set of zigzags and make a rising traverse to the glacier.

Climb a 50-65° ice gully on NW slopes of NE ridge to the highest col in the ridge, ca.5600m. Ascend the NE ridge, mostly ice climbing but there are four rock steps. The most difficult of these is at ca.6300m on rotten rock, III-IV with one pitch of V, allow 3-4 days for the ascent.

NE. face (French route); M.Barrard, L.Desrivieres, G.Narbaud, J.Ricouard; 18 August 1973. TD/ED.

This is reported to be an outstanding climb. Ascend moraines on W side of Gl. Llanganuco to slopes below the glacier tongue which falls from the NE ice face. Ascend the glacier on the left side to the first bergschrund, ca.5300m. Pass this and climb 60° snow slopes to the higher bergschrund, turning a prominent rocky outcrop on the left. Keeping right of a steep snow arete on the left side of the face continue upwards, trending left as the angle eases to 50° to gain the rock band at its narrowest point, ca.6300m. Make a rising traverse leftwards for one pitch, V+, and then climb 20m of A2 upwards to the top. Old fixed ropes in evidence. Continue easily to the summit, two days.

S. ridge; A.Peck, R.Taugwalder, G.zum Taugwald; 2 September 1908; This first ascent is somewhat disputed. PD+/AD-.

From Garganta normal route camp I, ca.5900m, go towards the S face of the N summit, cross a small bergschrund bordered by small seracs and climb the 40° slopes directly below the visible summit. Gain a plateau at the foot of the long S ridge and climb this directly to the top, 6-8h from the camp II.

Huascaran Sur, 6768:

E. icefall; J.Agullo, J.Angles, T.Bros, J.Prunes, R.Biosco, R.Pajares; September 1980.

Climb to the Garganta from the E, crossing through the right side of the changeable ice fall and then up the left centre of the N slope, easier ground.

NE. face (Anqosh face, French route); B.Grison; 14 July 1985. ED 1.

This route was ascended by Buhler and Wood shortly after the first ascent and they noted that it was exposed to stonefall. Follow the Chopicalqui base camp approach up the E side of Q. Anqosh, cross the Llanganuco glacier moraine and reach the Chopicalqui moraine camp, 5h. Traverse W below a toe of rock and pick a way through seracs, 4-8h.

In the middle of the face a rock pillar juts from the wall. Cross a bergschrund and 45° slopes, to a second bergschrund below a narrow ice gully right of the pillar. Climb this through a 200m rock band and over a snow arete to the first icefield. Continue up a series of steep ice grooves and faces, separated from one another by large fins of fragile snow and sections of mixed ground. Reach a 150m rock band capping the entire face, traverse right as this becomes seamed with ice runnels to mid-height. Climb a 10m left-slanting off-width crack through the steepest section and the cornices above. This gains the Spanish ridge ca.6400m, 2-4 days.

NE. face (Anqosh face, Slovenian variation); P.Kozjek; 14 July 1991. TD+.

This variant is easier than the French route in the lower part, with fewer rock problems. It is extremely exposed to stonefall in the link between the central and upper snowfields, ca.5800m, which should be climbed early in the day.

Approach as for the French route to the glacial bay left of the central rock pillar, 31/2 -4h from Chopicalqui moraine camp. Cross the first bergschrund in the centre and the second on the right. Climb the right-hand narrowing couloir, 60° , until it becomes necessary to climb diagonally left on 25m of IV rock to gain ice smears leading to the central snowfield, 1h. There is a small bivouac site here on ledges protected from stonefall by overhangs. Ascend the centre of the 55-65° central snowfield, 2-3h. At the top take a 50m/75° snow tongue off to the left (rather than climbing more directly on steeper ice) which leads to the upper snowfield. Traverse right to a 65° snow arete and follow this to join the French route ca.6100m, 2-3h, skirting right past the worst

Huascaran Sur & Norte - NE faces

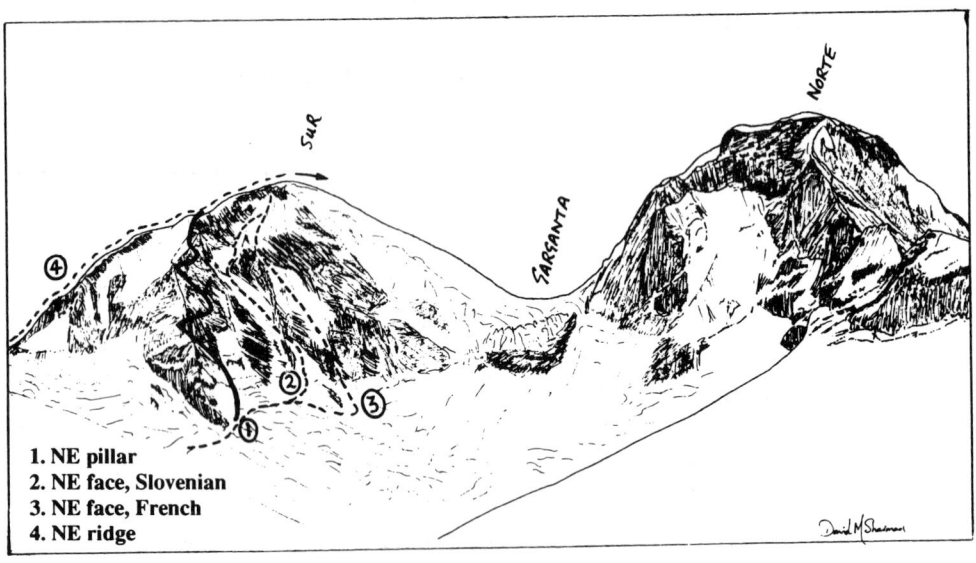

1. NE pillar
2. NE face, Slovenian
3. NE face, French
4. NE ridge

of a short mixed section, 10m/V. Two days total.

NE Pillar (The Road To Hell); M.Kovac, B.Lozar, T.Petac; 21 July 1993. ED.

This takes the easiest route up the wide pillar left of the Slovenian variation to reach the NE ridge 570m from the top, after 1300m of independent climbing which links left-slanting ramps with short rock sections; mostly 60-85°/V-VI. Starting at the right side of the pillar follow a line of snow ramp diagonally left to gain the left side at half-height. Traverse right across a snow shelf, turn a tower on its left (VI+, 90°, A1) and climb snowfields direct to the ridge, 21/2 days. Follow the ridge to the summit.

HUASCARAN MASSIF

NE. (Spanish) ridge; P.Acuna, F.Mautino, A.Perez, S.Rivas; 18 July 1961. TD+.
From Chopicalqui col, 5426m, cross into the upper part of the Matara glacier and climb broad snow slopes to reach the serious NE ridge, cornices and snow mushrooms, 2-4 days up.

E. face (Austrian); S.Hasitschka, E.Koblmuller, E.Lackner, C.Pollet, R.Schulz; 26 July 1972. ED-.
Climb Gl. Matara and N central side of E face, on a great sweeping icefield to ca.6300m.
Traverse right to weaknesses in granite rock wall ca.6650m (stonefall hazard).
Climb the steep, rotten, icy wall in 14h and continue up easier slopes of SE ridge to summit, 2-4 days.

E. face (Austrian direct); F.Six, A.Indrich; 8 August 1979. ED.
This unrepeated line was climbed in very dry conditions. It takes the centre of the E face directly. After passing the bergschrund ca.5500m via a 70° ice gully move left to gain the crest of a rock buttress seamed with ice.
Climb this to avoid severe stonefall hazard in flanking gullies. Gain the foot of the vertical summit wall ca.6400m and climb rock, V, and rotten ice to the summit plateau. An attempt to make a rising traverse left over icy slabs failed, and the headwall was finally surmounted via crack system on the right, 6 days ascent.

E. face (ANZAC route); P.Coradine, R.Ryan, R.Schneider, G.Wyatt; 24 June 1971. TD+.
Go up Gl.Matara and climb avalanche cone below S central side of the E face to reach the left end of the lower rock wall. Pass rightwards through these buttresses on a snow ramp to reach a mixed ridge, mainly 50-60° snow.
Climb this to reach a rightwards curving sickle-shaped snowfield ca.6400m, one day from bergschrund.

Huascaran Sur - E face

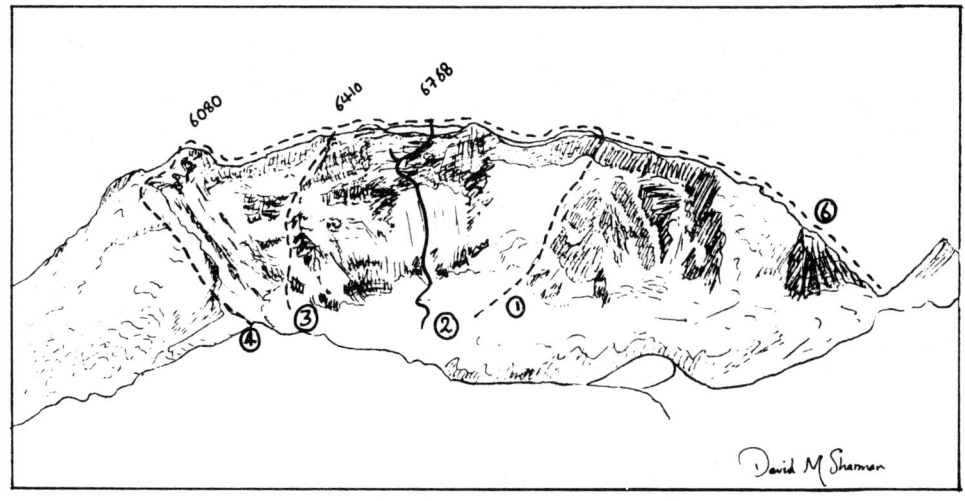

| 1. Austrian | 3. ANZAC | 5. Sw glacier |
| 2. Austrian direct | 4. SE ridge | 6. NE ridge |

Climb rightwards on the sickle, 65° , and then 250m of progressively more difficult ice and granite to join the SE ridge, two days from the bergschrund. Continue up SE ridge to summit, three days. A minor variant begins slightly to the right (N), climbing ice gullies from the high point of the glacier, to reach the snowfields.

SE. ridge; B.Jenkinson, M.Jones, J.Strang; 21 June 1971. TD.

Go up Q. Matara to a good bivouac at ca.5050 below the SE ridge. Climb up past dangerous crevasses to reach the ridge proper, first snow then rock and ice. There is overhanging rock ca.5800, also a restricted bivouac site (rock ledge or snow cave) a little lower. Turn the overhang to the S and climb dangerous snow slopes to P6080. Bivouac site beyond in crevasse. Climb the ice face above to P6410, a tent platform. Climb the narrow, steep, double-corniced snow ridge to the S summit's plateau. Four days from above Q. Matara to summit.

SW. glacier, SE. ridge; F.Ayres, H.Kendall, W.Mathews, D.Michael, I.Ortenburger, L.Ortenburger; 29 July 1958. D+.

From Q. Ulta ascend steep ravine to SW glacier or, easier, ascend the N bank of the Q. Qeshururi via Tumpa and cross boulder alluvium to the SW, Pamparaju, glacier. Ascend SW glacier adjacent to SW ridge to col between the high peak and P6410. The col is reached by a horizontal traverse across the steep NE slopes of P6410. Traverse, partly in bottomless snow, and partly along the edge of the exposed granitic E face, up the SE summit ridge, turning minor peaks on the E, 2-3 days ascent. It is equally possible to climb the SW ridge itself to the SE ridge. Join it from the glacier at the gap after the first of four steps. Turn the second and third rocky steps on the right. Pass the forth step by 50-60° ice on the left. Continue up the ridge.

W. arete (Shield route); W.Broda, S.Merler, B.Segger; 15 June 1969. D+.

Approach as for Garganta route but traverse SE on glacier and climb through seracs to gain knife-edge W ice arete, ca.5900m.

Climb this, or 50-60° , 400m, mitre-shaped W face on the left, to summit. One or two days return from base of arete. This is a good route if the Garganta icefall is impassable.

W. slopes (Garganta route); H.Bernard, P.Borchers, E.Hein, H.Hoerlin, E.Schneider; 20 July 1932. PD.

This climb is not suitable for unguided novices as the route finding is often complex and an awareness of glacier techniques vital. The crux is passing through the changeable Garganta icefall: enquire in Huaraz about the current solution. Follow the high street eastwards out of Musho, keep on the main path and pass a eucalyptus plantation. Take, a small path on the right (cairned) which goes up the left flank of the valley to reach the foot of a moraine. Half way up bear right towards a quenal grove and climb up the path to the base camp, 3h, often called camp Raimondi. To reach the moraine camp go right to some large smooth slabs and climb them easily, following cairns. Cross a stream and climb a grassy gully to reach the foot of a large smooth slab. Above the path goes up to the right and crosses three streams. Follow cairns across a moraine system then more, open, slabs, set up camp here, or use the platforms a little higher at the edge of the glacier, 2-3h. (Alternatively follow cairns directly above the base camp, towards the N side of the Garganta icefall, and reach the 'Russian' moraine camp in 11/2h. Above either try to pass the icefall on the N side, or make a difficult traverse below the icefall to join the normal route, 5-8h.) Climb wide slopes directly up towards the base of the serac zone which forms the crux of the climb, 3-4h. Normally it is best to climb just to the N of rocks at the S side of the seracs, although some years a way can be found at the far left. Once above traverse E towards the windswept Garganta col and set up camp I ca.5900m, 4-5h, 30-45° . Broad serac strewn slopes lead up to the summit, 8-12h, 30-40° . The greatest difficulty is bypassing occasional large crevasses. If this presents a problem then try traversing E, where a solution can normally be found. It is reported that windslab sometimes forms. If the Garganta icefall is unjustifiable then try the W arete.

P5600:

Unknown route on ice and rock pinacle between col 5426 and P5666; J.Anglada, F.Mendez, J.Pons, J.Bescos, F.Guillamon, J.Regil; 16 July 1961,

HUASCARAN MASIF

P5666:
NW. slopes of minor peak E of Huascaran-Chopicalqui col; J.Bescos, J.Regil; 18 July 1961.

Chopicalqui, 6354:
Unfortunately details are sparse regarding a number of fine-looking lines on this peak. The WNW spur, NW ridge, and SW ridge are all worthwhile. Deep snow on the summit slopes causes most failures for parties on the SW ridge. The name means 'by the side of the centre'.

W. face (Strah in Sreca); F.Knez, M.Freser; 12 June 1982.
A direct route up the centre of the 1000m face over 50-60° ground in two days to reach the NW ridge. Sticks to the left hand side of the central avenue, climbing the easiest and least threatened line up snow and ice.

WNW. spur; M.Rolland, J-J.Rolland, A.Roberts, H.Sigayret; 2 July 1981. TD+.
This route ascends the prominent 1000m high spur which is well to the right (S) of the NW ridge, and ends at the ice tower of Chopicalqui Norte, 6050m.
Approach as for the NW ridge to the glacier. Cross the bergschrund on the left of the spur and climb rocks on the crest, III/IV, to a bivouac. Then climb 650m (12 pitches), of ice with some mixed ground, on the left side of the spur until a second bivouac site below short steep rock walls. Delicately traverse right, V+, from ca.5700m to the crest and climb this to large snow slopes below the NW ridge. Ascend these rightwards to the summit avoiding the N peak if desired, 2-4 days from base camp. The route is objectively very safe.

NW. face; E.Dossin; 24 July 1982. TD.
This bold route takes the snow fluting which ascends directly to Chopicalqui Norte.
Approach as for WNW spur and climb gullies through right side of icefall to reach the bergschrund at its highest point, ca.5700m. Climb the widest central furrow to the N summit, 60-70°.
The first ascent was solo in one day, immediately after the route was swept by an avalanche. 2-3 days to true summit from base camp.

NW. face; D.Tic, M.Romih; 25 May 1986. TD.
Approach as for the NW ridge and climb the leftmost flute on the face proper tp reach the ridge just right of the serac which caps the nose of the NW ridge. Continue as for the NW ridge, passing Chopicalqui Norte to reach the summit. Generally 60° but some vertical sections, 800m in all.

NW. ridge; A.Cooper, B.Everett, J.Janney, W.Philips; 12 July 1969. (first ascent beyond Chopicalqui Norte by Czechs in June 1980). D+/TD-.
A splendid route usually combined with a descent by the SW ridge to create an immaculate traverse. Allow three days to return to the road.
From Chopicalqui base camp by Llanganuco road scramble up rock and grass slopes to the ESE. Pick a way up easy rock slabs to the left to gain the glacier, 3h. Climb the glacier towards the foot of a minor rock peak, and the rocky continuation to the foot of the NW ridge, bivouac site, 2h. Climb snow slopes to a col at the base of the ridge which is a 60° wall, capped by serac. Climb up to, and pass this serac to reach the ridge crest. Traverse the narrow ridge on the southern side to gain Chopicalqui Norte, 6050m. Abseil onto the joining ridge which is usually best climbed on the NE side, 55°, to reach the main summit.

HUASCARAN MASSIF

NW. ridge variant; A.Bouyssiere, J.Lacaze, C.Mourembles; 26 July 1977.
Climb difficult rocks of the NE spur of the lower buttress to ca.5700. Climb snow, ice, or mixed

Chopicalqui - N face

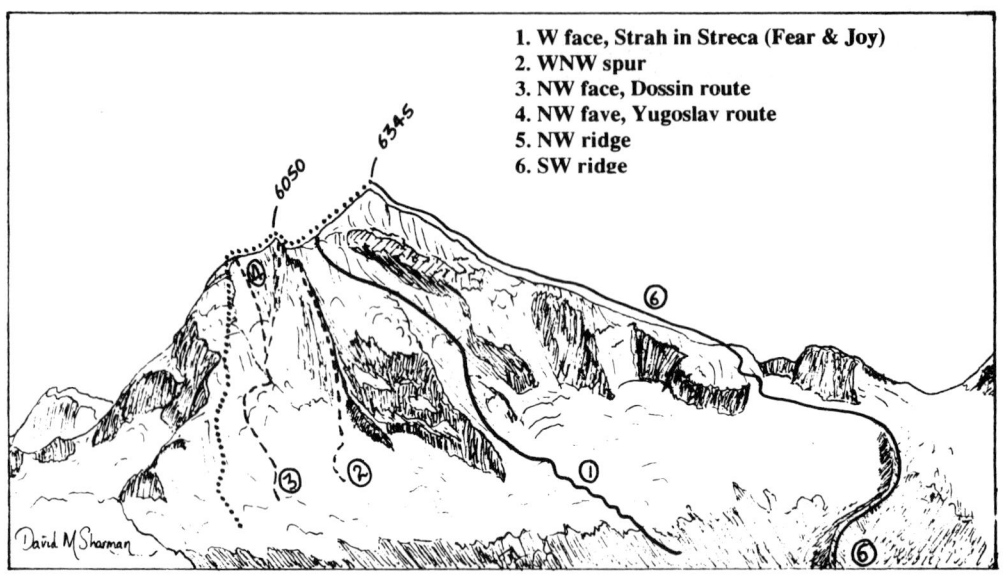

1. W face, Strah in Streca (Fear & Joy)
2. WNW spur
3. NW face, Dossin route
4. NW fave, Yugoslav route
5. NW ridge
6. SW ridge

ground to the main ridge.

NNE. face; V.Lant; end July 1977. Unknown solo in 2 days.

E. ridge; X.Chappaz, R.Desmaison, A.Vagne, M.Arizzi; 25 August 1982. TD+ ?.
From the head of the Q. Ulta cross the Chopicalqui E glacier and begin the E ridge from the col. Enormous fragile cornices and mushrooms, rotten rock, and abandoned fixed ropes. Several days. Significant objective hazards.

SE. ridge; M.Clarbrough, G.Wayatt; 20 June 1969. TD-.
From Q.Ulta climb SE ridge, joining SW ridge near the summit. Cornices can be avoided by climbing steeper ground on adjacent faces. (Original descent by NW ridge.) Three days.

S. face; Y.Uejima, H.Kamuro; 8 August 1979. TD ?.
From the glacier above the Q. Matara gain the base of the face. On the right climb through the serac belt which guards the lower face. Follow an ice gully to a snow flute which reaches the SE ridge. Follow this to the summit. Appears to present a few anxious days.

SW. ridge; H.Hoerlin, E.Schneider, P.Borchers, E.Hein; 3 August 1932. PD+/AD-.
The normal route on the mountain, often with deep snow, and consistently under-estimated.
From the most SW hairpin of the Llanganuco road, by a distinctive split moraine, follow a path S up a small valley to reach a campsite, 20 mins. Slightly up-valley find a cairned path leading up the right-hand (W) moraine crest. After a few metres drop down the other side into a rubble-covered glacial valley and follow cairns to regain the path on the far side. Ascend a steep moraine crest to a camp site, 31/2 -5h. Go up to gain the glacier, and ascend it towards the minor peak P5666. Trend left before this, climbing a series of plateaux to col campsite ca.5600m, 3-4h.
Avoid some large crevasses in gaining the broad lower slopes of the ridge proper, 50° . Pass a group of seracs on the left - crux, and follow a narrow exposed crest on to the summit. Some risk of slab avalanches. The seracs are normally fronted by a large crevasse. If this seems impassable

try looking at the extreme left end, abseil a few metres and climb up. The col ca.5600 may be gained from Q.Matara by climbing SE glacier and steep ice slopes, 1961 variation.

SW. face; M.Barrard, P.Vallencant; 22 July 1977. Unknown route on 'SW' face ?

P5575:

SW. slopes; D.Drake, G.Holdsworth; 14 August 1969.

From Q.Ulta go onto the E glacier of Chopicalqui and cross it to SW snow slopes and ridge.

CONTRAHIERBAS MASSIF

This seldom-visited massif is actually a single glacier-covered slate mountain. Access is now easy on the road up Q. Ulta which goes over the newly completed Punta de Shilla to Chacas. This may lead to a reassessment of the area, many hard lines surely await discovery.

P5166:

Unknown route from Q. Ulta; P.Schiml, H.Ziegenhardt; June 1977.

Contrahierbas, 6036:

NNE. ridge; S.Rohrer, K.Schmid, H.Schweizer; 28 May 1939.

From Q. Ichik Ulta climb up diagonally across N glacier of Pca.5675 and NW glacier of P5960. Bypass P5960 on the W and gain NNE corniced summit ridge, cornices overhang to the E. Ascent 11h from NW glacier edge ca.4850.

NW. face; F.Ayres, H.Kendall, W.Mathews, D.Michael, I.Ortenburger, L.Ortenburger, G.Whitmore; 20 July 1958.

From Q. Ulta gain L. Artesa and climb up to the NW ridge just right of P5490. Descend a slatey rock cliff on the NE side to the NW glacier and climb the easy NW snow face to the summit. One day return from a camp on NW ridge, ca.5350m.

Cajavilca I, 5775:

N. ridge; L.Irwin, J.Ricker; 27 July 1966.

From Yanama go to NW glacier edge ca.4850m (camp ca.4650m). Ascend ice avalanche threatened slate pavements to NW ridge Cajavilca II, 5675m.

Climb mixed snow and rock ridge to summit and traverse up snowy N ridge to Cajavilca I. One day return from camp.

Cajavilca III, 5419:

N. slopes; L.Irwin, J.Ricker; 22 July 1966.

From camp ca.4650m above Yanama ascend N glacier and snow slopes, one day return.

COPA MASSIF

The broad plateaus of Copa and Hualcan form the backbone of this massif. It drops gently to the West, but more sharply on other sides. The northern ridgeline rears up to the difficult Ulta, and the south-eastern ridgeline forms the clump of small peaks by Paccaraju, a good place for a short trip amongst easy routes. With the exception of peaks East of Paccaraju, the massif is composed of granite.

Access is by road to Q. Ulta in the North, or to Q. Honda in the South. All base camps can then be reached by a short walk.

P5325:
Unknown route from Q. Ulta; H.Handel, S.Hohenreiter, P.Schiml, H.Ziegenhardt; June 1977.

P5375:
S. ridge from col ca.5300m; E.Erdmann, C.Schiel; 8 July 1961.

Ulta, 5875:
Many attempts on this steep pyramid are unsuccessful. It is named for the tadpoles which teem in the many small ponds nearby.

NW. face; P.Dawson, D.Cheesmond; 18 August 1977.
A snow rib falls directly from the summit ridge. To the left is a huge oval cirque flanked on the left by the N ridge. On the right are ice flutings, the one nearest the rib runs almost to the summit. Climb this, steep snow and ice at the bottom leading to mixed ground, and at the top go right to avoid the summit cornices and climb three pitches up the W ridge.
NE. face; K.Bogne, G.Kampfe, R.Hechtel, D.Liska; 8 July 1961.
From Q. Ulta climb NW hanging glacier to col, ca.5300m, between Ulta and P5375. Ascend NE glacier and snow rib on NE face.
Climb steep ice to reach the N ridge, proceed to summit up snow slopes.
E. ridge; 'Waldo'McQuoid and party; 1981. TD. No further details of this Irish ascent.

Chugllaraju, 5575:
A corruption of the word for a steeply pointed grass hut.

NW. face; K.Bogner, E.Erdmann, C.Schiel; 12 July 1961.
From Q. Ulta ascend moraine to camp ca.4700m at edge of chaotic NW glacier. Go up this and climb avalanche-prone glacier slopes under W face of Ulta.
Climb NW face and 30m ice pinnacle at the summit, 15h return from camp.

Cancaraca, 5512:
W. ridge; G.Bianchi, C.Nembrini, F.Robecchi; 27 July 1973.
From Q. Ulta and Wallkacocha cirque climb rock and ice of W ridge.

Cheqiaraju, 5286:
The throat mountain after its position between Ulta and Hualcan.

N. slopes; M.Angeles, F.Ayres, L.Ortenburger, G.Whitmore; 3 August 1958.
Climb from Q. Ulta.

COPA MASSIF

E. side; M.Angeles, E.Bauer, D.Brown, C.Heller, H.Kendall, J.Lomont, P.Morales, O.Zuniga; 3 July 1960.
From Auquiscocha cirque.
SW. ridge; A.Bell, H.Clark, D.Teegardin; 27 December 1971.
From Auquiscocha gain Pariacaca-Cheqiaraju col, and climb SW ridge.

Pariacaca (or Tullparaju, or Kunkaraju), 5106:

N. ridge; G.Whitmore; 3 August 1958.
Climb from Cheqiaraju over rock needle ca.5130.
E. ridge; G.Gottesheim, H.Losch, H.Jesacher, K.Lapuch; early June 1979.
Climb from Auquiscocha in one day, IV.

P5250:

S. slopes; E.Angeles, D.Noordijk, F.Scheve, A.van Royens, R.Vermeer, J.van Royens; 23 June 1973.
Q. Honda, Q. Illauro, Q. Wichjanka approach and S slopes of this point 3km NE of Hualcan.

P5300:

W. side; F.Driessen, J.van Royen; 24 June 1973.
From Q. Wichjanka climb SW ridge, W.face, and steep upper NW ridge of this point 3km E of P5250. One day return from Q. Wichjanka.

Hualcan, 6125:

This mountain is named for a type of broad frilly lace collar which can be a part of local costume. The East side of the mountain is strangely unexploited, but now very accessible via the new road.

S. ridge; S.Rohrer, K.Schmid; early August 1939.
From W glacier gain S ridge at a point 1km N of P5850 by climbing inside corner of hanging glacier on W wall of S ridge.
Climb S ridge to summit and continue to Hualcan Oeste, 6104m, via an easy ridge.
SW. ridge Oeste; J.Slaymaker, D.Ciochetti; 7 July 1975.
From a campsite by lakes at the upper end of Q. Hualcan go up moraines on the left side of the glacier. Go up the left side of the glacier then cross to the right to climb a 50-55° snow face right of a mixed section. Bypass a serac barrier on the left and gain the base of the SW ridge, past a bergschrund on the right, or a steep wall on the left. Follow the crest past more difficult sections before reaching the summit of Oeste, 6104m, 6-7h. Follow the almost level W ridge to reach the main summit. Descend by S ridge route.

P5645, (Hualcan Sur II):

NW. side; E.Angeles, M.Angeles, D.Giobbi; 22 July 1971. PD ?.
Approach via Q. Hualcan, ascend NW glacier and slopes. Final pitch on 50° slopes on NE side.
SW. side; M.Angeles, V.Angeles, H.Walther, H.Zogg; 16 June 1962. PD ?.
Climb from the SW, approaching from Chancos

P5500:

This minor snowy point between Copa and Hualcan was first climbed from the W by the 1932 DOAV party, and is probably the place where Hoerlin went to live alone for two weeks to make cosmic ray measurements in 1932.

COPA MASSIF

Copa Norte, 6173:
N. slopes; unnamed Peruvians with DOAV party; 1932. PD.
Originally descended in error in fog by Peruvian porters with the 1932 DOAV party. Really a W slopes variant.
S. ridge; H.Abrons, I.Ortenburger, L.Ortenburger; 30 June 1964. PD-.
Traverse from main summit Copa.
From 6188m descend to the N on easy but crevassed slopes. Keep to the crest on the edge of the E face, pass under a minor summit and climb the N summit skirting the last slope to the left, 2-3h.
W. slopes; P.Borchers, E.Hein, H.Hoerlin, H.Kinzl, E.Schneider, and a number of Ancashino porters; 1932. PD.
Approach from Hda. Copa. Climb initially gentle W glacier slopes to high plateau ca.5450 (vague col area ca.P5500) and ascend slightly steepening NW slopes.

Copa, 6188:
Supposedly Copa looks like a laborer's cheap felt sombrero. Regardless it does possess an easy route to the top of a 6000m peak, one which is easily skied and suitable for accompanied trekkers. The East slopes are as yet unexploited.

SE. face; D.Anderson, J.Humphrey, J.Richardson; 11 July 1962. AD/D ?.
From Q. Paccharuri ascend a moraine crest to glacier just below Nev. Vicos, ca.5000m, and climb this to its rightmost corner. Climb a short section of icy slabs and then seracs to gain the top of a high hanging glacier and ridge ca.5600m. Go up the S ridge past a short mixed step. Descend as for W slopes.
W. slopes; E.Hein, E.Schneider; 26 September 1932. PD-.
The best base camp is 15 minutes before the lake, at the highest trees. From the ruined houses at L. Legiacocha walk to the N of the lake and climb a 45° snow couloir between rocky crags. This gives access to the gentle N side of the W ridge which has a steeper S face.
Climb easily past some crevasses, and seracs ca.5700m, to an easy bergschrund before the steeper summit dome, 6-9h, continue on up S ridge of the N summit if desired.

Vicos (Paccharuri), 5325:
These minor tops on the S ridge of Copa provide a beautiful traverse to those based near Legiacocha.

S-N traverse; A.Gamarra, A.Morales, J.Mariategui, T.Matellini, J.Torres, J.Vidal y Vidal; 16 July 1952. F.
From Legiacocha go around the lake to the S and cross easy slabs to a col ca.5000m on the S ridge, with a rocky peak to the S.
Climb easily up the beautiful snow ridge past both summits, 4h. Continue along the ridge and descend across the glacier to the lake, 2h, or descend 40° NNW slopes directly (first ascent line). Excellent views from the ridge.

Bayoraju, 5460:
SE. ridge; D.Anderson, J.Richardson, C.Staples; 1 July 1962. PD ?.
Either make a long traverse after approaching as for SW slopes Paccharaju, 5-7h from huts, or traverse screes W of lake and climb glacier direct to col ca.5200m on SE side. Climb SE ridge to summit.

COPA MASSIF

Paccharaju, 5744:

This cirque contains a number of good easy routes, all possible in one day from old Hidrandina huts by the lake. The walk to the huts is easy, 1km after portada on Q. Honda road turn left up the excellent trail which is incised in the cliff to the left of the obvious waterfall (from which the mountain and valley derive their names). Follow this obvious trail to the blue lake in 3 1/2 h. The main peak is just out of sight from the huts, and has two fine S summits as well as the N summits.

SW. ridge variant; G.Feichtenschlager, D.M.Sharman; 28 July 1991. PD.

A fine climb with a pleasantly exposed ridge section. Approach as for SW slopes but once onto the glacier climb to first S summit via a gully at the right end of the seracs, 150m, 50°, 2h. Then climb SW ridge to the higher, second, rock-capped S top - the final section on W side via 200m 50° ice, 1-2h. Continue to main summit in 1h.

SW. slopes; D.Anderson, L.Carter, J.Richardson, H.Carter, P.Carter, R.Goody, J.Humphreys, H.McDade, C.Staples; 4 July 1962. F.

Walk from the huts to the spillway, and then up easy grass and moraine to the glacier edge at the highest point, 2h, in line with P5220. Traverse N and E along the glacier shelf below the seracs, before picking a way through crevasses to join 40-50° SW ridge immediately below summit, 3-4h.

Paccharaju Norte I, 5665:

SW. face; D.Anderson, L.Carter, J.Richardson; 4 July 1962. F.

After approaching as for SW slopes main peak climb this in 1/2 -1h from col with main peak on short 45° slopes.

Paccharaju Norte II, 5600:

S. face; R.Goody, J.Humphreys, C.Staples, P.C arter, J.Richardson; 5 July 1962. F.

Approach as for SW slopes main peak. Climb easy S slopes or traverse from Norte I, a few hours only.

P5220:

W. side; H.Carter, L.Carter, H.McDade; 8 July 1962. F.

The rocky high point on S ridge Pacharaju. Easy climbing in 3h from glacier edge, choosing final route to give desired amount of scrambling. This ridge continues S. Many excellent rock climbs and scrambles can be constructed at all levels of difficulty by climbing directly opposite the huts. The traverse of the ridge to the prominent point is suitable for trekkers.

Atlante, 5465:

SE. side; A.Ketchin, G.Ziegler; 3 August 1968. PD ?.

Appears to be a good fun traverse, starting at Portachuelo de Honda, over Mancaraju, 5350m (J.Graafland, F.Kleine; 23 July 1965) and the summit before continuing down W ridge and back under the S face to the pass in one day return.

Chaqchipuncu, 5280:

Some of the peaks on this ridge group to NNE of Atlante were climbed by the Japanese party of 1966, e.g. Yacuhuarmi, 5259m.

PERLILLA MASSIF

The summits of the Perlilla massif rim a bowl set into the top of a broad plateau ca.5200m. Once onto the broad platea it is reported that there are few difficulties in gaining any of the summits lining the rim . Deep snow often appears the principal obstacle and most routes are an easy day out. Ideal trekking peaks, or for skiing around, but to a certain extent devoid of other interest.
The massif is formed of sedimentary and metamorphic rocks and there are various mines scattered nearby. Mina Tomalamano to the South is a very rich silver lode which has been worked since 1928 and looks set to continue. The ore from this mine used to be transported by burro, down the Q. Honda, to Vicos but now is transported over the Partachuelo de Honda to the eastern side of the range - these are also the prical approach routes.

Portachuelo, 5340:

N. ridge; J.Filsinger, J.Hough, S.Turner; 29 June 1963. F/PD ?.
After 1-2h scrambling along the ridge from Portachuelo de Honda gain the short N glacier and cross this to climb the N ridge, 1-2h.

P5205:

E. slopes; Colorado Mountain Club party; early June 1963. F.
From Q. Honda ascend Mina Tomalamano valley and glacier on S side of peak to Copap plateau. Climb short E slopes and E rock ridge in one day return.
W. ridge; F.Chamberlin, R.Neave, R.Strader; 13 July 1963. PD ?.
From S glacier climb a steep couloir to gain W ridge col. Climb subsidiary W peak (ca.5000m), traverse W and ascend snow couloir on N side of peak. Descend E ridge etc. in one day return.

Pacarish, 5276:

E. ridge; F.Chamberlin, R.Neave, J.Petroske, R.Strader; 15 July 1963.
From Q. Honda ascend Mina Tomalamano valley and glacier beyond S cliffs of P5205 to gain Copap plateau. Cross plateau to climb SE glacier and E rock ridge.
W. buttress; H.Bussey, G.Poush; 24 July 1973.
From Copap plateau climb the rocky W buttress.

Copap V, 5300:

NW. slopes; F.Chamberlin, E.Gibson, R.Lagaci, R.Neave, S.Turner; 5 July 1963. F.
From Q. Honda ascend Mina Tomalamano valley on the S side of P5205. Climb easy NW snow slopes of this snow dome to summit. One day return from Q. Honda.
S. slopes; D.Bamford, R.Rowlands; August 1973. F.
Follow the Q. Honda-Chacas trail to 1km E of Rinconada and cross to the N side of the valley. Follow the river until the base of the first glacial tongue after Copap V. Climb up the moraine to the NW of this to gain the snow plateau ca.5200m. Climb the S slopes to the top in one day return. This approach can be used to reach other routes above the plateau, which are also short easy climbs.

Copap IV (Condormina Sur), 5566:

Unknown route from Q. Honda; J.Hough, S.Turner; 3 July 1963.
NW. ridge; M.Duport, P.Jaunin, L.Rentchnik, P.Staub; 19 July 1971. F.
Approach as for S slopes V. Climb short NW ridge from Copap plateau ca.5200m, 2h.

P5410:

E. slopes; D.Bamford, R.Rowlands; 4 August 1973. F.
From the Copap plateau climb the easy E slopes.

PERLILLA MASSIF

Copap III (Condormina Norte), 5551:
W. face; M.Duport, P.Jaunin, L.Rentchnik, P.Staub; 20 July 1971. F.
From the Copap plateau ca.5200m climb flutings on short W face. Also easily traversed N-S.

Copap II (Yanatsilca Sur), 5567:
S. ridge; N.Benton, H.Steyskal; 21 July 1971. F.
Climb this snow ridge from the col with Copap III. Continue down N ridge if desired in one day return.
W. face; M.Duport, P.Jaunin, L.Rentchnik, P.Staub; 18 July 1971.
Climb the W face from a camp on the plateau ca.5200m.

Copap I (Yanatsilca Norte), 5579:
N. ridge; N.Benton, A.Hamilton, B.Gestell, A.Pines, B.Reenstra; 20 July 1979. F.
Climb ridge from col above plateau.
S. ridge; N.Benton, H.Steyskal; 21 July 1979. F.
Traverse from Copap II.
W. face; M.Duport, P.Jaunin, L.Rentchnik, P.Staub; 18 July 1971. F.
Climb the W face from a camp on the snow plateau ca.5200m.

Perlilla, 5587:
S. ridge; M.Ishinabe, A.Kurihara, H.Miyahara, Y.Ohe, T.Suzuki; 14 July 1966. F.
From Q. Honda ascend to Copap plateau as for S slopes V and climb the S ridge from the S col, in a short day from the plateau.

Purisima, 5177:
N. slopes; R.Aranda, H.Carter, E.Henostroza, G.Henosrtoza; 30 June 1968.
From Q. Rurichinchay ascend Yanamayu. From the E side traverse around to the N. Climb steep ice and rock on N slopes. One day return from camp ca.5000m above Yanamayu.

CHINCHEY MASSIF

The Chinchey massif is right next door to Huaraz, a feature which undoubtedly has played a part in the extensive development of the area. This accessibility means that the valleys are especially suitable for short trips, perhaps to acclimatise or to climb a specific route. Conversely the maturity of the area means that any one valley can easily satisfy a longer stay. Quebradas Llaca or Ishinca are most popular for acclimatisation, and Quilcaywanka for longer periods.

The geography of this important massif is complicated. It has been arbitarily divided into three chains which, broadly speaking, nestle inside one another. To the East is the Pacific divide chain of Chinchey-Tullparaju-Cayesh-Maparaju. The long arc of the Esparta-Tocllaraju-Pallcaraju-Pucaranra-Churup chain and the isolated Urus peaks form the centre, from which juts the chain of Ishinca-Ranrapalca-Vallunaraju. The geology is equally complicated but, crudely, the north-western peaks are granite and the others are metamorphic. There is little sense in trying to detail the many approaches. It is better to select your routes and then read the trail information.

Chinchey-Tullparaju-Cayesh-Maparaju Chain

Chinchey Norte III (Utsuraju), 5500:
SW. face; J.Feliu, F.Lusarreta, L.Saez de Olazagoitia; 17 June 1967.
From Ls. Vinouyo in Q. Honda go up moraine and glacier to climb steep avalanche-prone SW face in 5h from a high camp ca.4900m.

Chinchey Norte II (Ayukaraju), 5647:
N. ridge; R.Kirch, A.Landa, F.Lusarreta; 30 June 1967.
From Ls. Vinouyo climb the glacier on the W slopes of Chinchey Norte II and III through dangerous seracs. Climb N ridge in 9h from a camp ca.5100m.

Chinchey Norte I (Pamparaju), 5987
S. ridge; J.Feliu, R.Kirch, A.Landa, J.Lorente, F.Lusarreta, A.Rosen, L.Saez de Olazagoitia; 20 July 1967.
From Q. Honda climb moraine and rock buttress N of Pucaranra to avoid hazardous icefalls (this is a useful option for adjacent routes). Traverse E to past the Chinchey-Pucaranra col to gain and climb SW wall and deep snow and cornices of S ridge, 11h to summit from base of face.

Chinchey, 6222:
The northern routes on the Chincheys should be approached from Q. Honda, but the most popular W ridge is best approached via Q. Quilcaywanka. The eastern slopes hold their snow well but only two ascents have been made on this side. The name comes from the word which some areas use for 'puma'.

NW. face; C.Stark, P.Weidman, D.Webster; 15 July 1977.
Best approached from Chinchey-Pucaranra col.
N. ridge; W.Brecht, H.Schweizer; 2 August 1939.
From L. Vinouyo in Q. Honda ascend very active glacier to Pucaranra col. Climb W snow and ice slopes to a broad shoulder on the N rige, ca.5850m. Above climb past short steep ice walls to the summit, or traverse out onto the NW face and climb this to the W ridge right of cornices, 9h ascent from col, 2h descent. The N ridge was gained from the E, Q. Rurichinchay, in 1973: climb broad flutings above bergschrund to reach shoulder well left of cornices.
W. ridge / SW. slopes; M.Emslie, H.Simpson, W.Wallace; 17 August 1958. AD.
From old Hidrandina huts at L. Tullparaju follow the path towards Cuchillacocha and ascend to halfway up the zig-zags to the right of the Cuchillacocha outlet stream (not the more normal zig-

71

zags on the left side). Take a path leading rightwards through quenal woods, beyond follow cairns up moraines to reach tent platforms by a small lake ca.5100m at the snowline. Cross the flat glacier towards the Pucaranra-Chinchey col, some stonefall danger from Pucaranra, 4h. Climb the heavily crevassed 30° slopes S of the ridge to reach the short 55° summit pyramid, 6h. It is generally best to hug the ridge crest to avoid the worst of the crevasses. This route can be gained from Q. Honda via the Pucaranra- Chinchey col if desired.

W. face; R.Boyd, B. Wagstaff, K. Gerdes, P. Tamm; 26 June 1975.
Climb W face from high camp at Pucaranra-Chinchey col, no details, second ascent by Italians, 18 August 1975.

Puntancuerno (Chinchey Este), ca.6000m:

E. face / NE. ridge; A.Tordoya, A.Ortega; 21 August 1983. D.
From the village of Mallas, NE of Chavin, walk up Q. Rurichinchay to a base camp at Yuraccocha, ca.4600m, 6-7h. Ascend moraine to glacier base, 1 -2 h, and go up convoluted E glacier to the right side of the face, 6h. The face is rocky, rimmed by the NE ridge: climb up the junction of the two, 1h, 150m, 65°, to reach the shoulder above ca.5900m. The major difficulty is the dangerous 400m traverse along the NE ridge to the summit mushroom, 7h.

Tullparaju, 5787:

The name comes from 'tullpa' which means a small fireplace formed of a few stones. It is an alternative name for practically every mountain clump in the Cordillera Blanca and here the South peak has another name meaning 'where the rooster crows'.

W. ridge; D.Bernays, L.Patterson, C.Sawyer; 24 July 1962.
From L.Tullparaju approach as for W ridge of Chinchey and cross the glacier to base of W ridge, ca.4900m. Climb the initial 45° pyramid and then the sharp 60-70° snow slopes of the W ridge to a minor summit ca.5600m. From this to the top the ridge is diabolically corniced, 10-12h from glacier edge.

Gallohuaganan (Tullparaju Sur), 5456:

NNW. ridge; G.Dionisi, P.Fornelli, L.Ghigo, G.Marchese; 3 July 1958. PD ?.
From L. Tullparaju ascend as for W ridge Chinchey to climb NNW ridge on NE side: an exercise in glacier crossing.

Chopiraju Central (Andavite), 5513:

Chopiraju means 'the centre (of the) mountains'. It certainly does feel at the hub if it is a clear day on top of any of these summits. Andavite is Spanish for 'work of a lifetime' which was presumably the comment of an exhausted mine labourer.

W. ridge; G.Dionisi, P.Fornelli, L.Ghigo, G.Marchese; 2/3 July 1958. F.
From L. Tullparaju climb NW glacier to easy W ridge, and also to the summit of Este. This is a long approach on a bad glacier, better to traverse from Oeste, 5h, good views from summit. Este was possibly climbed in 1957 by R.Lambert to view Cayesh.

Chopiraju Oeste (Tururu), 5475:

W. ridge; probably L.Patterson, C.Sawyer; 24 June 1962. F.
Go up the left side of Q. Cayesh and begin climbing up the large scree cone spilling from the left end of the W ridge, just right of red rock pinnacles. Pass a bowl of quenal trees and more scree to reach the W ridge, 2° h. Ascend gentle snow slopes turning crevasses and seracs on the left, 2h. Continue to other summits if desired: an excellent route. It is also possible to climb to the ridge from near L. Tullparaju on grass, trees, and loose rock: A.Ames, V.Albino; July 1963.

CHINCHEY MASSIF
N. face; M.Wheeler, P.Weidman, D.Webster, C.Stark; 27 June 1977.
Quite technical climbing requiring a bivouac.

Cayesh, 5721:
The steeple of Cayesh rears forth, as if calling climbers to worship. Such prominent mountains demand much and Cayesh has a disproportionate number of hard routes, and bears witness to an even greater number of failures. The West face is now littered with abandoned pitons and slings as testimony to this. This little peak has a most appropriate name, that of a tiny back gnat with a ferocious bite which infests the valley in the rainy season.

E. face; M.Richey, C.Boyd, N.Pothier; 19 July 1983. ED 1/2 ?.
A challenging route taking the easiest line up this remote face. The lower half of the face below the summit is a large overhanging rock bay. It is bounded on its right side by a snow ramp which leads to a rock wall and then the upper icefields. Access is either by the Q. Rurec or from the beautiful Q. Qarwaskancha (Carhuascancha) via a pass E of Milpocraju.
Cross the compact E glacier of Cayesh to the base of right- wards diagonalling broad ice ramp, ca.4600m. After 350m the ramp ends and another set begins leftwards into rock. Begin climbing the steepening compact rock to gain access to ice columns which penetrate the rock band where it overhangs, ca.5200m. After about 150m the icicles give way to an ice gully and a traverse right to the first icefield.
From its right-hand corner climb steep rotten rock in a difficult traverse right to the second icefield. At the top of this climb a rock ramp and ice runnels to cornices which overhang the face by some 10m. To the left icicles rise through this ceiling for two delicate pitches which gain the N ridge 120m below the summit. Cautiously traverse to the top, 4 days.
The best descent route appears to be to descend the unstable S ridge for 150m of vertical height. At this point down-climbing and abseiling lead to the top of the Italian fixed ropes, which are bright yellow 12mm anchored ropes, and which allow safe descent of the W face. The Abra Villon pass could be crossed to regain the E side of the range.
W. face / S. ridge; L.Crawford, D.Ryan, L.Stewart; 21 July 1960. TD ?.
From the last campsites in Q. Cayesh follow a path which ascends diagonally to cross the L. Cayesh outlet stream just below the lake. Continue up moraine crest, then slabs, to gain the glacier at plateau level, 2h. Traverse easily across glacier to the base of the W face, 1h.
Beginning below the subsidiary peak to the S climb the lines of snow flutings and ramps leftwards up the face to reach the S ridge at its low point. Climb double cornices of S ridge on steep rock and ice. Four days return.
W. face (German route); M.Roeper, J.Steinsberger; 4 July 1988. TD+.
Climb a 60° icefield at the beginning of the Czech route and then a prominent ramp rightwards to the Italian fixed ropes, IV, four pitches. Follow these yellow ropes up for one pitch until they turn right. Traverse left to a dihedral, VI-, to reach easier mixed ground with some 70° ice. Make a rising traverse leftwards on this, crossing the Czech route to reach the sloping bivouac site shared with the American route, four pitches, IV. Some ice leads to three difficult but solid rock pitches up a large inside corner right of the American line, VI-, and the airy ridge one pitch S of the summit. Abseil descent, 2-3 days return. Friends and knifeblades useful on this and adjacent climbs, which catch the sun and are easily escaped from .

CHINCHEY MASSIF
Cayesh - W face

1. British _____
2. American ••••••••

3. Italian yelow rope o o
4. Czech __•__•__

5. German __ __

W. face (Czech route); B.Husicka, P.Hapala; 2 June 1986. TD.
A route of extreme difficulty on the right side of face. This is reportedly the line taken by the New Zealanders S.Allen, S.Dawson; 14 July 1973 (only completed to the ridge). Five pitches of icy mixed ground lead to steep and compact rock, V+. Four pitches of this gain the left end of steep ice (the NZ found it neccessary to abseil left in order to gain a gully at the side of the ice), 2-4 days.

W. face (American route); C.Fowler, J.Arnow; 28 July 1988. TD+.
On the left flank of the face climb steep snow and ice slopes by the start of the British route. Climb loose rock rightwards under the summit, IV/V, occasional 80° ice patches to reach a junction with the German route at the bivouac site.
Climb a buttress of good rock above, V+/VI-, (left of the German route) to a hanging belay below the summit ridge, 2-3 days return, 650m. Although this is probably the most direct route on the face the rock is often serious - poorly protected and loose.

CHINCHEY MASSIF

W. face (British route); J.Gore, T.Moore; 14 July 1986. TD/TD+.
This route is of a different character to the other W face routes, linking ice ramps on the left side of the face to create a line which is more serious in nature. Cross the glacier plateau towards the left flank of the W face, 2-3h.
Climb a snow couloir, 45-55° , turning to ice, 60-65° , in five pitches to just under the col with the snow ridge abutting left side of the face (bivouac site). Go right towards a rocky diedre and climb this, IV+, or mixed ground further right, III+. Go left and climb a rock pitch to the right of an ampitheatre and directly below a serac, V+, A2. Skirt the serac on 85° ice and climb mixed ground to bivouac ledges, 12h. Continue up 65° ice and then a rock pitch, IV, traversing right on a small platform to avoid a serac. Climb a 60° ice wall to the short summit ridge, 6h. Abseil descent, 2-3 day return to glacier.

P5420:
SE ridge; Japanese party; 1978.

Milpocraju, 5300:
SE. ridge; R.Fear, W.Lahr, B.Steele, A.Watson; 12 July 1972.
From Q. Rawarushka climb S glacier above Milpoqocha to col with the minor peak to the E (Milpocraju Chico). Climb SE ridge of steep snow, cornices, some rock. 13h return from camp ca.4400m.
SSW. spur; unknown first ascentionists. D+ ?.
This obvious and elegant spur lies between the W face and the watershed of the S ridge. At the head of the Q. Cayesh climb the moraines to the right of the jumbled glacier, and follow cairns to two smooth boulders and the glacier. Ascend the crevassed glacier towards the base of the ridge which is gained from the E, bypassing some seracs.
Climb the slopes to the left of and on the crest, 50-70° . Climb the W side of the 80° summit ice tower, 6h, 500m. Descend S face by abseil.
W. face; P.Gigliotti, M.Marchinni; June 1986. TD ?.
A variant 200m left of the '85 route. It probably follows the '85 route to the snowfield and then goes directly to the summit.
W. face; R.Thorns, A.Hinkes, R.Payne, I.Peter, S.Derwin, J.Gore; 13 June 1985. TD-.
An elegant line traversing the main part of the W face. Best approached as for W face Cayesh, although also possible as for SSW spur. Negotiate the crevassed glacier and a 50m loose rock wall to gain 100m of mixed ground before a snow slope. Then 10 pitches of a narrow 60-80° gully leads to the summit ridge. A final pitch, IV, gains the top, 1-2 days.

Jatungarbanso, 5057:
From Q. Rawarushka ascend rock slabs and then scramble along rock pinnacles of N-S ridge (or easy S snowfield) and return in one day. (N.Adams, H.Carter, E.Henostroza, G.Henostroza; 5 July 1969)

Maparaju, 5326:
The SW ridge is one of the best easy routes in the range, and can be recommended to trekkers with the usual caveat that they should be accompanied by a guide or other experienced mountaineer.

E. face; M.Richey; early August 1980.
From Q. Carhuascancha and Q. Rawarushka, climb the obvious N-S diagonaling snow-and-ice ramps to gain the SW ridge 200m below the summit: one day return from the valley.
SW. ridge; J.de Paz, L.Stewart; 16 July 1960. F.
Near the head of Q. Cayesh an abandoned mule path zig-zags up rock and scree to the glacier edge of the Abra Villon pass, passing abandoned coal workings, 2h from last camp sites, well

cairned. Climb glacier 50m to col and then gentle slopes of SW ridge to top, 1 -2h. Traverse on down NW slopes to descend the icefall at head of Q. Cayesh if desired, although not recommended (4 h, PD in ascent).

Urus and Esparta-Tocllaraju-Pallcaraju-Pucaranra-Churup Chain

El Caballo, 5300:

A point on Urus-Tocllaraju ridge with easy scrambles for acclimatisation.

Urus Este, 5420:

The SE side of Urus Este provides another of the Cordillera Blanca's standard 'trekking' routes. This popularity is well deserved.

NW. ridge; D.Leppert, J.Schmidt; 14 May 1964. PD-.
An easy rock scramble and snow climb to join SE side route.
SE. side; V.Day, E.Henostroza, A.Jamanca, T.McCormack; 18 July 1957. PD-
From Q. Ishinca base camp climb directy up a moraine crest under the Urus glacier. This curves right and then easy rock slabs lead towards the glacier which is climbed until in front of a small rock buttress. Turn left up the E ridge and climb a short ice slope under the summit, 5h up.
S. ridge; D.Bespflug, D.Jack; 17 November 1974.
It is possible to climb the harder E ridge direct.

Urus (Central), 5495:

SE. side; A.Morales, C.Morales;3 April 1954.

Urus Oeste, 5450:

SE. side; G.Apotheloz, D.Bach, A.Bezinge, G.de Rham, J.Fatton, C.Jaquet; 3 August 1963.
Climb S side from col between Oeste and Central, 1-2h from a camp ca.4900m.

Esparta, 5390:

SE. slopes; R.Davies, J.Graafland; 1 August 1965.
From the Mina Esparta area climb SE slopes to the SW of the three summits.
SW. ridge; P.Ritzema, K.O'Connell; 15 July 1978.
Climb SW face and ridge from Aquilpo Sur col.

Aquilpo Norte, 5560:

E. face; S.Matsushima, K.Yamaguchi, Y.Yoda; 12 July 1968.
Climb E face from Q. Honda above Rinconada.

Aquilpo Sur, 5520:

NE. ridge; J.Graafland, F.Kleine; 28 July 1965.
Climb NE ridge from Mina Esparta area.
SE ridge; J.Fullop, S.Turner, R.Watne; 14 July 1963.
From Mina Esparta area gain S col and climb S ridge and slopes. One day return from glacier camp.

CHINCHEY MASSIF

Chaco (on S side Q. Honda), 5320:
E. face; L.Gilardoni, E. Angeles; 18 August 1975. One day return.
SE. face; various; 29 June 1963. One day return.

Tocllaraju, 6032:
The pyramid of the 'noose mountain' is most commonly attempted from Q. Ishinca by the NW ridge route. This route sees many failures and the W face route has a greater success rate. A worthwhile alternative approach is from Q. Honda to the N.

NW. ridge; W.Brecht, H.Schweizer; 31 July 1939. PD+/AD-.
From Q. Honda and Cancahua reach Mina Esparta area. Ascend N glacier to col ca.5300m and climb NW ridge, 4-5h from col. Alternatively approach to camp ca.5300m as for W face. Then climb up and to the left, skirting seracs on 45° slopes to reach shallow col above. Follow gentle slopes to the first bergschrund, and steeper slopes to a harder bergschrund, 65°, often impassable. Climb 45° slopes and short E ridge to the summit if it cannot be taken directly.

N. ridge; L.Ortenburger, K.Ross; 30 June 1959. PD+/AD-.
From N glacier climb N ridge, about 100-150m below summit cross below the upper part of the N face to gain E ridge, thus avoiding a serac/cornice above. Climb this to top, 6-7h return from a glacier camp. This route is essentially the Q. Honda solution for NW ridge.

W. face; F.Fauve, G.Rivier; 27 July 1978. D-.
From Q. Ishinca base camp walk along the path on the N side of the sandy plain. Cross a stream and follow cairns up the valley to the E between two large moraines. Turn N up the steep crest of a moraine which can be followed to gain the glacier to the right of rocky cliffs, 2° h. Ascend the gentle glacial slopes to camp ca.5300m, 3-4h total. Traverse rightwards under the W face and climb a line on the S end which skirts the upper serac barrier on the right to join the S ridge 100m from the summit, 5-6h from camp. Descend via NW ridge.

W. face direct; G.Calcagno, M.Carara, G.Lafranconi, C.Zappelli; 15 July 1980. D.
From camp ca.5300m traverse rightwards and cross the bergschrund at its highest point on the N side of the face, right of mixed ground, 2h.
Climb 55° ice slope above and pass through the serac barrier with difficulty, 150m, 70-80°. Go up a snowfield to gain the S ridge just below the summit, 8-10h, 10 pitches. Descend NW ridge. The seracs have been avoided by traversing left to the NW ridge.

Palcaraju Oeste, 6110:
SW. ridge; P.Baltazar, C.Fernandez, M.Romero, F.Suazo; 12 May 1954.
From Q. Ishinca scramble a long way over moraine and glacier to col ca.5300m and then SW ridge. A more pleasant approach is the traverse of Ishinca.

Palcaraju (Cuchilla), 6274:
Palcaraju means the 'branching' mountain and its limbs can easily be approached from all sides. Despite this it is not a popular peak.

N. side; W.Brecht, S.Rohrer, K.Schmid, H.Schweizer; 7 June 1939.
From Q. Honda gain Paqliashcocha. climb onto N glacier between Palcaraju and Tocllaraju and ascend to NW glacier basin.
Climb up N side of W ridge. Traverse across N face to ascend 50m steep ice before reaching NE ridge near summit.

CHINCHEY MASSIF

NW. face; H.Abrons, D.Doody, T.Frost, H.Hultgren, H.Kendall, J.Kendall, I.Ortenburger, L.Ortenburger, W.Mathews; 10 July 1964.

From NW glacier basin climb the fluting which ascends to NE ridge near summit, then climb ridge.

S. face; Y-C.Sonnenwyl, P.Morand, E.Loretan; 17 July 1980.

From Q. Cojup follow route as for S approach but continue to traverse E until under the S face. Climb a system of couloirs to reach the SE ridge (bivouac site under cornice) and climb this to the top. Descend as for S approach, 2 day round trip. It is also possible to climb the SW face direct. Cross the bergschrund below the summit, 75-80° ice, and ascend 400m of 50-55° ice to the top, 8-12h from the glacier edge.

S. Approach; K.Baker, G.Holdsworth, L.Irwin, J.Ricker; 3 August 1965.

From the Cojup base camp below Perolcocha go up the small valley to the NW following the stream and right side. Scramble N to the glacier and ascend snow platforms and ice fall, beneath the W peak initially, traversing to the col between W and main peak.

Climb N face above col joining W ridge near summit. One day return from camp at ice edge, ca.5000m, under Ishinca-Palcaraju col. The W ridge can be climbed in its entirety from the col, this is difficult on steep ice; after a direct start to gain the col, 70-75°, 700m, 8h. (P.Poljanec, Z.Trusnovec; 31 May 1987)

Palcaraju Sur, 5900:

N. ridge; N.Jaeger; 20 June 1977. TD (see below).

Traverse the ridge from Palcaraju on 50-80° ice. It is also possible to climb the 45° snow of the WNW face direct.

SE. ridge; N.Jaeger; 20 June 1977. TD.

From the col with Pucaranra climb this and continue to main summit. Begin by slanting up to the right by rocks on the N side, IV. Reach the slender ridge and pass cornices and ice towers by steep snow slopes to S. Pass the summit ca.5900m and continue on past other minor points to the main summit, easier ground, 10h, 500m.

Pucaranra, 6147:

The orange rocks which are exposed on the SE ridge give this mountain its name. The SE ridge can be recommended as a fine two day expedition, never serious but requiring commitment.

E. (ENE) ridge; L.Ortenburger, K.Ross; 17 July 1959. AD/D ?.

From L. Vinouyo (Pucaranracocha) in Q. Honda climb glacier to Pucaranra-Chinchey col ca.5200m. Gain the crest of the ridge and climb a chimney to slabs. Turn a prominent gendarme on the left to reach a notch and then climb a short, steep rock wall ca.5950m. Climb ice through a yellow rock band to the summit. Ascent 12h, descent 12h, from col.

A 1976 party spent three days in climbing from the col and may have climbed a substantially harder line, descending by the SE face.

SE. face; C.Kogan, V.Moreno, A.Lambert, R.Lambert, C.van der Stratten; 23 July 1955. AD+.

From L. Tullparaju in Q. Quilcaywanka climb up glacier to Pucaranra-Chinchey col area as for the W ridge of Chinchey. Before reaching the col climb the 50-55° slopes to the S of the E ridge, avoiding the mixed ground at the top, 6h. Descend by this route. The face sheds its ice at the end of the season.

SE. ridge; B.Lauterburg, F.Marmillod, R.Schmid, F.Sigrist; 5 July 1948. AD+.

From Cuchillacocha spillway climb moraine on the right side of the lake, turn a small rock crag easily on the right, and reach the glacier, 45 minutes. Follow ramps leftwards through seracs on the glacier to gain a sheltered campsite immediately below a shallow col in the SE ridge, ca.5700m, 4h. Climb the ridge above to the easy orange rock band. Pass this, and the next one, to the summit, 5h. Descent from the col ca.5700m towards Chinchey would be unwise.

SW. ridge; K.Baker, G.Holdsworth; 17 August 1965.
From Perolcocha area of Q. Cojup climb true SW corniced ridge and SW face. Two days return with a snow cave bivouac at the top of the ridge, ca.5220m. There appear to be plenty of serac obstacles on the ridge.

W. face; M.Cohen, T.Parlane; 4 July 1975.
From Q. Cojup cross the glacier to climb steep ice couloirs on the N end of the face, avoiding overhanging seracs near the summit.
Climb an obvious avalanche chute to the bergschrund. The face steepens above, passing easy rock bands and reaching 70° before the couloir ends, bivouac site. Continue carefully to the top, two days return.

NW. ridge; N.Jaeger; 19 June 1977. TD.
From base camp in Q. Cojup go SE in the direction of a col between two moraines. Cross the stream flowing from L. Pallcacocha at cairns and pick a way through boulders. Go over the moraine col and up a small green valley towards the summit. Descend to reach the glacier in 2-3h.
Climb the glacier towards and up a 45° couloir enclosed by rocks. At the top of the coulouir make a rising traverse to the right to a notch betweeen two seracs. Climb a 70° ice wall and follow the slope to the NW ridge. Meet the ridge above a rocky spur, at the base of a very steep (65-70°) snow wall and follow it to the summit, 8-12h. Descend the route or the exposed SW ridge.
The entire NW ridge may be climbed direct from the col ca.5500m between Palcaraju and Pucaranra. Climb the difficult narrow ridge with cornices, ice, snow mushrooms, to the rock spur. Second ascent seiged over many days.

P5350:
This and P5340 are two small peaks on the Jatunmontepuncu- Pucaranra ridge which bear useful one day routes:

SW. ridge or N. face; G.Feichtenschlager; 26 & 27 June 1991. F & PD.
From col ca.5200m climb short snow ridge to pleasant summit in 40 minutes. Alternatively descend to flat N glacier and traverse to climb 60° 200m N face in 1° h.

P5340:
NE. face; G.Feichtenschlager; 26 June 1991. F.
From Cuchillacocha base camp climb grass and moraine to col ca.5200m, leaving a large rock buttress to the right, 2h.
Climb generally sound rock on the NE side to a tiny snowcap, II with a step of IV, 45 mins.
SW. face; G.Feichtenschlager; 27 June 1991. D.
At a small lake go directly up to the base of the face. Zig-zag up 60° glacier, climbing vertical seracs as necessary to gain the top in 3h.

Jatunmontepuncu (Bayo or Huapi), 5415:
This 'large gateway peak' boasts the excellent SW ridge which is open to anyone with a little determination, and worth the effort.

SW. ridge via E. slopes; A.Szepessy, M.Soni; 5 July 1948. F.
Above Cuchillacocha climb grass slopes and moraine to glacier, 2° h. Climb gentle glacier to low on 30° SW ridge and continue to top, 4h total.

SW. ridge via W. sloes; S.Leppish, A.Soriano, H.Vargas; 27 September 1957. F.

From Q. Cojup follow the approach path for Pucaranra to the col between two moraines. After this climb directly up the slope, over snowy crumbling ledges to the edge of the ice. Either climb a couloir on the left, between seracs, or pass these on the right to the gentle 30° SW ridge, 2-4h.

NW. ridge; L.Irwin, J.Ricker; 24 August 1965. F.

From Q. Cojup go up as for Pucaranra and climb rocky NW ridge, traverse down SW ridge in one day return.

Huamanripa (Choqo), 5243:

N. ridge; B.Anderson, T.Anderson, J.Braig, H.Clark, H.Goodro, D.Green, J.Wilkerson; 14 July 1969. F.

Ascend hillsides above Cuchillacocha to col with Jatunmontepuncu, 1° h. Scramble easily along rocky N ridge and traverse tops as desired. Other pleasant scrambles can be constructed in this area, e.g.

From Q. Huamanripa to Churup III, or Churup II from Q. Cojup (R.Megard, H.Vargas, A.Soriano; 4 August 1960), all at an easy standard. Huamanripa is a yellow medicinal herb which grows in profusion on the higher slopes of this area.

Churup I (Oeste), 5493:

Churup is a twice-corrupted way of describing the columnar crystals of mud and ice which crunch underfoot after a heavy groundfrost. The SW face is a good technical testpiece, never too hard but sustained until the end of the descent.

NW. slopes; A.Canaval, A.Miro-Quesada, A.Morales, C.Morales, A.Palacios, R.Thomas, possibly others; 8 August 1954.

Q. Cojup approach to Aqoshcocha (a small lake emptied by 1941 alluvion) and then NW side, 60° ice and steeper loose mixed ground.

S. face; M.Inokuchi, H.Yoshikawa; 18 July 1962. AD.

About 1° h after passing the portada of Q. Quilcaywanka turn left and ascend a small valley, and then a moraine crest to bivouac below the SE face, 6-8h.

Climb 200m of rock up the left side of the face to reach corniced SE ridge. Occasionally loose, V maximum, abseil descent. Can also be approached by traversing from Q. Churup.

SW. face; R.Fear, W.Lahr, M.Malotaux, R.Ridgeway; 15 August 1972. D+.

Skirt N around L. Churup and follow a cairned trail up rock slabs and moraine. Avoid a rocky crag and seracs to gain the base of the face, 3h.

Climb through the low rock band in the obvious steep centre-right couloir (75-80°, IV+ depending on conditions) for 200m. Above either traverse up and left to gain the W ridge left of large cornices, or continue straight up 60° flutings and the steep summit seracs just to the right of the summit (harder), 8-12h, 500m. Descend route, or SE or N ridges, abseils required.

CHINCHEY MASSIF
Ishinca-Ranrapalca-Ocshapalca-Vallunaraju Chain

Ishinca, 5530:
The SW ridge of Ishinca is another common 'trekking' route of no particular interest.

NE. ridge; W.Basset, J.Hough, C.Satterfield, S.Turner; 23 June 1965.
Gain N col ca.5300m from either Q. Ishinca or Cojup. Climb NE ridge to top past cornices and rock sections.

SW. ridge; P.Baltazar, C.Fernandez, C.Morales, M.Romero, F.Suazo; 12 May 1954. F.
From the Ishinca refuge descend towards the lake and go around it to the right before ascending moraine to the glacier edge, following a well worn cairned path, 1h. Gentle glacier leads to the col, 1° -3h, and then a further 1° -2h up the easy SW ridge to the summit tower. Here cross a bergschrund and climb a short steep section to the summit, 60°.

NW. slopes; J.Fonrouge, W.Lindauer, H.Salger, H.Schmidbauer, U.Staudacher; 1964. PD.
Climb snow and ice face in 4-5h from Ishinca refuge after an easy traverse of the moraine and glacier, 55° at top.

Ranrapalca - N & NE faces

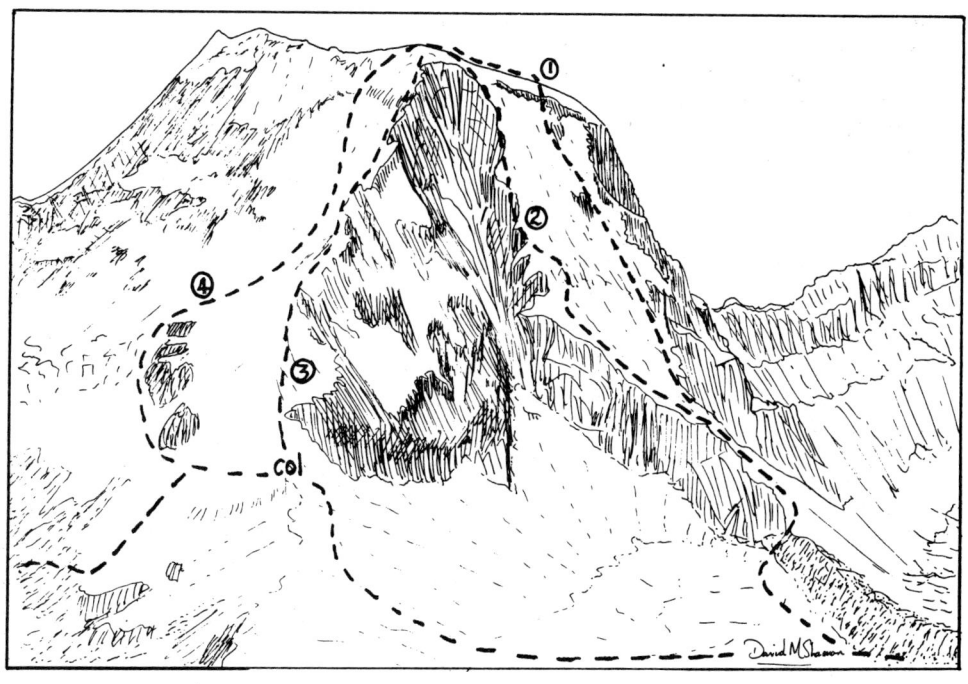

1. N face   2. N spur   3. NE ridge   4. NE slope

CHINCHEY MASSIF

Ranrapalca, 6162:

For a mountain named after a pile of stones it certainly contains some good mixed climbs. All the routes are reported to be worthwhile and the NE slopes and E ridge especially so. The summit plateau is quite large.

N. face; M.Johns, C.Slaymaker, M.Rourke; 22 August 1975.
Climb a snow ramp leftwards through the icefall and then ascend a 45-60° snow arete which slants right, passing by rocks before gaining the summit plateau, 10h up.

N. spur; J.Simpson, R.Potter; 30 July 1994. TD.
The N spur is the distinctive ice/rock ridge at the extreme left end of the N face. To the left is the huge central gully, to the right the snowfiels of the N face. Poor snow and ice conditions (neve penitentes, sracs, and unconsolidated sugar) may dictate a bivouac high on the spur to await freezing conditions, 1000m, TD, 8h.
From a bivvi on the right side of the Ishinca glacier approach col as if crossing to the NE slopes from Q. Ishinca (rock gendarmes). Follow 45° snow slopes leftwards to reach small rock band - 1 pitch loose rock - before gaining icefields above. Rising left traverse through unstable seracs to reach the far left end of the central rock band. This is climbed via a narrow ice gully to reach the base of the north spur. Climb spur direct on mixed ground. Airy and exposed climbing especially towards top, constant rockfall down 500m deep central gully. Exit face at small rock band on top of spur. Follow snowfields to junction with NE slopes/ridge and summit.

NE. ridge; W.Brecht, S.Rohrer, K.Schmid, H.Schweizer; 25 June 1939.
From Ranrapalca-Ishinca col climb steep rocky NE ridge to snow summit platform. Traverse 500m on crest of summit plateau to knife-edge summit.

NE. slopes; G.Dionisi, P.Fornelli, L.Ghigo, G.Marchese; 23 July 1958. D-.
The Ranrapalca-Ishinca col can also be gained from Q. Cojup. From the camp in the Cojup valley zig-zag up pathless grassy slopes to the W. Ascend left to a plateau and walk round it on the right towards Ranrapalca. On reaching a waterfall flowing down a slab turn the corner of a cliff on the right. Cross some swamps and enter a moraine cirque (cairns). Look out for a pair of moraines on the left of smooth rock slabs, and climb first the right one, then the left to reach L. Perolcocha. This is a good campsite, there are two other lakes to the NE and SE (the largest), 3-4h.
Climb the moraine on the right bank of the highest lake, and climb rocky scree slopes to the col, 40 minutes.
Climb the easy snow slopes on the left of the ridge then two short sections through seracs, 60°. Cross a bergschrund and climb the ice, or mixed, wall left of a small serac, 55°. Join the NE ridge and climb it to the summit snow platform. Traverse S to the knife-edge of snow which forms the summit, 5-7h. In recent seasons the mixed wall has been turned to easy, but loose, rocks in August

E. ridge; R.Ghilini, B.Prud'homme, J.Bouchard; 18 June 1977. TD+.
From Q. Cojup climb this difficult ice ridge, two days. Turn the first rocky step on the right, until it is possible to regain the crest by a couloir of shattered rock in the NE face. Continue up the ridge, mostly on the 65-70° snow and ice of the left side, past numerous cornices, steps, notches and towers, turning most on the right, 16h, 650m. A good climb, recommended.

S. face; N.Jaeger; 13 June 1979. TD+.
From Q. Cojup (Qojup) climb steep grassy slopes to the S of the E ridge. At the foot of the ridge cross the glacier to the base of the route, keeping to the left of a rocky spur and serac zone. Climb somewhat leftwards on a mixed 55° slope, of shattered rocks, to the right of a rocky ridge to a short wall, V, to gain the col between the summits. Climb the sharp corniced ridge to the main summit, 8-12h, 750m, descend by the NE slopes.

CHINCHEY MASSIF

SW. ridge; T.Aas, B.Hammeraas, E.Boehlke, K.Bjerge, H.Ekiksen, U.Geir-Hansen, P.Gren; 7 July 1971.

Approach from the W via Q. Llaca. Climb SW face to SW ridge, then avoid difficulties by a rib on the SE wall, and back onto SW ridge again above ca.5850m. Camp at ca.5300 at base of ridge, and at ca.5850m on the top of the rib. This leads to the summit of Ranrapalca Suroeste, 6000m. Continue traverse to true summit.

SW. face; J.Porter, A.MacIntyre; 21 July 1979.

Approach from the W via Q. Llaca and start up the right side of the SW face from the top of the glacier.

The face has steep rock capped by seracs on the right and a one kilometre wall of ice and seracs on the left. Ascend diagonally leftwards to the base of a leaning tower in the centre of the face, stonefall danger on the traverse. Climb the tower to a bivouac site, one day. Manoeuvre carefully through seracs and towers on hard ice to reach the summit plateau, 45-70° ice, V, 8-16h. Descend by the NE slopes although the first ascentionists descended the problematic W ridge. In 1985 Poles climbed direct to the tower.

W. ridge; Y-C.Sonnenwyl, P.Morand, E.Loretan; 22 June 1980

From Q. Ishinca base camp go back down the valley and up the tributary valley to the S, then a complicated glacier to reach the Ocshapalca-Ranrapalca col, one day. Bypass several immense crevasses and vertical steps on the W ridge to reach the summit on the second day.

Ucro, 5246:

S. side; A.del Arroyo, A.Soriano, H.Vargas; August 1954.

Climb from the dry lake basin of Aqoshqocha in Q. Cojup.

Rima Rima, 5203:

W. face; V.Ramirez, A.Szepessy; January 1950. F.

From the bridge in the Q. Llaca follow a path through trees and then cairns up towards the col in the jagged N ridge, 21/2 h. Scramble along the ridge, some shattered rock but no rope required by most parties,1/2h. The final section is very exposed to form a good training climb.

Ocshapalca, 5881:

The S face of this peak is supposed to resemble branching straws. The gullies to which this refers are being developed into a series of modern sport routes.

N. ridge; A.Miyashita, T.Sato; 10 July 1965. PD/AD ?.

From Q. Ishinca go up to L. Urayraju, 3h. Cross glacier to reach base of N ridge ca.5150m and climb on steep snow and ice of narrow ridge. 5h from a campsite at ca.5500m.

S. face; T.Casas, A.Obregon, J.Amils, J.Sunyer; 11 July 1989.

Climb a 50-60° snow and ice fluting to the right of Grassi's, passing 40m of steeper ice at the top. Reach the ridge at a point of red rock on the right of the summit, abseil descent.

S. face (Grassi route); B.Francou, J-M.Cambon, G.Grassi; 20 June 1982.

This route climbs directly to the summit. Begin just to the right of the summit and climb 60-65° ice to two difficult pitches of steeper (75-85°) mixed gullies, in order to gain the ice fluting which goes directly to the summit, 80° in places, 7-8h, 650m. Descend by abseil.

S. face (American route); R.Blatherwick, M.Richey; 9 August 1979.

To approach the S face routes walk to the huts in Q. Llaca and continue up the small valley towards the E. Take a small path on the right to ascend the crest of a moraine on the E side of the valley. At the top of this descend left towards the glacier following cairns, and circle up the heavily crevassed glacier to reach the face from the E, 3h.

CHINCHEY MASSIF
Ocshapalca - S face

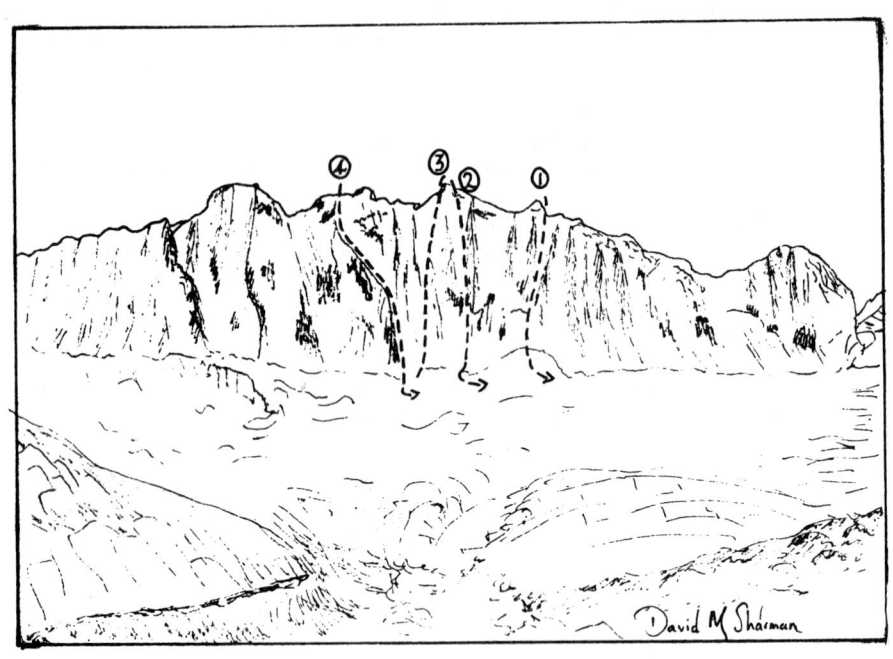

1. '89   2. Grassi   3. American   4. Swiss - French

From the glacier above Q. Llaca the route takes a direct line up the centre of the face just left of a rocky spur descending from the summit. An easy snow slope leads to the bergschrund. Cross this and climb 60° flutings and then a series of 75-85° ice pitches to gain the summit at a notch. Climb 100m of the difficult and dangerous ridge to the top, 7-8h, 650m, descend N side or abseil.

S. face (Swiss-French); V.Banderet, J.Ouellet, B.Balmat; 12 June 1982.

This route begins just left of the American'79 line and follows the prominent rocky spur which ascends leftwards.

Climb snow and ice, 60-65°, with some mixed sections to the final two steeper pitches below the ridge; 7-8h, 650m. Traverse dangerous ridge E to summit, descent by abseil or to N.

Yangyaraju I, 5675, (Este):
NW. ridge; D.Ciochetti, C.Slaymaker; August 1975.
SW. ridge; S.Colbek, D.Ewers, I.Jirak; 1 August 1963.
From L.Mullaqa climb SW glacier and steep SW ridge.

Yangyaraju II, 5630, (Central):
SE. face; S.Colbeck, D.Ewers, K.Heathershaw, I.Jirak; 31 July 1963.
From SW glacier reach col between Yangyaraju I and II, climb SE face.

CHINCHEY MASSIF

P5400:
SW. face; S.Colbeck, I.Jirak; 7 August 1963.
From Q.Mullaqa by SW glacier and SW face of this point on the W ridge of Yangyaraju II. One day return.

Yangyaraju III, 5450, (Oeste):
NW. ridge; B.Pfeiffer, J.Plimpton, J.Spezia; August 1974.
Q.Mullaqa approach. Traverse along broken dangerous W glacier edge to base of NW ridge. Climb NW ridge.
SE. face; J.Muck, I.Jirak; 18 July 1958.
From Q. and L.Mankaruri climb SW glacier to final SE mixed face. One day return.
W. ridge; D.Ciochetti, C.Slaymaker; 2 August 1975.
One day return from SW glacier basin.

Vallunaraju (Wallunaraju), 5686:
Vallunaraju is a double-headed mountain which has proved popular with trekkers and guided parties, or as an acclimatisation peak for others. The S summit is slightly lower although the estimated height of 5600m seems inconsistent. It is named after the ice cutters who still quarry ice from the glacier for use in Huaraz.

NW. face; M.Diaz, R.Gonzales, A.Ramos, H.Vargas; 5 June 1954.
One day return.
N. ridge; L.Ryan, R.Ryan; 5 July 1971. PD+/AD-.
From the hut in Q. Llaca walk around P5120 and head left up a moraine crest. 2h. Go up left towards a huge boulder, pass this on the right and climb mixed terraces to the col ca.5600m on N ridge leading to the Yangyarajus, 1h.
Climb N ridge with rock falling away to the left and snow slopes to the right, 2h. Alternatively cross NW face from SW slopes to N ridge col (1975). One day return from Q. Llaca.
E. side; G.Grassi; June 1982. AD-.
From the huts in Q. Llaca climb up the small valley to the NE keeping below rocky cliffs to the N. Climb up slabs rightwards by a series of ledges and continue N up moraine towards the col between the Vallunarajus, 2°-3h, 3km. Follow a series of loose rocky ledges to the col, then the easy S ridge, 4-5h, III/IV, 400m.
Alternatively ascend the E face direct at a similar standard on excellent granite, or climb to the S summit ca.5600m.
SE. face; M.Schenone, G.Ghigo, E.Tessera; 8 August 1987.
Climb this delicate mixed face in one day after approaching from the Q. Llaca.
SW. slopes; A.Szepessy, M.Szepessy; 1949 (ski ascent). PD-.
It is possible to drive to 4300m in the Q. Llaca, along a good trail which leads to a hut. This hut is used by the Huaraz guides, who should be approached for the key. A direct path runs from the hut to the glacier, 2h. Another runs from where the trail crosses the bridge, 2° h. Join the glacier by a col and loop way out to the left (to the N) to avoid the worst crevasses. Ascend towards the twin summit and climb whichever you want, steeper at the top, 3-5h from glacier edge.

P5120:
SE. ridge; A. del Arroyo, C.Morales, D.Morales, O.Morales; 31 July 1963.
Approach as for Vallunaraju E face to beyond the slabs, after which cross to the left towards the col in the NW ridge of P5120 which is on E ridge Vallunaraju Sur.
Climb the ridge to the top by way of terraces, 4-5h. Alternatively gain col from S side, or climb a harder line directly up the fine granite of the S face, V, 5h.

CHINCHEY MASSIF

Carhuac Este, 5110:

SW. ridge; B.Lauterburg, F.Marmillod, R.Schmid, F.Sigrist; 12 June 1948

Climbed whilst traversing Carhuac Oeste and San Cristobal.

HUANTSAN MASSIF
Map of Chinchey & Huantsan Massifs

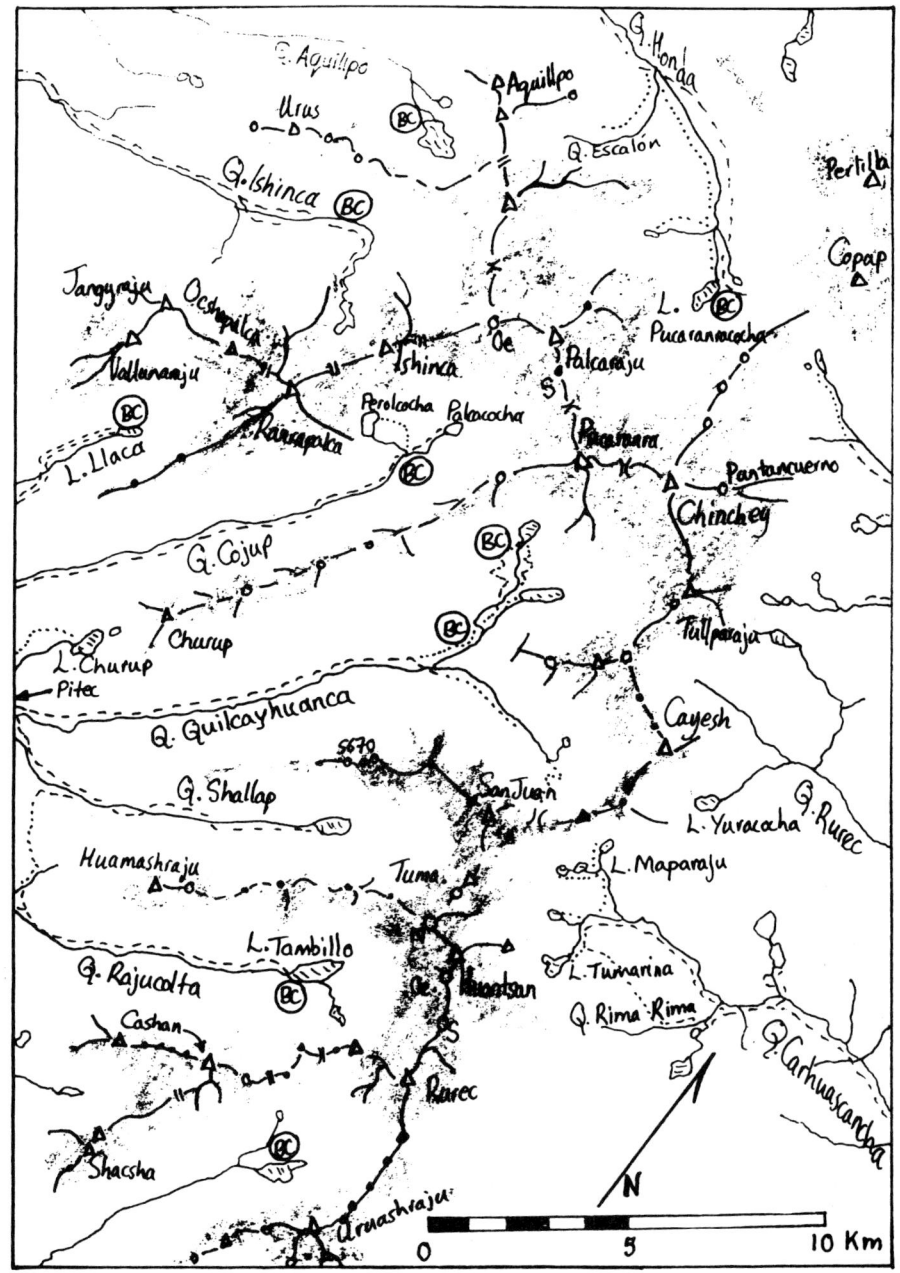

HUANTSAN MASSIF

This is the last massif with extensive glaciation and peaks over 6000m. To the South the Rio Santa valley becomes smaller and opens out to high rolling grasslands into which are set island-like minor massifs such as the Pongos. The grass, or pampa, laps along the South-West corner of the massif to the interesting spur of the Cashan and Shacsha peaks. The core of the massif is undoubtedly the great bulk of the Huantsans with their clutch of classic mixed routes which can be approached in a confusing number of ways. Other peaks of the continental divide include the easier Rurecs and Uruashraju in the South, or the substantial San Juan to the far North.
Approach to the northern peaks is generally via the Pitec roadhead.

From here Q. Quilcaywanka leads to the Abra Villon pass, or trails lead South to Qs. Shallap and Rajucolta. A road from Olleros leads to a ruined bridge at the entrance to Q. Rurec and the southern peaks. A few routes must be approached via Chavin and the beautiful eastern valleys.

This massif marks the southern end of outcrops of the great granite batholith, which surfaces only for Huamashraju, Cashan, and Shacsha.The other peaks are mostly loose quartzite and slate except for the metamorphic rocks and volcanic flows of Huantsan itself.

Quimarumi, 5459:

The E ridge of Quimarumi, the mountain of three stones, is a delightful little excursion, suitable for accompanied novices.

E. ridge; D.Bathgate, T.Burnell, L.Irwin, J.Ricker; 11 August 19660. F+.
At the lower end of Q. Cayesh two streams flow down from Q. Anqosh, in defiles which border a narrow spur. Scramble up this, or the eastern side of the eastern stream, and then walk up through pastures and rocky bluffs. Take the crest of the black moraine and traverse across a rockfall scar to the glacier, 31/2 h. cross the short glacier to the col ca.5200m, 1/2 h, and climb easy snow slopes on the S side of the ridge to the final pillar of shattered rock. Scramble easily up the exposed crest, one short passage of II, and reach the summit snowcap, 45 minutes. The first ascentionists appproached from Q. Shallap as for S ridge San Juan. The superior approach described was opened by D.McClung, J.Sanders, K.Newcomb, 12 July 1969.

San Juan, 5843:
San Juan is most accessible from Q. Cayesh and has some good middle grade routes.

E. arete; D.M.Sharman, D.A.Thomas; 4 August 1991. AD+.
Approach as for SW ridge Maparaju. Above the Abra Villon pass is the jumbled E glacier bay of San Juan. Wend through this with interest to gain an interim plateau below the E face, 2h from ice edge. At the left end of the E face cross a bergschrund (or easy rocks further left) and climb to the E arete. Follow this past a 50° gully and mushrooms to join the easy upper slopes of the S ridge, and thence the summit, 3h. Reverse route without abseil.
S. ridge; N.Clinch, R.Tidrick; 3 July 1957. D-.
There are a number of different approaches to this route, all with drawbacks. The approach from Q. Shallap is detailed for completeness although it is horrendous, and it is fortunate that this and adjacent climbs have alternative approaches. Walk around the N shore of L. Shallap and scramble up water-smoothed rocks at the NE corner, II. Above is a cliff with a number of waterfalls: it is possible to climb the left one (a jungle experience in the deepest, most vegetated gully) or to turn the cliff on the right side, II/III either way. Walk up the left lateral moraine past a rocky bluff, and cross onto the glacier at plateau level, 3-4h. Some parties prefer to ascend on the S side of the Shallap icefall. Walk across the flat glacier and ascend the crevassed mess which drops steeply from the San Juan-Tumarinaraju col, 3-4h, dangerous. Turn the rock tower at the base of

the ridge on the S side and then pass some mushrooms at half-height to enter the easy upper slopes, 6h to summit. If approaching from Q. Cayesh or Q. Carhuascancha via the Abra Villon pass it seems possible to climb rocks to join the ridge between the tower and mushrooms. This could also be gained in 1h from the Huantsan-Tumarinaraju col, 5369m.

NW. ridge; M.Emslie, D.Fabian, H.Simpson, W.Wallace; 14 August 1958. AD.
The best approach is as for E ridge Quimarumi from Q. Cayesh. Alternatively gain col ca.5200m in 2h from Gl. Shallap ice edge as for S ridge San Juan.
From the col ca.5200m climb across 45° snow terraces split by crevasses, keeping always to the S of the ridge. Turn a rocky tower and finish up S slopes to summit in 5-6h from col. Climbing the corniced ridge itself is longer and harder.

Tumarimaraju, 5670:

The sugar loaf shape results in a name meaning 'apex of a curve'. The E ridge looks hard but there are easier possibilities on the two summits.

E. ridge; R.Fear, D.Peterson; 3 July 1972.
Q. Carhuascancha approach to Q. Rawarushca. Ascend slopes beyond tiny lake W of L. Maparaju to edge of NE glacier, ca.4800m, then climb NE glacier to Abra Villon pass. Above is the 300m high ridge of 150m steep rock above a 60° ice flank. One day from glacier.

Huamashraju (Yanawaqra), 5434:

The W slopes of the female mountain are a good easy route.

Unknown route; J.Acosta, T.Cornejo, A.Yanac, G.Yanac; 5 April 1954.
Approached from Ls. Huarmiwakanan to climb rock route, NW ridge perhaps.
S. slopes; R.Cundiff, L.Duelsberg, D.Liska, G.Oetzel, H.Walton; 4 August 1967. F.
From Q. Rajucolta climb to S slopes and the summit, 4-5h.
W. slopes to SW. ridge; J.Cabana, A.Soriano; 15 April 1954. F.
At ca.4000m in the Q. Rajucolta (shortly after descending into the valley if approaching from Pitec) a stream flows down from a valley below Huamashraju, the Q. Huamashruri. Go up this valley to a lake, and then cross moraine and slabs to the glacier, 1 1/2-2 1/2 h from lake. Ascend the glacier to the right of rocks to reach the ridge in 2h. Turn left along the exposed SW ridge to the top, 1h.

Huamashraju Este, 5250:

S. side; Y.Hamano, N.Kaburaki, A.Murai, P.Morales; 19 July 1962.
Climb S snowwall then E to summit.SW. ridge; traverse from main peak.

Quimaraju (Quiso), 5406:

N. slopes; C.Stark, R.Webster; 8 July 1973.
From below Q. Shallap icefall climb moraine and rocks to a snowpatch ramp high beneath the summit, or traverse jagged and rocky NE ridge. Appears uninviting from any direction.
E. face; R.Cundiff, L.Duelsberg, D.Liska, G.Oetzel, H.Walton; 31 July 1967.
From Rajucoltacocha ascend SE glacier and rock E face.
SW. side; Y.Komatsu, A.Miyashita; 27 June 1967.
From Rajucoltacocha ascend SW glacier and SW side.

Pucashallash, 5130:

N. side; N.Adams, O.Aranda, H.Carter, E.Henostroza, G.Henostroza; 8 July 1969.
Climb this rock peak E of Huantsan from the Q. Rawarushca. The name comes from the red screes which are here.

HUANTSAN MASSIF

Huantsan Norte, 6113:

Huantsan Norte is separated from the main summit by a long narrow ridge. There are many approaches to this peak, which are mainly detailed under the NW ridge.

NW. ridge; T.de Booy, G.Egeler, L.Terray; 6 July 1952. D ?.

To approach from the E via Q. Rawarushca, go to L. Tumarina and ascend NE glacier above. Traverse around base of N wall and N ridge. Cross over col 5369m to W side. Go up NW glacier to base of NW ridge, ca.5500m.

To approach from the N ascend to Abra Villon pass from either Q. Carhuascancha or Q. Cayesh. Traverse through base of San Juan E glacier bay and under the serac-capped rock cliffs flanking the S ridge - 1/2 rom the W via Q. Shallap gain glacier plateau as for S ridge San Juan. Ascend icefall towards col 5369m, starting up the centre and finishing up the right side. Traverse to base of NW ridge. (D.Michael, I.Ortenburger, L.Ortenburger, E.Vargas, G.Whitmore; 17 August 1958). From ca.5500m climb steep spur to foresummit snow plateau, ca.5950m, and then ridge to N peak, avoiding difficulties by climbing on the E side. Col 5369m to summit is 5-7h.

SW. ridge; R.Auda, P.Bonnier, J.Bouquier, L.Coursol, P.Ferry, G.Martin; 8 August 1978.

This route climbs the SW ridge to the foresummit of the N peak, ca.5950m. The approach as described could be used to access other routes on the W side of the Huantsan group.

From the huts at L. Rajucolta (L. Tambillo) climb the small valley to the S to a meadow. The path continues up the left flank of the valley above the lake below. Continue towards, and skirt, a small rock cliff by the ruins of a base camp (cairns). Enter a small cirque on the right and leave it by a river which is followed to L. Awash (L. Hahuac), 4780m, 2-3h. Camp here and go up moraine to the glacier, 1h. Cross the glacier under the W face of Huantsan to climb the snow slopes on the right side of the SW ridge, avoiding seracs by going further right, 3-5h. Traverse NW ridge to true N summit.

W. face; K.Klinger, W.Sachatonicek; 6 June 1980.

From L. Rajucolta ascend the complex and broken glacier, as for the SW ridge, to the foot of the W face.

Climb 55° ice on the lower half of the 1000m face and continue up more snow and ice to the foresummit of the N peak, ca.5950m. Reverse route or downclimb NW or SW ridges.

Huantsan, 6395:

The bulk of Huantsan definitely dominates this massif. The summits are possibly the least climbed of all the 6000m peaks in the Cordillera Blanca. This means that if you bother to visit you may well have the area to yourselves. Oddly the mountain is apparently named for a grassy plant liked by pigs.

NNW. ridge; T.de Booy, G.Egeler, L.Terray; 7July 1952. D+/TD-.

Traverse from Huantsan Norte down a steep narrow snow arete to a saddle, ca.6050.

Climb NNW ridge on steep snow with some ice, 50-80°. At the top it is possible to climb near rock outcrops on the E side of the ridge, or to avoid some difficulties by climbing on the W side, 4-6h return.

NE. ridge; M.Batard, J.-M.Maire, G.Missilier, M.Parmentier, then others; 17 August 1974. TD+.

Thirteen people fixed ropes from 5200m on the first ascent which took two weeks.

Q. Wachektsa, Q. Huantsan approach. Climb E glacier to col, ca.5100m, between Huantsan and P5369.

HUANTSAN MASSIF
Huantsan - W face

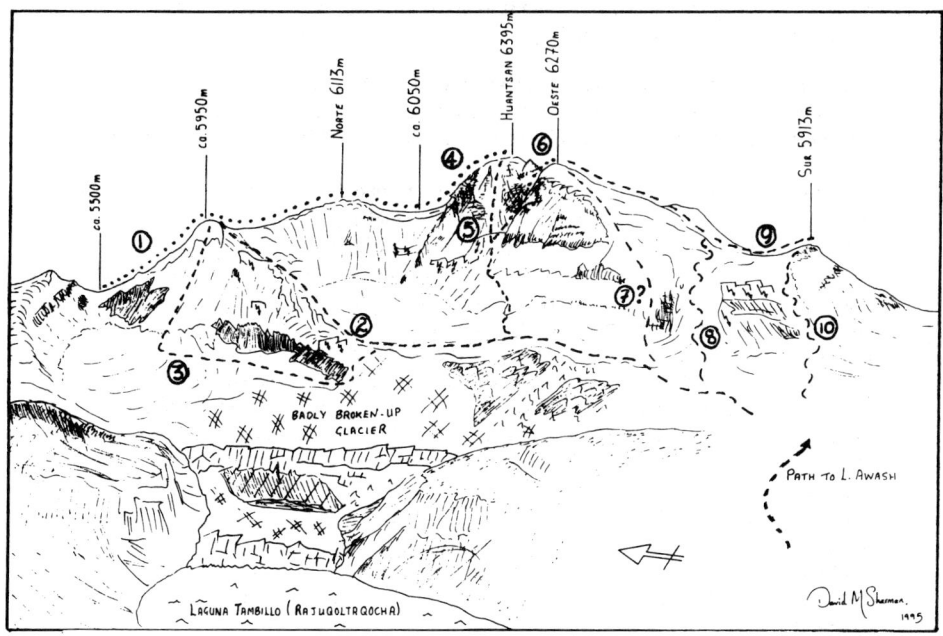

1. NW ridge	4. NNW ridge	6. N. Face	9. N ridge
2. SW ridge	5. W face	7. W face	10. W slopes
3. S face		8. SW slopes	

Climb E ridge, on the N side, except for sections ca.5650 and near the summit. This is sustained mixed climbing with the crux being the final rock band 200m below the summit. Reach the col just to the left of a prominent rock face.

Climb the arete above, traversing onto snow ramps on the N side, 35-40°, and reach a campsite at 5450m. Return to the N side and pass a bergschrund to reach a hanging glacier. Go rightwards up this and 50° snow slopes to reach a camp below enormous cornices at 5800m. Return to the exposed and snowy 45° crest of the ridge and climb it until a snow shoulder campsite at 6000m. Above is a steep mixed step. Go up snow for 100m and then climb diagonally right on mixed ground to reach a chimney in rotten rock, IV. Exit left on 50m of delicate ledges and continue up the summit ridge.

SW. ridge;

A steep rock and ice wall above the saddle with Oeste, it has repulsed many seasoned attempts at the top.

W. face; B.Young, K.Messer, M.Lehner; 2 August 1979. TD ?.

Approach as for SW ridge of Huantsan Norte to 5350m just below the face. Make a traversing ascent of two shields of ice separated by a short vertical step, and gain a tongue of rock which defines the central couloir, ca.5800m. Make a rising traverse up pillars and bulges of water ice for 200m to a bergschrund below a 200m rock band. Steep rock and difficult mixed ground leads left to the last icefield and the summit. The start is essentially as for N face Oeste.

HUANTSAN MASSIF

Huantsan Oeste, 6270:

N. face; J.Tarver, K.Starr; July 1984. TD- ?.

From Q. Rajucolta approach as for the SW ridge of Huantsan Norte and cross the glacier to the base of the N-facing ice slope leading to the col between the W and main summits. Twenty pitches of 55° snow and ice lead to the col and then the W summit. Descend to S in two days return.

W. face (Rochelais route); D.Blanchi, E.Beguin, J.Philippe Floras, E.Brochot; 23 July 1989. D.

Approach as for the SW ridge Huantsan Norte to below a rocky ridge which defines the left side of the seracs between the W and S peaks.

Climb snow slopes to the right of the ridge, passing easily through seracs, 60-70° maximum.

Leave a final huge serac to the left and exit onto open snow slopes leading to the S ridge. Continue to the top. Unrepeated ascent over five days return with 200m fixed rope.

SW. slopes (Italian route); L.Alippi, C.DiPietro, C.Ferrari, A.Galmarini, G.Giannantonio, D.Giobbi, L.Guidali, S.Liati, M.Mazzoleni; 20 June 1973. D-.

Approach as for the W ridge of Huantsan Norte. From the L. Awash traverse broken W glacier northwards through seracs to join the S ridge ca.6000m.

Climb this to summit. There is significant danger from serac avalanches. This can often be avoided by climbing W slopes of Huantsan Sur and traversing the ridgeline.

Huantsan Sur, 5913:

N. ridge; C.Di Pietro, A.Galmarini, D.Giobbi; 19 June 1973. D-.

Approach onto W glacier slopes from L. Awash, then traverse N on the ice avalanche prone W face to the col between the S and W peaks. Climb N ridge.

W. slopes; K.Kobayashi, A.Miyashita, T.Hayashi, Y.Komatsu, M.Nishigori; 23 June 1967. D-

Approach via Q. Rajucolta as for the SW ridge of Huantsan Norte. Climb up glacier margin at L. Awash. Climb over the very broken W glacier to summit avoiding dangerous and changeable seracs.

Rurec, 5700:

The Rurecs are the 'mountains on the inside' and the NW ridge awards good views of everything on the outside. The routes from Q. Shallap up the lesser Rurecs are easy acclimatisation routes.

NW. ridge; E.Angeles, H.Carter, D.Giobbi; 17 July 1965. PD.

From Q. Rajucolta ascend steep slopes to L. Awash as for SW ridge of Huantsan Norte, camp at the lake.

Climb up moraine on the E side and the very easy ridge of loose rock going SE. Ascend a snow dome and climb the very short NW ridge of Yahuaraju, 45° with some solid and easy rock before the summit, 3-4h. Descend the SE ridge and climb up gentle crevassed snow slopes to the summit of Rurec, 6-7h total. A good route.

SW. face; R.Renshaw, D.Wilkinson; 13 July 1979.

From Q. Rurec climb the straightforward 1000m snow face.

SW. buttress; S.Chaney, J.Lund, B.Wilson, S.Howe, R.Jones, J.Cristol, P.Cloud, D.Tody, J.Glidden; 9 July 1981.

From Q. Rurec climb the SW buttress in one day return by climbing snow and ice to reach the W ridge shortly before the summit.

HUANTSAN MASSIF

Yahuaraju (Rurec Oeste), 5675:

NW-SE ridge traverse; see NW ridge Rurec, PD.

NW. face; K.Klinger, W.Sachotonicek; 1 June 1980.

Start the approach as for the SW ridge of Huantsan Norte. From L. Awash climb onto the glacier to the right of the glacial tongue which descends to the lake, 1h.

From the glacier climb the 800m face of mixed ice and rotten rock, which is difficult in the upper part and up to 55° .

Rurec Oeste II, 5350:

N. slopes; I.Hamada, K.Hamada; 22 June 1967.

From L. Awash climb the N slopes of this minor peak _ km W of Yahuaraju.

Rurec Sur I, 5300:

W. side; F.Mohling, S.Chaney, D.Tody, J.Crystol, R.Thron, L.Krimen; 7 July 1981. F/PD.

One day return from Q. Rurec, including two pitches of moderately hard snow and ice.

Rurec Sur II, 5320:

W. slopes; H.Chanzy, Y.d'Aubigne, M.Emslie, W.Wallace; 8 August 1958. F.

From a camp in Q. Rurec ca.4900m go around the N side of L. Tararhua, climb W slopes and glacier to summit in one day return. The easy open W sides of Rurec Sur I, II, and III offer a large variety of pleasant routes on 30° slopes.

Rurec Sur III, 5300:

W. side; W.Dixon, J.Lasner; 10 August 1957.

From L. Tararhua an easy climb in one day return.

Uruashraju, 5735:

The 'columnar mountain' is named for the vertically folded rocks. The Q. Pumahuacanca routes are good value and could be combined with the walk from Olleros to Chavin.

NW. face; A.Schoon, A.Schoon, M.Scott; 8 July 1981.

From L. Tararhua climb NW face in one day return, the base of the face can be reached by crossing Uruashraju's NW spur.

S. ridge; J.Packa, D.Ciochetti, D.Langmade, C.Slaymaker, M.Rourke; 27 July 1975. PD.

Follow the Olleros-Chavin trail to a bridge over the Rio Negro before Qollotococha. Cross the river and follow a good path past huts and up into the Q. Pumahuacanca. Cross the river and go up to a hut below by the glacier edge, 7h from Olleros. Cross the easy glacier to gain S ridge col ca.5300m, 1h.

Climb the narrow, exposed, ridge to the top, 45° maximum, 21/2 -3h.

W. ridge; D.Giobbi, C.Mauri; 17 June 1966. PD.

From L.Tararhua climb NW glacier to W ridge col ca.5300m. Alternatively cross easy Pumahuacanca glacier and climb to reach the W ridge bypassing seracs on the left sided. Then climb W ridge to join S ridge and ascend the exposed crest to summit. Climb 60-70° ice on W of summit block, 7-8h to summit. Some possibility of avalanche danger on this line when warm, fohn-like, winds blow.

It is also possible to climb Uruashraju Chico, 5400m from this col in 3h (C.Giobbi, D.Giobbi, M.Angeles; 29 July 1964).

HUANTSAN MASSIF

Pumahuacanca, 5563:

N. side; H.Clark, A.McKeith; 24 June 1969.

From Q. Rurec climb slopes to the col, ca.5200m, to the N of the summit. Climb NE flank of NE ridge on mixed ground to NW summit. Traverse on steep water ice to highest SE peak, One day return from high camp ca.4900m on NW slopes.

P5130:

Unknown route on E side of southernmost rock summit of Pumahuacanca ridge; A.Miyashita; 20 May 1966.

P5373:

W. slopes; F.Kojima, A.Miyashita; 22 May 1966.

From Q. Pumahuacanca climb the W slopes of this, the southernmost peak on the S ridge of Uruashraju.

Cashan and Shacsha Spur

Abeja, 5377:

N. side; Y.Komatsu, Y.Yokochi; 21 June 1967.

From L. Awash above Q. Rajucolta climb N. side, or E ridge of this point 2km W of Yahuarraju.

Abeja Sur, 5300:

Possible ascent; M.Angeles, F.Martin; 20 August 1957.

P5100

SE. side; W.Dixon; 20 August 1957.

From L. Tararhua climb S / E side of this point 1 1/2 km N of L. Tararhua, on SE ridge of Abeja.

Pucamataraju, 5224:

E. ridge; G.Agnolotti, G.Pettigiani; 18 May 1978.

From L. Tararhua climb to the E col and then the delicate, corniced ridge to the sharp summit 1/2km SE of Cashan Este, in one day.

P5120:

S. side; J.Lasner, W.Dixon; 5 August 1957.

(rock point 1 1/2 km NW of L. Tararhua on SE ridge Cashan Este)

Cashan Este, 5723:

A cashan is a spine or thorn; the name refers to the needle-like summit as seen from Huaraz. Such elegant peaks deserves good routes and this pair have many fine lines.

NE. face; J.Levy; 10 July 1981. PD.

From the old Hidrandina huts below L. Tambillo in Q. Rajucolta follow the path up the grassy Q. Pumahuacanca (there is another quebrada of the same name nearby). The path turns right and follows cairns across moraine to an obvious snowfield, 3 1/2 h. Cross the snowfield and ascend a rightwards sloping 45° snow ramp to exit onto the snowy W ridge and then the top, 3h.

E. ridge; R.Soaper, B.Wilson, C.Griffin, H.Steyskal; 12 July 1981.

Approach through the Q. Rurec and camp at ca.4800m, above a small lake E of P5120.

From the campsite follow cairns up the moraine to its highest point, 45 mins, and continue up the glacier towards the prominent E subsidiary peak. Pass N of this on wide snowfields and gain the E ridge 200m below the summit, 3h. Traverse the ridge, bypassing its high seracs on the N side, and go up a steep 60° snowfield past a short mixed section to the summit, 3h, 7h in total.

This route can also be approached from the Q. Rajucolta. From the huts beside L. Rajucolta (L. Tambillo), ca.4300m, cross a small stream and climb S up a steep couloir edged with cliffs. On reaching a plain follow a cairned path to the right and then the right side of a stream towards a small group of isolated rocks.

Climb scree then moraine and cross a stream to the right on smooth slabs. Continue up scree slopes on the right, and then rock pillars and snow slopes to the ridge, 4-5h.

SW. side; B.Lauterburg, F.Marmillod, R.Schmid, F.Sigrist; 17 June 1948.

Approach via Q. Jauna and Q. Cashan. Climb SW glacier to 50° W ridge of summit ice pyramid, 10h return from high camp ca.5000m.

Cashan Oeste, 5701:

NE. ridge; P.Millar; August 1980.

From Q. Rajucolta climb the steep granite of the NNW face of the second minor summit E of Cashan Oeste. Traverse delicate and exposed ridge to main peak, passing ice towers and descend by the NE face. Two days round trip.

W. side; D.Anderson, L.Carter, J.Miller; 4 July 1967.

Ascend to camp at L. Tururucocha from Macashca by Q. Paria, or by traversing from near Pitec. Climb up rocky slabs to the right of a conspicuous rocky spur and gain the W glacier ca.4600m. Go up to the SW ridge at a small col, climb this and bypass a prominent bergschrund with a traverse across the 45° W face to near the NW ridge. Climb ridge and W face to fore summit. Climb along corniced ridge to the top, 50-60° ice, 2 days return from glacier edge.

Shacsha, 5703:

It is possible to climb Shacsha in one long day from Huaraz if you are fit and organised, alternatively it could be combined with Cashan and a few days of pleasant walking on the grassy plateau. The mountain has two distinct summits, the South is 5697m high and more accessible. It is named for the local equivalent of a Morris dancer.

NE. ridge; H.Chanzy, Y.d'Aubigne, M.Emslie, H.Simpson, W.Wallace; 6 August 1958.

From Q. Rurec ascend E slopes to a col ca.5400m on the NE ridge. Climb NE ridge, bypassing a minor summit on the NW side (ca.5500m). Two days return from a high camp ca.4900m.

S. ridge; H.Martens, J.Maardalen; July 1988. PD+.

Follow the Olleros-Chavin trail and take the fork into Q. Rurec. The bridge over the Rio Negro is washed out but the river is fordable. Follow the trail up the wide valley until it narrows at the second grassy terminal moraine, 1h from ford. Cross the stream and climb a hillside to the NW to eventually reach the slabs and moraine beyond some small lakes, 21/2 h. Alternatively approach as for NW slopes. Cross the moraine to a small rock tower below P5300, 1/2 h. Traverse easy glacier S of this, along a shallow col, to the bergschrund at the base of the ridge, 1h.

Climb 45-50° W flank of S ridge to S summit, 2-3h. Traverse W below the summit to the main summit if really desired. P5300 can be easily climbed from this approach.

NW. slopes; D.M.Sharman; 14 August 1991. AD.

Either approach as S ridge or, quicker, take the path which leads N from the outskirts of Olleros. It climbs to a broad ridge and turns E along the N slope of the crest to lead directly to Shacsha, 4h. Gain the glacier on the right, as for S ridge, and traverse left ca.5200m where it is possible to climb through seracs to gain slopes below the NW ridge, 2h.

Climb these 45° slopes to near top, 2h. Go right at the top and up the left side of a rock tongue to the actual N summit, 60° , 50m.

YANAMAREY MASSIF

The Yanamarey are a group of low peaks situated just North of the Olleros-Chavin road. All the routes are very easy, and those noted below are by no means exhaustive: many other lines have been taken by locals on family holidays. The best approach is from Qerococha which is the breathtaking lake by the Chavin road, buses go to Chavin most days. Yanamarey means black pestle, both the small hand ones and the larger water driven wheels introduced by the Spanish.

Yanamarey (Yanamarey Norte), 5262:

N. ridge; D.Anderson, E.Angeles, V.Angeles, D.Bernays, H.Carter, L.Carter, J.Duenwald, G.Henostroza; 13 July 1967.

From the swampy Q. Araranca climb N glacier and icy N ridge in one day return from the valley.

Yanamarey Sur, 5220:

S. slopes; G.Hartmann, E.Reiss; 20 July 1965.

Climb S slopes in one day return from the Punta Cahuish tunnel.

Yanamarey de Cahuish, 5115:

SE. ridge; A.Cram, L.Cram; 26 June 1966.

From Punta Cahuish tunnel go W, bypass a tiny lake and go up snow to pass. Ascend SE ridge in one day return.

Pukaraju, 5346:

S. face; D.Bernays, G.Henostroza; 23 July 1967.

From Qerococha go up the deep valley off Q. Yanamarey and climb the S face couloir in one day return.

NW. ridge; M.Conway, G.Moseley; 1973.

From Q. Yanamarey climb the NW rock ridge.

P5141 (Conde):

N. side; A.Cram, L.Cram; 28 July 1966;

From W side of Punta Cahuish tunnel ascend N slopes beyond tiny lakes to climb the N ridges on loose red rock.

PONGOS MASSIF

A rather jumbled cluster of low peaks to the South of the Olleros-Chavin road. All the routes are reported to be easy, and can be accomplished in one day from the valleys. The usual approach is from Catac over excellent horse country. The name 'pongos' is a corruption of 'doorway'. The other name for this range is 'queshque' which is a puya that is smaller than the giant Puya Raimondi.

Pongos Norte I (Jatunllacsha I), 5680:

N. side; E.Angeles, M.Angeles, D.Giobbi; 6 June 1964,
From Q. Pamparaju ascend N glacier ampitheatre and climb N side close to NW ridge.

Queshque, 5463:

SW. face; T.de Booy, C.Egeler; 5 June 1952.
From Ls. Queshque climb SW glacier and SW face.

P5403:

S. side; W.Hummel, R.Rocker, F.Wibmer; 27 May 1971.
Climb this a minor peak 100m W of Queshque as for SW face Queshque taking in another minor peak ca.5360m on S ridge of Queshque.
SW. ridge; P.Schiml, W.Weber; 27 May 1971.
From the SW glacier climb the SW ridge of Queshque passing two other minor points, ca.5380m and ca.5330m on the ridge.

P5420:

SE. ridge; D.Fritz, H.Guner; 27 May 1971.
Climb this minor point on the ridge just NE of Maretaca from Q. Queshque.

Maretaca, 5365:

W. ridge; P.Schmil, D.Schwenkglenks, F.Wibmer; 17 May 1971.
From Q. Queshque go over to, and climb, W ridge. Also take in a snowy point ca.5250m to the S.

P5300:

SW. ridge; D.Fritz, H.Guner, W.Humel, R.Rocker, P.Schmil, D.Schwenkglenks, W.Weber, F.Wibmer; 2 June 1971.
From Q. Queshque climb the SW ridge of this, the highest point between Huamashraju and Maretaca and traverse other minor points.

Huamashraju, 5303:

E. side; D.Felber, E.Schill; July 1967.
Climb the E side of this snow peak from Ls. Queshque.

Pongos Norte III (Jatunllacsha III), 5600:

SE. ridge; D.Fritz, W.Hummel, P.Schmil, F.Wibmer; 23 May 1971.
From a camp in Q. Queshque ca.4500m climb the S glacier and SE ridge of this peak, 600m NE of Pongos Norte I.

P5300 (Luyacpani):

Unknown route; J.Diamond, A.Jamanca, J.Terborgh; 9 July 1963.
S. ridge; D.Fritz, W.Hummel, P.Schmil, F.Wibmer; 22 May 1971.
From Q. Queshque ascend this, the first snowy peak N of col ca.5000m by its SW glacier to the S ridge and climb along it past three minor summits.

PONGOS MASSIF

Cayacpunta, 5250:

S-N traverse; D.Fritz, W.Hummel, R.Rocker, P.Schmil, F.Wibmer; 28 May 1971.

From Q. Queshque ascend SW glacier and climb up SW rock slopes to join S ridge. Traverse minor peaks and rock summit then descend N ridge over other minor points

Pongos Sur III (Ichik Pongos), 5580:

NW. slopes; H.Guner, R.Rocker, D.Schwenkglenks, W.Weber; 25 May 1971.

From Q. Queshque climb NW glacier and snow slopes.

Pongos Sur I, 5711:

N. ridge; D.Fritz, H.Guner, W.Hummel, R.Rocker, P.Schmil, D.Schwenkglenks, W.Weber, F.Wibmer; 3 June 1971.

Climb N ridge from Q. Queshque.

E. ridge; E.Angeles, M.Angeles, D.Giobbi; 10 August 1964.

From Q. Raria ascend S glacier and climb S face and E ridge to summit, considerable serac danger.

W. side; T.de Booy, G.Egeler, L.Terray; 10 June 1952.

From Q. Queshque climb W glacier, then the W face, SW ridge and SW face as appropriate.

All the points on the SW ridge of Pongos Sur I were climbed by the 1971 Naturfreunde party. A selection are noted below The approximate altimeter heights have been crudely adjusted to relate better to the heights used elsewhere.

P5410 (Caracuta):
Climb the mixed N ridge of a minor peak ca.5270m to the SW and go up the SW ridge to the top.
P5227 (Acoraju):
Climb the N ridge from Q. Queshque and traverse adjacent points if desired.
P5089 (Acorumi Norte):
Climb N ridge from Q. Queshque and traverse points on the ridge to the SW if desired, ca.4990m, ca.5013m, ca.5010m.

RARIA MASSIF

Another group of lesser peaks in the far South. Because of a frequent tourist bus service to Pastoruri it is possible to climb here for just one or two days, on the many easy routes, not all of which are detailed below, but all of which had been climbed by the early 70s. The name Raria is interesting as it may be a badly corrupted version of either 'high place' or 'lonely place'. An exciting alternative is that it antedates Quechua as it has atypical vowel combinations.

Raria Norte, 5590:

S. slopes; M.Angeles, D.Giobbi, D.Solano; 2 August 1963.

From Q. Waiyaku ascend S glacier of Raria massif to col and descend snowfield to the base of S snow and ice slopes. Climb these and final ridge to top. Alternatively climb the peak easily from Q. Raria in 4-6h.

Raria Sur (Tantash), 5530:

NE. ridge; H.Gasser, D.Solano; 10 June 1959.

From Q. Waiyaku ascend S glacier of Raria massif to col with Este I. Descend far snowfield left to col ca.5200m with Norte. Climb the rocky NE ridge.

Raria Este I, 5460:

S. ridge; E.Angeles, M.Angeles, D.Giobbi; 3 August 1963.

From Q. Waiyaku ascend SW glacier towards col with Este II. Climb SW snow slopes and S ridge, or broad N ridge of Este II, 5380m.

Waiyaku (Huarapasca), 5430:

The Waiyaku peaks are only a few hours from the road and the summits can be gained in 4-6h over the easy, 30-45° , glacier slopes typical of the area.

CAULLARAJU MASSIF

The last peaks before the Huayhuash, the first to be seen as you crest the Conococha pass on the road from Lima. From Conococha they are supposed to look like a white gull spreading its wings in flight.

Approach is from the road at Pastoruri (frequent tourist bus services from Huaraz) or the mining road up Q. Tucu. All the routes are reported as being easy day trips.

Quenuaracra, 5353:
N. face; S.Gloggner; 25 July 1977.
From Q. Huicsu climb scree and then 40° snow slopes in one day return.
S. face; Eugenio Angeles, D.Giobbi; 12 July 1962.
Approach via Q. Quenuaracra and S glacier to climb S face.

Quenuaracra Chico, 5147:
NW.-SW. traverse; M.Angeles, D.Giobbi; 16 July 1962.
From S glacier of main peak traverse in descent to valley. Also climbed from SW in June 1967.

Caullaraju Este, 5686:
N. face; Eugenio Angeles, M.Angeles, D.Giobbi; 14 July 1962.
From Quenuaracra S glacier traverse to N glacier ca.5200m and climb steep snow of N face.
NE. ridge; S., H., & P.Gloggner; 30 July 1977.
If neves penitentes of NE face prove troublesome then climb this rock ridge in one day return from Q. Huicsu.
W. side; V.Angeles, D.Flores, R.Matsuda; 22 May 1966.
Approach via Q. Quellish.

Caullaraju Central, 5636:
N. shoulder; Eugenio Angeles, M.Angeles, D.Giobbi; 18 July 1961.
From a lake ca.4900m in Q. Ocullo climb to the N shoulder and thence the summit. Continue traverse to Oeste I if desired.
N. slopes variation; E.Chrobak, R.Gutkowski; 8 July 1973.
Climb from Q. Huicsu to a high camp ca.5100m on edge of the Caullaraju Central plateau. More directly scree slopes lead to the long flat summit ridge in one day return.

Caullaraju Norte, 5420:
N. slopes; E.Chrobak, R.Gutkowski; 9 July 1973.
From Q. Huicsu climb to a camp ca.5100m on the Caullaraju Central plateau. Climb N slopes.
SW. side; H.Gasser, H.Pattis, D.Solano; 22 June 1959.
Q. Peceipallca approach to ascend its main tributary, the Q. Yantacuta, and begin climbing from the SW.
W. ridge; Eugenio Angeles, D.Giobbi; 15 July 1960.
From Q. Ocullo ascend to base of W glacier ca.4900m and thence climb corniced W ridge. One day return from ca.4900.

Co. Yanawanka, 5180:
NE. slopes; Eugenio Angeles, D.Giobbi; 14 July 1960.
From Q. Ocullo take the S fork (another Q. Yanawanca) to the w glacier area. Climb the NE rock slopes in one day return from the valley.

CAULLARAJU MASSIF

Caullaraju Oeste I (Shumaqraju), 5582:

N. slopes; Eugenio Angeles, M.Angeles, D.Giobbi; 20 July 1961.
From a camp ca.5280 on the Caullaraju Central plateau go towards col ca.5200 connecting the peaks and climb N slopes to summit.

Cruz de Plata (Caullaraju Oeste II), 5603:

NW. side; H.Gassner, K.Keplinger, H.Pattis, U.Staudacher; 21 June 1959.
Approach via Q. Peceipallca and climb NW side.

Caullaraju Oeste III, 5500:

NW. ridge; F.Anzio, G.Verganni, A.Vinci; mid-March 1952.
Approach from Q. Peceipallca to middle basin (Q. Yantacuta) of W glacier of Nevado Cruz del Plata. Climb W glacier and NW ridge of peak.
S. slopes; Eugenio Angeles, M.Angeles, D.Giobbi; 19 July 1962.
Approach from the SW to camp ca.5100m on S glacier. Then climb this, and Oeste IV, in one day.

Caullaraju Oeste IV, 5460:

S. slopes; Eugenio Angeles, M.Angeles, D.Giobbi; 19 July 1962. See S slopes Oeste III above.

Tucu, 5479:

NW. slopes; Eugenio Angeles, M.Angeles, D.Giobbi; 23 July 1963.
Approach by road up Qs. Pachacoto and Ingenio to Mina San Anton (Santon) and thence Q. Pastoruri. Climb to a camp ca.5050m by NW glacier edge and continue to summit.

Huicsu, 5487:

NW. ridge; H.Gasser, H.Pattis, D.Solano; 4 June 1959.
From Q. Rajucolta climb NW rock ridge.
W. face; F.Niedermaier, A.Muller, S.Gloggner, P.Gloggner; 31 July 1977.
From Q. Huicsu follow the glacier which gradually steepens to 40°, one day return.

Huicsu Sur, 5437:

E. ridge; P.Morales, M.Sotomayer, D.Gambini; 1967.
Climb E rock ridge from Q. Tucu.
SE. slopes; Eugenio Angeles, M.Angeles, D.Giobbi; 26 July 1963.
Climb SE slopes and descend E slopes. The first ascentionists approached by the Huicsu-Tucu col ca.5100m to the head of Q. Tucu, but it is also possible to approach up Q. Tucu.

Condorjitanka, 5392:

SE.-NE. traverse; Eugenio Angeles, M.Angeles, D.Giobbi; 25 July 1963.
From Q. Tucu climb scree slopes and N face of Condorjitanka Chico. Continue up SE ridge of main peak and descend NE snow slopes in one day return from valley camp ca.5000m.
SW. ridge; H.Gloggner, S.Gloggner, F.Niedermaier; 27 July 1977.
From Q. Huicsu climb rotten rock and then 150m of 50° ice to reach summit ridge, one day return.

Rajutuna Norte, 5349:

NW. slopes; Eugenio Angeles, D.Giobbi; 26 December 1959.
Approach from mine road and Mina Tucujirca on the W flank to climb NW slopes and W wall.

CAULLARAJU MASSIF

Rajutuna, 5360:

W. slopes; A.Gruft, H.Gruft, E.Henostroza; 2 October 1963.

Approach W slopes from Mina Tucujirca. Climb N summit the same day if desired.

Rajutuna Suroeste, 5137:

N. slopes; J.Acosta, C.Maguina, Alberto Morales, M.Sotomayor, H.Varillas, S.Villanueva, Apolonio Yanac, J.Morales and others; 28 May 1957.

Climb N slopes of this minor peak from Mina Tucujirca.

APPROACH INFORMATION
Map of the Cordillera Blanca

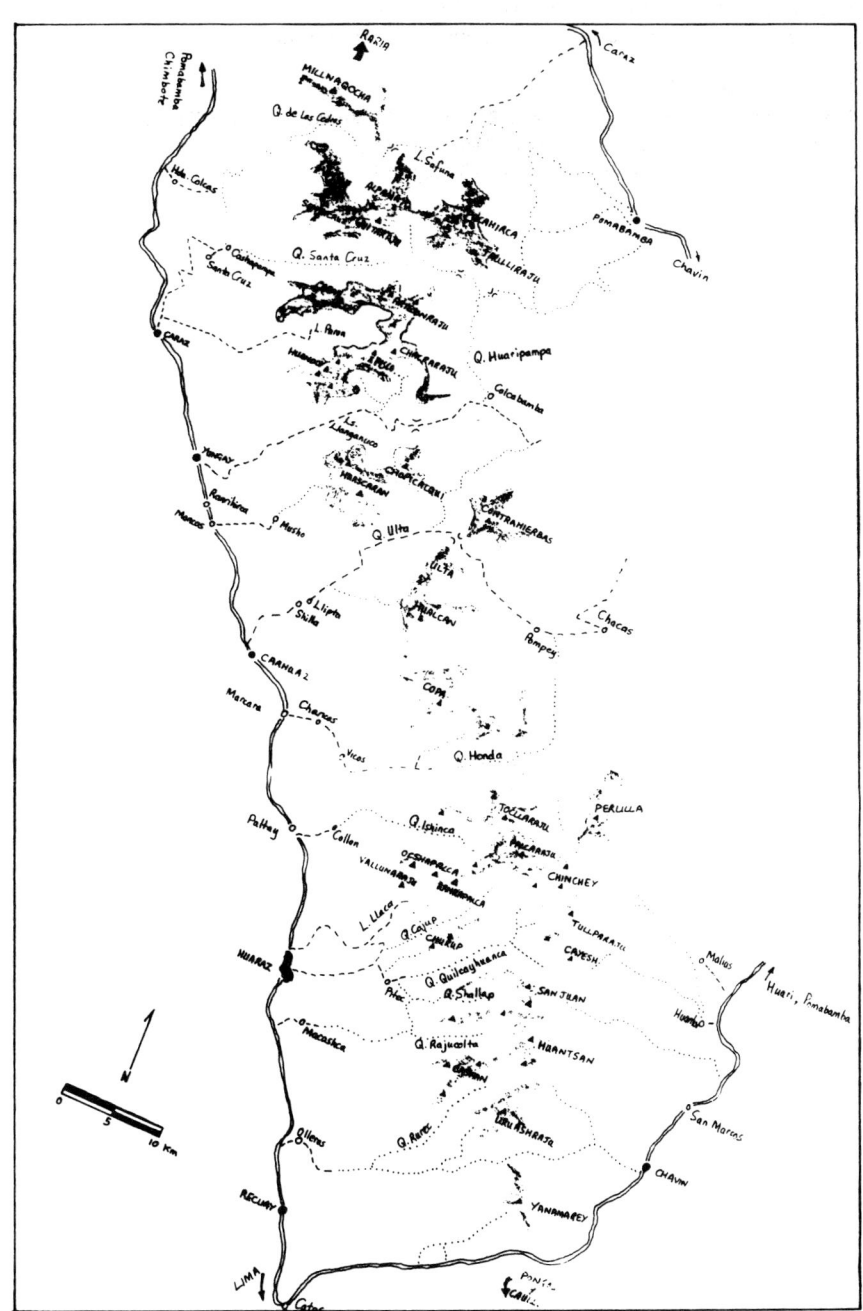

APPROACH INFORMATION

This section draws heavily upon Jim Bartle's excellent trekking guide **Trails Of The Cordilleras Blanca & Huayhuash Of Peru**. Sadly this is no longer in print, and is extremely scarce. A second edition is promised for 1996, but in the absence of another trekking guide to which climbers can be referred for approach information a very limited description of the important approaches is made below. This book is not intended as a trekking guide. Climbers are expected to be more self sufficient than walkers, and so are largely left to their own devices in making their way up valleys. Often the key problem is choosing the right path out of the roadhead villages and across a maze of fields. Once the steep sided quebradas (valleys) have been entered very little route finding is required.

Quebrada Tayapampa

At the head of the Quebrada Tayapampa lie a series of small lakes, the Lagunas Safuna and Laguna Pucacocha. A meadow below the latter is the normal base camp for the N side of the Pucahircas. It used to be possible to drive to Laguna Safuna along a rough dirt road suitable for four wheel drive vehicles.

The road should be followed 30 km N from Pomabamba past the one shack village of Larel to the one shack village of Palo Seco. A 'Corporation Peruana del Santa' sign marks the start of the 27 km rough road up to the three houses known as Huilca. If you are walking there are a variety of other, better, paths to reach Huilca (from either Laurel or Pomabamba, ask directions at Pomabamba). After Huilca the road crosses the stream on the bridge 100m upstream and reaches the Ls. Safuna 5.5km later. The best campsites are at the lower lake.

The trail up Quebrada Tayapampa leaves the Safuna road after the road crosses the stream, climbs past several cascades to a large meadow (good campsite) where it recrosses the stream. Then go steeply up to the right past another waterfall. Above follow the middle of the canyon past tiny Laguna Kaiko to a crude cabin above Laguna Pucacocha.

Quebrada de los Cedros

This trail is used to reach the N side of Alpamayo and Santa Cruz, the S side of the Millwaqocha massif, and by taking a side track up to Laguna Yuraccocha the W side of Santa Cruz is reached. It is a long walk of 50km to the campsite at the head of the valley.

On most days collectivos leave the market in Caraz for the village of Cashapampa, a dusty ride which takes about three hours. From Cashapampa take a complicated 8km walk to the village of Cholin. I do not have room to explain it here, so ask - or simply traverse the farmland along the base of the Cordillera. At Cholin fill your water bottle as it is the last water for 12 km. Climb out of Cholin along the obvious red trail heading steeply north. This turns right when the grade lessens, traverses the ridge to east, switches back northeast over the ridge, passes through old Inca terraces and a flat area, then begins a long series of switchbacks. After these the trail turns left and crosses an enormous landslide then two small muddy creeks (7km to Cullicocha). More switchbacks, another creek, another ridge and then a fork. The left hand fork goes on another 3km of moderate climbing to reach Laguna Cullicocha.

By walking along the right fork for 15km you reach Laguna Yuraccocha. The trail enters Quebrada Yuraccocha high above the river and stays on the ridge for several kilometres before descending steeply to some meadows. It then ascends the moraine below Nevado Santa Cruz Sur to Laguna Yuraccocha. There are old Ingemmet huts halfway up the moraine.

APPROACH INFORMATION

The trail to Cullicocha wanders on until it reaches the lower end of the lake. The best campsite is at the north end of Cullicocha's outlet tunnel, by Azulcocha. After this follow the trail over granite to the pass into Quebrada de los Cedros. Two ridges later the path descends a series of switchbacks at the bottom of which the trail forks. The left fork goes to the village of Alpamayo. The main trail goes to the right, descends to the east to meet the river, and then follows the right side of the river. The path and river turn right at the top of the valley. Then cross a stream near the lower end of the high moraine near Laguna Jancarurish, a small barren pea green lake. Go up the moraine and stream to the large flat grassless Alpamayo base camp.

Many parties use a base camp up the branch of Quebrada los Cedros which flows towards Santa Cruz, ca.4450m, by rock walls. Obviously a good site for Santa Cruz, but also good access to the glaciers which come off Quitaraju and Alpamayo. Just above the campsite follow gully up to ridge (the one coming down from Loyaqjirka), steepish for the last 100m. From there it is a gentle descent over easy benches to the Alpamayo glacier. This base camp is useful for parties who wish to climb both on Santa Cruz and Alpamayo.

Quebradas Santa Cruz & Huaripampa

When people refer to the Quebrada Santa Cruz they are often referring to an extremely popular trekking circuit which takes in the valleys of Santa Cruz, Huaripampa, and the Llanganuco lakes. Climbers can use combinations of different parts of the circuit to reach various base camp sites.

Climbers will normally walk up the Quebrada Santa Cruz and camp in meadows between Artesonraju and Taulliraju, or then turn left up the Quebrada Arhuaycocha to Alpamayo base camp. This walk begins at the village of Cashapampa. Cashapampa is reached by taking the camionetta (pick-up) service from the market square in the town of Caraz. This journey takes 2 or 3 hours and runs most days, leaving to go up at about 10am, returning about 2pm. The Cashapampa road is a side fork of the road to the village of Santa Cruz where the camionneta may stop for an hour or so. If you arrive at the straggle of houses which form Cashapampa at midday then it is usual to arrange for burros and arrieros in the afternoon, camp overnight on the field, and depart early the next morning so as to avoid walking up through the gorge in blistering afternoon heat.

Leave Cashapampa by the track on the opposite side of the 'square' from the small shop. After 100m turn right where there is an old sign and go up a small walled lane to an irrigation channel. Follow this upstream to the wall at the entrance to the valley. The gate in the wall is seldom locked. An extremely well worn path is followed for 3 hours across rock slides on the south side of the entrance gorge. It then descends to follow the river bank and 6 hours after leaving Cashapampa the first lake is reached, Ichicocha, and then the second, Jatuncocha. There are pleasant campsites at the east end of Jatuncocha. The path across marshy meadows leads to the base of the hanging valley of Quebrada Arhuaycocha where two alternatives are normal. *To reach Alpamayo base camp take the path which goes straight up into the steep entrance to the side valley, swings right to avoid marshes, and then back to the centre to campsites under stands of quenal trees, 6h from Jatuncocha. Do not use the trees for firewood as they have suffered very badly from the depredations of climbers.* The other main base camp is 2h further up the Quebrada Santa Cruz. Follow the path upstream to meadows from which both Taulliraju and Artesonraju are visible.

Both these camp sites give access to the same groups of peaks and it is mainly a matter of preference which is chosen. The one in Santa Cruz is less frequented by climbers, but is often visited by trekkers who go on to cross the pass at Punta Union (just follow the path for 2h - this is the way to reach the Taulliraju glacier) and descend the Quebrada Huaripampa to the village of Colcabamba.

APPROACH INFORMATION

It is just as pleasant to walk in to these campsites, or into two relatively unexplored areas accessed from the Quebradas Ranincuray and Paria, from the east side of the range, up the Quebrada Huaripampa. The drawback is finding a regular and reliable transport across the range to reach Colcabamba. It is best to ask in Yungay about the trucks or buses which travel (irregularly) every few days up the road from Yungay and across the Portachuelo de Llanganuco to Yanama. If there are enough of you then you could hire one on your own. This spectacular truck ride takes most of one day. You are dropped at the roadside by a pair of houses just 10 minutes walk uphill from Colcabamba (if you have walked out this way then it is possible to sit by this roadside for a day or so, waiting for a vehicle). In Colcabamba there is a small store, inn, and restaurant. I once drank the most superb coffee, ground and roasted over a fire by the lady who runs the inn - truly excellent as I'd just walked down from Alpamayo with a huge rucsac.

Just below Colcabamba cross the river to the northeast bank, or wait 1km to the bridge. *If you wish to go up the Quebrada Ranincuray then stay on the southwest side of the river by Colcabamba.* Then follow the path, remaining in the valley and not taking the side path which climbs up and east to a silver mine. The path crosses and recrosses the river before passing by the Lagunas Morococha (6h, 15km from Colcabamba). *Where the path crosses the river it is possible to turn west and follow a path up into Quebrada Paria, 10h.* The path then winds steeply up through grass and rock slabs to reach the pass of Punta Union after another 1.5h. Many campsites are possible along the way. Once over the Punta Union then simply drop down to whichever base camp suits best.

Lagunas Llanganuco

The valley of Llanganuco has two superb blue lakes nestling in it. It is also the way to reach routes on the south side of the Huandoys the east of the Huascarans, and Chopicalqui. The two normal base camps are the Pisco base camp and the Chopicalqui base camp. Just before the lakes is a toll booth where visitors pay a daily rate for entering the Parque Nacional de Huascaran. Foreigners pay more than Peruvians, students pay less if they have valid ISIC cards. It is possible to lie about how long you are entering the park for, but if you do so you are cheating the environment of much-needed cash.

The most reliable way up is to use the tourist buses which depart from Huaraz every day or so for day tips to the lakes. You will have to pay the driver extra to take you the extra 1km to the entrance to Quebrada Yanapacha where the Pisco base camp is only 300m from the roadside. The bus driver may be unwilling to take you the extra 3km up to the zig-zag which marks the drop-off point for the Chopicalqui base camp. Other ways up are to use the trans-range buses and trucks which go to Yanama (see Quebrada Santa Cruz), or to hire a pick-up truck in Yungay which normally costs $50 or so. I have had success on three occasions hitching up and down this road, but the standards of driving I experienced were terrifying.

Laguna Paron

This is the access to the south side of Artesonraju. The approach is very simple - a vehicle to the power station and then a short walk along the north shore of the lakeside to camp at the east end.

In some years a tourist bus visits these lakes on day trips from Caraz. Otherwise it is necessary to hire a pick-up ($50 or so) truck to get up to the Hidrandina power station. Hire this in Caraz by asking in the market place. Coming down it is often possible for pairs to hitch a lift on Hidrandina vehicles which saves trying to arrange when transport should return to collect you..

APPROACH INFORMATION

Quebrada Ulta

Not many climbers visit this area these days so if you do climb then you are likely to be on your own. A number of extremely hard routes on the south side of Chopicalqui and Huascaran are accessible, as well as on Ulta itself. This valley is a useful way of crossing the range.

A road runs up Quebrada Ulta, past the villages of Shilla and Llipta above Carhuaz through the tunnel in the passage de Ulta, and down to Pompey and Chacas on the east side of the range. From these villages it is possible to travel north by a looping road to Yanama, or more easily south to Chavin and hence back to Huaraz. There is a weekly bus service from Huaraz - Carhuaz - Chacas, and occasional trucks go from Huaraz - ask near the new fish market.

It is possible to walk up the valley, or up the side valley of Auquiscocha which goes to climbs on Ulta and Hualcan.

Quebrada Honda

It is normally best to hire a camionetta in Huaraz to take you up into the quebrada as the walk uphill from Vicos holds no real interest. *(When walking downhill from the gate it is possible to follow a fairly obvious footpath which cuts directly across the road's sweeping zigzags).* It is possible to arrange for burros in Vicos. If you are taking a camionetta it is best to arrange for burros by making a preparatory daytrip to Vicos by one of the regular buses. The gatekeepers cottage is right by the gate so it is normally possible to get a car or burros in without making prior arrangements. The main trail up the quebrada to Laguna Pucaranracocha is extremely obvious as it has borne heavy traffic to the mine workings beneath Copap. It keeps to the north/east side of the river and takes 7h to reach campsites at the lake outlet. More interesting paths take the other side of the river and it is from these that the paths into the side valleys lead to climbs on Tocclaraju and Palcaraju.

The road up to Laguna Pacharuri is blocked by fallen boulders just after the turn off from the main trail. From here it is only a 4h walk to the old Ingemett huts at the lake, following the very obvious trail.

Laguna Legiacocha

This is where the base camp is for Copa. Take one of the many buses from Huaraz to Chancos where you can arrange for burros if required. This is advisable as the path is very easy to miss, and the climb very short and steep, 10-12h. This is why no further description is given.

Quebrada Ishinca

This is a popular base camp from where a decent number of middle grade routes can be easily accessed. The approach is short and only the miserable base camp stops this being a perfect valley.

Unless you arrange for a truck in Huaraz you should take the bus to the village of Paltay. From this a murderous flog up the road takes you to the village of Collon in about 4h. Unfortunately there is no regular bus service to Collon. In Collon you can arrange for burros, but they are normally quite expensive and often horses are the only (expensive) beasts available.

Take the trail from the roadend in Collon. After 200m there is a fork. Take the lower trail which descends to cross a small stream. Soon it crosses the main stream, turns right and passes through

APPROACH INFORMATION

farmaland to the gate which is normally locked (key in Collon). From the gate follow the path through a lovely quenal forest and then meadows to the base camp by the lake outfall, 8h from Collon. The campste is sandy andtoo many climbers have left garbage around.

Laguna Llaca

Some smashing climbs on the south face of Occshapallca are usefully combined with easy and quick access.

Occasionally tourist buses visit this Quebrada, but normally you will need to arrange a pick-up truck. Make sure that the driver has arranged for the gate at the bottom of the quebrada to be opened. It is a long walk up. The guides have access to a hut which can be used as a base - ask at their office by the Plaza de Armas. This is the area the guides use for their own training courses.

Quebrada Cojup

Not many people visit this quebrada despite the variety of good, easier routes which are available, as well as some extremely hard lines on Ranrapalca.

The easiest approach is to get a ride up the Quebrada Llaca road to Km 15 where a trail descends 1km to the *portada*. This is normally locked, ask in the village of Unchus (1h from Huaraz) as to who is the current *duena de la jabe*. Once in the valley follow the trail up the south side of the valley to a rocky meadow where it crosses the stream and continues along the other side to the old Ingemett camp just before Laguna Palcacocha, 14h from the portada. There is no trail to Laguna Perolcocha. Instead climb straight up the canyon wall to the northwest, starting 500-1000m below the Ingemett camp, until you reach a large meadow. Then bear left and walk directly towards Ranrapalca to reach the lake, 3h. There are campsites by all the lakes, and good sites along the main valley floor.

Another approach is to walk up the road to Pitec (see Quebrada Quilcayhuanca) and follow the meadows north (not going up into Laguna Churup) until you strike the portada after 4km. Both these approaches are easier than the direct walk.

Quebradas Quilcayhuanca & Cayesh

This is a very pleasant valley for which you should allow two days to access. At the head of the valley are a number of routes of all grades. The problem is that the routes are quite spread out and so it is difficult to site a base camp which serves them all, yet retains reasonable approach lengths. The best campsite is where the paths diverge, just above the Cayesh turn-off. The problem with this is the long slog up to Cuchillacocha for climbs on Pucaranra. Like many others this valley is badly overgrazed as a result of the system of semi-communal ownership of grazing land which encourages each of the community members to graze as many animals as possible.

The road up from Huaraz to Pitec takes about 5h to walk up, 3h to walk down, and 2h to drive. Driving up is a very good idea. If you wish to walk up then be prepared to get lost several times on a confusing number of parallel paths through the densely populated farmland around Unchos and Llupa. Follow the motor road until you reach Llupa, but then take the well worn narrow path which takes the crest of the ridge; the road winds away on the right, occasional meeting the path. Pitec is a small straggling village away to the right of the roadhead.

Follow the clear trail to the portada into Quebrada Quilcayhuanca. This is always locked, and confusingly the gatekeeper's cottage is not the place where the key is kept. The key is kept down in

APPROACH INFORMATION

Unchos. After the gate just walk straight up the valley to where it divides (9h) to go right up Quebrada Cayesh or straight on up to Laguna Cuchillacocha and Tullparaju. There are many excellent campsites.

If you turn right up Cayesh then you will probably have to wade the river. There is a little brush bridge but it is hard to locate. Once across the river there is a maddening struggle to find indistinct animal paths in dense brush. It takes 3h to reach the head of the valley where the path reappears to zig zag up the hillside on the right to the old coal mine and the glaciated Abra Villon pass to Quebrada Carhuascancha.

If you go straight ahead the trail to Laguna Cuchillacocha will fork left and zigzag up the left side of the valley to reach meadows and old Ingemett huts near the lake, 4-5h. Another steeper path drops down on the other side of the stream to meet the Tullparaju path higher up.

Alternatively the path to Laguna Tullparaju turns right past old Ingemett huts at the point where the Cuchillacocha path starts ascending. Then it goes through a small ravine and up the north side of the outfall stream. It is quite clear, 1h, no campsite at the lake.

Quebrada Churup

From Pitec make a 2h hike to this small lake. Always stay left (west) of the outfall stream. From the roadend follow the moraine up to the left and not until level with the lake do you begin traversing over to it. This is because of granite cliffs below the lake. Poor campsites.

Quebrada Shallap

It takes one day to walk up Shallap from the roadhead at Pitec. The portada is always locked, and I have not been able to find out where the key is kept. From Pitec follow the Quilcayhuanca trail and split right along the obvious road. Follow this road, which turns into a smaller but still distinct path and contours around all the way to the portada, 1h. Follow the trail easily up the quebrada to reach the end in 4h. Read the climbing descriptions for S ridge San Juan.

Quebrada Rajucolta

If you want to climb on Huantsan then this is probably your best approach and base camp. The obvious approach is up the valley from Macashca which is a long gentle trog up the south side taking a path through good farmland. However the approach described below is easier to organise.

Start from Pitec as for Quebrada Shallap, but continue to skirt the edge of the farmland, following the path which contours around beyond the entrance to Quebrada Shallap, reaching the portada after 2h. This path peters out a little as it crosses a small spur, but by following your nose and being careful not to lose too much height you will succeed. On the last occasion I visited the portada was locked and the caretaker did not have the key. Follow the path up the quebrada for 6h to reach old huts at Laguna Tambillo. The best campsites are set down in the quebrada from the lake. Read the climbing descriptions for the SW ridge of Huantsan Norte.

APPROACH INFORMATION

Quebrada Rurec

There are actually two Quebrada Rurecs, one on the west side of the Huantsans and another on the east. This description is for the western quebrada which is useful for Shacsha, Cashan, and Rurec. Buses run regularly from Huaraz to the town of Olleros. It is possible to stay in Olleros but I make a point of never lingering here as it is the place where a British hiker was murdered by Sendero Luminoso terrorists in the late 1980s. He was staying in the town hall, and when the terrorists came to assassinate the mayor the mayor scarpered and the unfortunate Briton became a substitute victim.

Follow the Olleros-Chavin road & trail and take the fork which descends 100m to cross the bridge over the Rio Negro into Q. Rurec. The bridge over the Rio Negro is washed out but the river is fordable. Follow the trail up the wide valley until it narrows at the second grassy terminal moraine, 1h from ford. *Here cross the stream and climb a hillside to the NW to reach Shacsha.* Otherwise continue up the wide valley to reach the large Laguna Tararhua, 7h from Olleros.

Quebrada Yanamarey

Take the bus which goes every day to Chavin. At the west end of the Laguna Querococha get off the bus and follow the path around the north shore, over a swamp, and cross the inlet stream to meet the main path (which goes down to the road at the east end of the lake at Km 25). Follow the main path up the valley to the old Ingemett huts, 3h.

The Eastern Quebradas

I make no claim to be able to advise on approaches on this side of the range. I am told that in general the valleys are steeper and more rugged. They are certainly rarely visited by climbers or trekkers. As a consequence the locals are less used to having a dozen *gringo* climbers arrive unexpectedly and ask to hire burros and arrieros. Not only will they simply not know what to charge (leading to concerns by both parties that they are being ripped off), but they often do not have burros to spare from carrying out fieldwork. A complicating factor is that Quechua is spoken more widely than Spanish. This suggests that it is well worth investing in a decent cook who can assist you in the business of arranging these sorts of things. It will also be worth allowing extra time.

Grading

As far as possible I have evaluated the difficulty of routes in an effort to help you select suitable climbs. I have used the UIAA system of alpine grades which I feel to be most appropriate as the Cordillera Blanca is essentially a super-alpine range. Below is a brief explanation of this system.

Overall Grade

The overall grade is indicated by a french adjectival grade running from the easiest, Facile (F) and Peu Difficile (PD), through Assez Difficile (AD) and Difficile (D), to harder routes at Tres Difficile (TD) and then the open ended upper reaches of Extrem Difficile 1, 2, 3... (ED 1, 2, 3...).

The adjectival grade takes into account such factors as the length of the route, problems of descent or retreat, technical difficult, and objective dangers such as exposure to rockfall. Thus a very fierce and sustained technical route which is short and safe could have quite a low grade whilst a technically easy climb which is long and continually exposed to serac fall might be awarded a higher grade. The grade is given for the normal conditions on the mountain. The difficulties will be increased by poor conditions: fresh snow on rock routes, or insufficient or poor quality ice on ice routes.

As an approximate guide to difficulties F would be suitable for novices and D is the point at which technical climbing becomes common. A TD would have some serious pitches and normally require a bivouac above any high camp, whilst on ED routes retreat is frequently problematic and there will be pitches of great difficulty.

Pitch Grading

Sometimes the difficulty of individual sections is indicated. Free rock climbing is graded with Roman numerals using the UIAA system, e.g. V. For aid pitches the letter 'A' is used in conjunction with a numeral from 1 to 5. A1 designates extremely simple aid climbing and A5 involves difficult and insecure placements. Only the inclination is used for snow and ice, e.g. 50-65° . A combination of all of these methods is used for mixed ground. Variations within a grade are noted with + and - signs. e.g. V+ or TD-. If the grade of a route is uncertain then I have indicated this with a query to allow you to treat this with due caution. e.g. D+ ?.

Graded List

Below is a graded list of representative climbs in the Cordillera Blanca. In case you are completely unfamiliar with the UIAA grading system some of the routes are paired with similar climbs in other alpine regions. Whilst these are not meant to be exact comparisons hopefully they will allow you to deduce a common reference point. By 'similar' what I mean is that a party who would be technically competent on one route should be able to cope with the technical difficulties of the other.

All routes in the graded list are routes of good quality. Additionally a star system is used with *** being the best. The symbol + indicates that a route is popular with guided parties

		NE ridge traverse, Millishraju, F-
		(Aonach Eagach ridge, Scotland / Midi-Plan traverse, France)
+	***	N-S traverse, Vicos, F
		*W ridge, Jatunmontepuncu, F
+	*	SW ridge, Maparaju, F
		(Hochstedder Dome, NZ)
+		W slopes, Huamashraju, F

		E slopes, Caraz I, F
+		SW ridge, Ishinca, F
		(normal, Mt Blanc du Tacul, France / Kaindlgrat ridge, Wiesbachorn, Austria)
+		SE side, Urus Este, PD-
+	*	SW ridge, Pisco Este, PD
+		SW slopes, Vallunaraju, PD
		(normal, Grossglockner, Austria)
+	*	W slopes, Copa, PD
		(Bosses ridge, Mt Blanc, France / normal, Mt Delebeche, NZ)
+	**	Garganta, Huascaran Sur, PD
+	**	SW ridge, Chopicalqui, PD+/AD-
		(N face, Wildspitze, Austria)
+	***	S ridge, Huascaran Norte, AD-
		(W Buttress, Denali, Alaska)
		SW slopes-W ridge, Chinchey, AD
+	*	W ridge, Quitaraju, AD
		(Linda Glacier, Mt Cook, NZ)
		E ridge, Rinrihirca, AD+
		N ridge, Artesonraju, AD+
		(Tasman-Silberhorn traverse, NZ)
+	***	Ferrari, Alpamayo, AD+
		(N face, Tour Ronde, France)
		SE ridge, Pukaranra, AD+
	**	SE face col, Pucarashta Oeste, D-
	**	N face, Quitaraju, D-
		(N spur, Chardonnet, France)
+	*	NE slopes, Ranrapalca, D-
		(Palavicini, Grossglockner, Austria)
	*	SE face, Artesonraju, D
		(Brenva spur, Mt Blanc, France)
	**	French, Alpamayo, D+
		(Jaeger, Mt Blanc du Tacul, France)
		NE face, Santa Cruz, D+
	*	NE face, Huandoy Norte, D+
		(Swiss, Courtes, France)
		S face, Pucarashta Central, TD-
		(Orion face, Ben Nevis, Scotland)
	*	S face Occshapalcca, TD+
		(Gabarrou couloir, Mt Blanc du Tacul, France)
	*	E ridge, Ranrapalca, TD+
		(N face, Ortler, Austria)
	**	American or German routes, Cayesh, TD+
		(Bonatti Pillar, Petit Dru, France)
	***	Quebec/Fowler variants, Taulliraju, TD
	**	SW face, Santa Cruz, TD
	*	Slovenian variant, NE face, Huascaran Sur, TD+
		(Caroline face, Mt Cook, NZ / Shroud, Grand Jorasses, France)
	**	Jaeger route, Chacraraju Este, ED1
		(normal N face, Droites, France)
	*	NE face, Huascaran Norte, ED1
		S face, Pucarashta Este, ED1
		(Orion Face direct, Ben Nevis, Scotland)
	***	Paragot route, Huascaran Norte, ED 1/2
		(Walker spur, Grand Jorasses, France)
	**	Fowler-Watts route, Taulliraju, ED 2/3

Languages, Abbreviations, & Glossary

Names

Names cause considerable trouble because of the many different ways of writing and spelling them. The names of people have generally been written with initials and dominant surnames. Compound Quechua-Spanish place names have evolved from their original easily recognisable roots to those in use today. This process of evolution has yet to set firm as Quechua is only slowly becoming a written language. Additionally any one point (especially mountains) can have many different names bestowed by various communities. The most common or appropriate has been used and major alternate names noted in parenthisis. Accents and other diacritic marks are not used as I cannot keep up with typing them for every language from Spanish to Slovenian via Japanese.

Quechua In Peru

The Quechua language spoken around the Cordillera Blanca is of the Quechua B family of dialects. This is probably fairly similar to the original Quechua which evolved around two thousand years ago amongst the fishing communities near Lima. It varies markedly from the later Cuzco Quechua A dialects; as much as Portugese does from Spanish. Quechua A was relatively recently superimposed by the Incas as an administrative language and is thus far more homogenous.

Peru has formally adopted Quechua as a second language using the Cuzco dialect as a model form. If written correctly this results in fairly Germanic spellings which are disliked in Huaraz. Accordingly the Ancash/Chavin region has chosen to use a more Latin system for rendering the local dialects, although even this rule is not strictly applied. Therefore I have tried to spell place names in this Latin form, which should be pronounced as if Spanish. Locals will hopefully recognise your attempt and help correct the inevitable mistakes. When pronounced correctly Quechua sounds quite stacatto and harsh.

Many of the place names reflect the concerns of people trying to extract a hard living from the unyielding Andean environment. The basis for some are noted in the text. Those seeking detailed further information should consult the Diccionario Quechua Ancash-Huailas or should look to the Quechua Phrasebook (see bibliography).

Spanish

Few Peruvians speak English or another of the major languages so you will need to be able to communicate in Spanish. As an absolute minimum you can pick up enough Spanish on the plane journey to Peru, but I recommend that you do try and learn a liitle more than this. Your attempts will undoubtedly be greatly appreciated - good luck.

Glossary & Abbreviations

arriero		donkey driver
AGMP		Peruvian Mountain Guides Association
burro		donkey
ca.	cerca;	approximately
Co.	cerro;	hill.
colectivo		A 'bus service operating more or less regularly on a more or less defined route. Often a minibus or pick-up truck which leaves from a market town and visits a string of villages.

camioneta	The pick-up truck which colectivos usually use, and which you share with animals, crops, local children, and farm men and women going to market.	
DAV	Deutsche Alpenverein;	German Alpine Club.
DOAV	Deutscher-Osterreicher Alpenverein; German-Austrian Alpine Club. (Since divorced to to form the national clubs of the DAV and OAV).	
Gl.		glacier.
guardian		effective anti-theft device.
h		hours.
km		kilometres.
L(s).	laguna(s);	lake(s).
m		metres.
mins.		minutes.
Nev.	nevado;	mountain.
OAV	Osterreicher Alpenverein;	Austrian Alpine Club.
P		unnamed high point.
PNP	The new name for the police.	
PIP	An old name for an investigative branch of the police (the detectives).	
Q(s).	quebrada(s);	valley(s).
R.	rio;	river.
UIAA		International Union Of Alpine Associations
UIAGM		International Union Of Mountain Guides Associations

Useful Addresses & Books

Mountain Sickness - prevention, recognition & treatment
Peter H. Hackett M.D.
ISBN 0-930410-10-6

Quechua Phrasebook
Ronald Wright & Nilda Callanaupa
ISBN 0-86442-039-0

Diccionario Quechua Ancash-Huailas
(with a companion grammar)
Gary J. Parker & Amancio Chavez
Ministerio de Educacion, Peru, 1976

Mountaineering In The Andes, a sourcebook for climbers
Jill Neate
ISBN 0-907649-33-5

South America On A Shoestring
Geoff Crowther
ISBN 0-908086-75-X

Medicine For Mountaineering
James A Wilkerson
Mountaineers Of Seattle

Medical Handbook For Mountaineers
Peter Steele
Constable

South American Handbook
ISBN 0-900751-25-8

South American Explorers Club
Av. Rep. de Portugal 146
Casilla 3714
Lima 100
Peru   tel.. Lima 4250142

South American Explorers Club
126 Indian Creek Road
Ithaca, NY 14850, USA
tel.: (607) 277-04888

114

Mountaineering History

adapted from Mountaineering In The Andes by kind permission of Jill Neate

Possibly the first European to penetrate the range was C.R.Enock who, in October 1903, persuaded several Indians to accompany him in a hair-raising attempt to cross the snow covered Abra Villon pass ca.5200m, between the Chinchey and Huantsan massifs, with a view to establishing a trade route from Huaraz in the Santa valley to Huari on the eastern side. Six months later Enock, with an Italian and some Indians, made the first attempt on Huascaran, from the West side, being turned back at ca.5100m by the first large crevasses. However he did estimate the height of the peak accurately as ca.6800m. Enock was followed by the determined little American academic Annie Peck who, in the course of many trials and tribulations in the years 1904, 1906, and 1908, finally reached the summit of the lower North peak of Huascaran at her fifth attempt. Her exaggerated estimate of the height of the peak, made in an attempt to wrest the women's altitude record from Fanny Bullock Workman, and acrimonious remarks made by her guides inevitably cast suspicion on her ascent, but this has never seriously been in doubt. The only other known travellers in the early twentieth century were all Germans - geologist G.Steinmann, geographer Wilhelm Sievers and botanist A.Weberbauer. Their publications contributed greatly to the scientific knowledge of the cordillera but their journeys were confined to some valleys and passes, and there was no overall impression of the range until the arrival in 1932 of the first DOAV expedition.

Apart from surveying and other scientific aims, largely carried out by Dr. Hans Kinzl and resulting in one of the best mountain maps ever produced, the aim of the 1932 expedition was to ascend the most prominent peaks in the range. The party was led by Philip Borchers, accompanied by Erwin Schneider, E.Hein, H.Hoerlin, W.Bernard, B.Lukas and Dr.Kinzl. Their first objective was Champara but, hampered by fresh snow, they achieved only several lesser peaks. Next, an attempt on Contrahierbas was stopped by a breaking cornice and avalanche danger after an impromptu bivouac. After waiting for conditions to improve the climbers decided to attack Huascaran by its West slope, through the steep ice fall to the saddle (Garganta) between the North and South peaks. At last, at 4p.m. on the sixth day, after struggling through thigh-deep snow above the Garganta, they reached the summit of the massive South peak. Two weeks later they ascended the East peak of the massif, Chopicalqui, a very fine ice pyramid which is steep and never easy. The party was now depleted by sickness and other work, but Hein and Schneider achieved the ascents of Artesonraju and the difficult and dangerous Huandoy Norte; the latter was attempted from three sides before it finally succumbed. Finally they set up equipment to measure cosmic rays on Copa, Hoerlin spending three weeks at 5500m and above. All told, members of the expedition climbed five summits over 6000m and a further fourteen over 5000m.

The second DOAV expedition in 1936 was led by Dr.Kinzl, with Erwin Schneider and Arnold Awerzger. Their main objective that year was the exploration of the Cordillera Huayhuash but first they explored the northern part of the Cordillera Blanca. Based in Yungay, their first exploration was to the most northerly of the big peaks, Champara, a massive peak with a broad flat snow summit and steep flanks; this was climbed via the West ridge. Next the remote valley of Quebrada de los Cedros and Alpamayo was explored and Quitaraju climbed via the West ridge. Lastly Schneider and Hammerle, a local hacienda manager, set out to cross the Llanganuco pass and return through the Santa Cruz valley. They made a bold and successful attempt on Pucahirca Sur but their trip was dogged by bad weather, they were robbed, and finally they ran out of food three days before reaching civilisation again.

Dr.Kinzl was out again in 1939 in the southern part of the range with new companions who repeated the Peck route on Huascaran Norte and made first ascents of Contrahierbas, Hualcan, Chinchey,

Tocclaraju, Palcaraju, and Ranrapalca. Hans Kinzl's last major expedition in 1954 was again to the Cordillera Huayhuash. The beautiful books and precise maps he produced on the two ranges testify to his dedication to the geography of Peru. An Honorary Member of the Sociedad Geografica de Lima, holder of the Peruvian Order of Merit for Distinguished Services and many European honours, he was the sage of Alpine and Andean glaciological studies. In 1953 an area between Copa and Hualcan, where he studied cosmic rays for many weeks, was designated 'Glaciar Kinzl'. He died in 1979 before completing his last great work, a history of Huascaran.

There was no further activity until 1948 when Frederic Marmillod and four companions from the Academic Alpine Club Zurich spent two months in the range. Their first major climb was Cashan Este, from the West through deep glacier snow and crevasses and up the final ice pyramid via the exposed North-West ridge. Next they attempted Pucaranra by a rib on the East face but were forced to give up by the steepness and bad conditions. Ten days later they ascended the peak by the steep and difficult South ridge, bivouacing at ca.6000m during the descent. The same day two other members climbed Jatunmontepuncu by the then very corniced West ridge. Santa Cruz was tackled next by two ropes, one on the North ridge and the other on the North-East face; the latter having to bivouac only one pitch below the summit. An attempt on Alpamayo came to an abrupt end when a breaking cornice carried the climbers down 200m, fortunately without serious injury. The expedition closed with an attempt on Caraz I via the South glacier and East ridge, broken off after several hours of struggling through hip-deep powder snow.

During the 1950s the Cordillera Blanca rapidly developed into an international playground, with expeditions every year by climbers from more than a dozen different countries worldwide. Since then the number of climbers visiting the range has rivalled even that of the Himalaya; consequently only the highlights are dealt with below.

Once called the world's most beautiful mountain, Alpamayo is an outstanding peak in the Santa Cruz massif. The Swiss attempt was followed in 1951 when a Franco-Belgian party, misled by darkness, claimed an ascent of the peak although they had only reached the North end of the summit ridge, via the North ridge. The true South peak was climbed in 1957 by Gunther Hauser and three companions via the steep, corniced South ridge. On the third ascent in 1966 a British party repeated the ascent of the North ridge and traversed the summit ridge. Several variations followed but the next major events took place in 1975, i.e. the ascent of the South-West face and the first complete traverse of the mountain. The South-West face was climbed by an Italian party led by Casimo Ferrari, starting from a camp in the Quebrada Arhuaycocha. Fixed ropes were used in the ascent to a col ca.5300m in the South ridge, where another camp was placed in full view of the face. The ascent of the 350m high ice-fluted face took four days, most of the way in shade and using fixed ropes. The traverse of the mountain was the work of two Americans, D.Manning, and B.Carson, who ascended the East ridge and, using a 80m rope, belayed for twenty-five pitches along the 1 1/2 km heavily corniced ridge, before descending the North ridge. This took four days overall.

Elsewhere in the Santa Cruz massif the difficult Taulliraju, first climbed in 1956 by Lionel Terray, resisted several further attacks before the second ascent was finally made in 1976 by three Japanese climbers via the South face. Steep and difficult rock, vertical ice and storms kept them on the wall for six days. Another fine peak, Quitaraju, received a new route in 1969 when a party of Germans climbed the ice wall and rock buttress to the sharply corniced South-East ridge, and thence to the top, descending via the North face. This continuous climb lasted five days with two of the four bivouacs being in snow caves on the ridge. Confusion over Pucahirca Norte was not cleared up until 1961 when Japanese climbers ascended the highest point in this group, proving that a 1955 American party had climbed the slightly lower adjacent peak. It took two strong Italian expeditions to overcome Pucahirca Central. The 1960 team established three approach camps on the South-East snowfield but the final attack up the South-West ridge failed about 30m from the top on account of sheer. rotten ice. The following year persistent snowfall kept the ridge in bad condition but finally two beautiful days allowed the ridge to consolidate and the climbers managed to complete the ascent. although the final 20m ice wall required several hours of work.

The horseshoe-shaped Huandoy massif contains some of the most exacting peaks in the Cordillera Blanca. including the the twin summits of Chacraraju and the four summits of Huandoy itself. The highest peak, Huandoy Norte, was climbed in 1932 by members of the DOAV expedition as mentioned above. In 1952 Huandoy Este was climbed by an American expedition, by two routes simultaneously. after a tragic start to the proceedings when one member of the party succumbed to pulmonary oedema. The pair attempting the North face found the route fairly easy, notwithstanding the loose rotten rock. The other two made a rapid ascent of the far more difficult North ridge, at times heavily corniced on one side and too steep to cling to on the other. In 1955 a German group from Munich were remarkably successful. Their climbs included Caraz I, via the 60° icy eastern slopes to a summit so sharp that only one climber could stand on the top at a time. However, bad weather prevented an ascent of Piramide and climbing difficulties ended an attempt on the rugged granite spire of Nevado Aguja ca.250m below the summit. At the time the isolated Piramide (de Garcilaso) could only be approached by rafting across Laguna Paron and it was not until 1957 that it was climbed by Gunther Hauser's party.

The ascent of Chacraraju Oeste in 1956 provided what Lionel Terray called his most difficult ice climb. Terray's party climbed the rock and ice of the steep North-East face to the col between the two summits. which are connected by a fantastically sharp ridge over one kilometre long.

From there they followed the heavily corniced East ridge, the most difficult obstacle being a rock wall near the summit. American climbers made a new route from the North in 1964, the final 250m being over very steep ice covered rocks to the final ice flutes. Terray returned in 1962 to climb the East peak. This was achieved via the South-East ridge with several detours onto the South-East face. Despite being a hard route which required three intermediate camps, the climb was accomplished quite quickly and three ropes reached the top.

Perhaps the most extravagant climbs in this region have been those on the 900m rocky and overhanging South face of Huandoy Sur. The face was attempted in 1968 by Don Whillan's four man expedition. but was abandoned after several narrow escapes while making a difficult traverse threatened by avalanches. They were soon followed by a French party who also failed, as did a strong Italian party in 1975. However the folowing year three lines were achieved on the face. The first was made by Japanese climbers who took a direct line near the centre of the face. Next came the Italians who followed the Japanese to halfway and then traversed left to pick up the British traverse line. Finally a French party under Rene Desmaison made a direct ascent to the Italian ramp. All three routes were extremely hard seige climbs, involving precarious intermediate camps and much unstable and vertical aid climbing.

Huascaran. by virtue of its great height is one of the most popular mountains in Peru with over twenty routes on its massive walls. This has been at some cost and dozens of mountaineers have died on Huascaran. including all fourteen members of a Czech expedition who were overwhelmed by an avalanche triggered by the earthquake on 31 May 1970, which led to the complete destruction of the town of Yungay and killed an estimated 80,000 people in the region. The first difficult route to be put up was by an American party in 1958 when they climbed the South-East glacier and ridge on the South peak. The long North-East ridge succumbed to a Spanish party in 1961 and ten years later an ANZAC team plugged the obvious gap of the huge East face to show the way to adjacent Austrian routes in 1972 and 1979. At the same time the 1971 team also made the first traverses of the South peak. A few years before this a Canadian group deviated from the normal Garganta line to capture the important West arete Shield route. The South peak was brought up to date with Benois Grison's bold solo of the North-East face in 1985 and the parallel Slovenian route by Pavle Kozjek in 1991.

Huascaran Norte was also a hive of activity beginning with the superb line of the Paragot route on the North face in 1966. The French returned in 1972 for the adventure of the North-East ridge, and then in 1973 for an elegant solution to the North-East face. The Italians solved the problem of the North-West ridge in 1974 and various eliminate lines followed between this and the Paragot route. Characteristically the most direct path up the North face was taken by Casarotto in 1977, in a twenty day epic solo during which he dropped his sleeping bag and ran out of food. Other hard routes were pioneered on this wall by the Spanish in 1983 and Swiss in 1986 to give some of the most sustained climbing in South America.

Chopicalqui was largely ignored until 1969 when the first traverse occurred by the South-East and North-West ridges. Many other hard routes followed up the sweeping icy faces, an exception being Desmaison's seige of the tortuous East ridge which resulted in an alarming film. The Anglo-French ascent of the West-North-West spur in 1981 is an example of a safe but difficult line, whilst the Dossin solo of 1982 is more daring, climbing a runnel in the North-West face immediately after an avalanche as he did.

South of Huascaran is the difficult pyramid of Ulta where Dawson and Cheesmond profited from previous failures to claim the North-West face. Many minor and easy routes have also been acieved on adjacent massifs but strangely many major lines remain untouched in this area.

Cayesh is a spectacular icy blade spearing from the Chinchey massif. This was first climbed in 1960 by an independent minded New Zealand party via the steep West face and doubly corniced South ridge. This route was well ahead of its time and a similar attempt by New Zealanders in 1973 failed to reach the summit, but was achieved in 1980. A rash of routes were put up on the unrelenting faces of the blade in the early 80s; they all share difficult technical climbing but the East face route by Mark Richey and some methadone inspired Colorado companions is massively committing and surely in a class of its own. Elsewhere in the Chinchey group Jaeger's remarkable solos stand out. His rapid ascent of the North-West ridge of Pucaranra in 1977 was shortly followed by a large group of Italians seiging the same line over many days. Also in that year Jaeger's companions took the striking East ridge of Ranrapalca, and earlier in 1971 the long South-West ridge had fallen to a Norwegian party. Nearby and clearly visible from Huaraz is the South-West face of Churup Oeste, this was climbed in 1972 and has since been the scene of many minor epics. The other important developments around Chinchey occurred on Ocshapalca. The American pair of Blatherwick and Richey climbed the central runnel of the South face and the 80s saw three other lines up adjacent gully systems: all are in the modern idiom, being hard day routes with abseil descents.

Still further South is the huge bulk of Huantsan where the adventuresome team of Terray, Egeler, and de Booy approached from the East to traverse the North-West ridge, over the North peak, to the main summit. In 1958 an American party pioneered a shorter approach from the West, but it was not until 1967 that Japanese ascended the South summit. Steady development followed with an international seige of the North-East ridge of the main top in 1974, and a Harvard party claiming the West face in 1979, as highlights.

Among the most remarkable climbs in the Cordillera Blanca in recent years were those made by the prolific Dr.Nicholas Jaeger in 1977 and 1978 which deserve collecting together. On Alpamayo he made an early repeat of the South-West face, choosing to descend the North side. He also made rapid solo ascents of; Santa Cruz (N ridge), Ranrapalca (SE face), Pucaranra (NW ridge), Palcaraju (SE ridge), and Huascaran Sur (SE ridge). In 1978 Jaeger made five more solo ascents; Taulliraju (S face), Abasraju (E face), Santa Cruz (SE face), Huandoy Este (SW face), and Chacraraju Este (S face). During his visits to Peru Jaeger also spent sixty days alone at 6700m on Huascaran, making physiological observations and writing a book about his experiences. The thirty-two year-old Frenchman disappeared on Lhotse in April 1980, and the northern slopes of Huascaran above the Garganta have been named in memory of his neatly suited figure which had become familiar on the streets of Huaraz.

The late 70s saw a new route bonanza on the slopes of Santa Cruz. Jaeger's companions took the North-East face direct, Austrians the South face and South-West ridge, and in 1980 Americans the West ridge and Swiss-French the gloomy South-West face. More routes followed in the 80s but the focus had shifted to the inspiring cathedral of Taulliraju. Apart from Jaeger's 1978 route the French also found the South-South-East ridge; the easiest line on the mountain. The North face was taken in 1979 as a Canadian shot and the following year Italians climbed the West buttress of the South-West face, later to be publicised by the Lowe second ascent. Soon the English pair of Mick Fowler and Chris Watts climbed up the neighbouring East buttress, a route that was to defeat many parties before a New Zealand second ascent by a variant in 1989. The French returned in 1988 for the steep couloir in the face of the South buttress which was shortly followed by Charlie Fowler straightening out the Quebec variation on the Italian buttress, and going on to solo a traverse of the peak in eleven hours. In 1991 a British team filled in gaps on the Pucahirca-Pucarashta South wall to bring the Santa Cruz massif to impressive maturity.

A similar series of gaps were filled in the Huandoy massif during the 70s and 80s. The South faces of the Caraz group received a series of hard lines, as did the flutings of Piramide, however it was the furrows of Chacraraju which were to provide the most concentrated series of test pieces. The Japanese started in 1976 by climbing direct to Terray's South-East ridge route on Este, but the obvious adjacent couloir fell to Jaeger in 1978 when he raced straight to the top. The Richey-Brewer partnership countered with the next major runnel along; attitudes (and gear) were definitely changing. The West summit direct was the work of the Bouchard-Meunier couple, complete with collapsing ice mushrooms and broken ribs in an impressively committing style. The companion runnel went in 1983 to Desmaison's team after Astier had picked off a line in 1979 and Yugoslavs another in 1982. Later, in 1986, a Czech pair climbed the North-East face direct and suffered a fatal accident abseiling the Bouchard-Meunier. Many routes were claimed on the short South face of Pisco Oeste during this period and it seems that at least all the obvious lines were done. Soloing was popular at this time and Astier also took in the North-East face of Huandoy Sur in 1979 whilst Alex Lowe climbed amongst the beautiful feathery formations of the South-East face of Huandoy Este. Huandoy Norte now hosts many quality routes: one of the first went to a seasoned American team which ascended the North-West face in 1971. Another facet, the North-East face, was cunningly solved from Llanganuco by a French pair in 1974, before Poles took the safest line up the dominating East face in 1976. In 1987 a powerful Slovenian trio climbed the North face direct to create probably the hardest alpine-style ascent in the Cordillera Blanca. A 1400m route with pitches of VII- it is certainly a sign of things to come even though there are many untouched corners with plenty of potential at the lower grades.

Peruvian mountaineering in the Cordillera Blanca

It is certain that some mountains surrounding the Cordillera Blanca were climbed in pre-colonial times but as yet there is no clear evidence to suppose that the Incas attempted Huascaran and her companion peaks. After the Spanish conquest many mines were opened in the area and prospectors ranged widely, some onto the slopes of Huascaran and others to explore the possibilities of high passes for trade networks.

The first unaccompanied Peruvian mountaineers were the porters of the 1932 DOAV expedition who accidentally descended a new route on Copa when they became lost in fog, however intentional modern Peruvian climbing in the Cordillera Blanca has its origins in the disastrous 1941 alluvion which decimated Huaraz. In response to this the government formed an Office Of Lake Control which began the long work of identifying and draining lakes with unstable moraine dams. One of the first lakes to be drained was in Quebrada Llaca and in 1950 a team of the project workers attempted nearby Nevado Vallunaraju. Carrying a large metal national flag, and bundles of grass to light a signal fire on the summit, they climbed the moraine where two of the team wisely dropped out with siroche. Undaunted the remainder continued over the glacier and only abandoned their attempt below the final pyramid. The subsequent revelries were only slightly marred by their being snowblind for a few days due to no eye protection whatsoever on the climb.

Despite this setback they tried again in 1951 - with improved equipment. Not only did they acquire glacier goggles but also boots and alpenstocks to replace the sandals and steel crowbars of the previous year. Unfortunately they failed again but the seeds of active alpinism had been sown.

Some, such as Alcides Ames, continued to work on the lakes' problem (the office eventually evolved into Hidrandina) and made extensive traverses around the base of mountains in the course of glaciological research. Others, such as the Angeles brothers, gained international reputations as solid, dependable porters and served with foreign expeditions year after year. Whatever course they chose they continued to improve their techniques in the course of many adventures. Stories abound from this period along the lines of,"...and then there was the time I was hanging upside down in the crevasse with a hemp rope and potato-sack rucsac.." as they ranged widely with their primitive equipment.

Six of these pioneers, including the three Yanac brothers, made the first all-Peruvian ascent of Huascaran. Developing a taste for foreign travel one went on to climb Aconcagua in a record time. During this period the porters formed an association to represent their interests in the Cordillera Blanca. In 1978 this association was to provide the nucleus for a Swiss project to establish a fully-fledged guiding profession.

With the arrival of this newer, younger generation of 'professionals' came a marked disinclination on the part of the noisier types to attempt anything original. However the more subdued Augusto Ortega teamed up with Americo Tordoya who was the star of the Lima University mountaineers. In 1983 they made the first ascent of Puntancuerno (Chinchey Este). The surveyed height of 5959m seems too low and so this was probably the last virgin 6000m peak in Peru.The ascent was also notable for being one of the few on the eastern flank of the range, and for being the first Peruvian route to involve strung-out technical climbing. Sowing a fatal desire for glory and a disdain for safety precautions Tordoya travelled to Chile later in 1983 where he was tragically killed in an avalanche. Other talent is developing in Peru such as Renzo Ucelli who has repeated the Paragot route on Huascaran Norte.

Acknowledgements

Often I have read accounts of how authors owe an enormous debt of gratitude to so many people. Well now I know how true this is. In fact I cannot really describe myself as the author of this guide. I am better described as the compiler; relying heavily on my predecessors efforts, and on so many people who have assisted with a snippet of information here, a clue there. I am afraid that I really cannot thank you all enough, or even mention you all by name. However contributions and support from the following individuals and organisations have been crucial:

Julio Cesar, Mrs Maureen Chesterton, Selio Villon Lopez, Mario Holenstein, Franci Horvat, Joco Razpotnik, Shane Winser, Jim Bartle, Pavle Kozjek, Noella Francey, John Phelan, Renzo Ucelli, Jean-Paul Glassier, Dr. Pete Davis (medical notes), Mrs Pat Johnson, Jerry Gore, Raul Sotomayor Alba, Val Pitkethly, Irma Angeles, H Jenny, Emilio Gloria, Alcides Ames, Ellen & James Wroughton, Mike Miller, Philippe Beaud, Marcos Zapata, Yolande Corvettio, Pedro Yanac, Juan Julio Vergaray T., Lucho Olaza, H. Adams Carter, Lindsay Griffin, Mick Fowler, Chris Watts, Simon Richardson, Margaret Daivall, Carol McDermott, Petra Schepens, Fidel Broncano Vasquez, Richard Pelly, Victorino Angeles, Don Montague, Hidrandina, Peruvian Mountain Guides' Association, Alpine Club Library, Royal Geographical Society, Expedition Advisory Centre, Summer Institute of Linguistics, British Embassy Lima, British Mountaineering Council, South American Explorers Club, Royal Navy & Royal Marines Mountaineering Club.

I would never have begun to climb in Peru, nor have been able to begin this guide without the example of John Ricker's classic guide to the area, *Yuraq Janqa*: I hope that this guide is seen by all as having been completely reliant for its basic historical information on Yuraq Janka. Jim Bartle has provided me with much useful background to the problems that Peru faces in general, and an understanding of the people and environment of the Blanca in particular. I am especially indebted to the late Jill Neate, and to Gerhard Feichtenschlager, Augusto Ortega, Franci Savenc and Charlie Fowler.

Much information was trawled from the invaluable *American Alpine Journal* and additionally I have attempted to sift through all the major mountaineering periodicals of the world. My thanks are due to all who have troubled to write for these publications, or to produce expedition reports and file them with their Alpine Clubs.

The map of Huaraz is based upon a map provided by the *Hostel Andino*. The sketch maps in the book are based upon those in *Trails Of the Cordillera Blanca & Huayhuash*. The detailed map of the range is based upon one published in the Japanese mountaineering journal *Iwo To Yuki*. Heights of mountains are based upon those quoted in *Yuraq Janka* unless otherwise noted.

Errors, Omissions, & Corrections

Please let me know if something is wrong, ambiguous or misleading, or should be added. I can be contacted at:

David Sharman
PO Box 412
Aberdeen
AB9 6JA
SCOTLAND

PEAK INDEX

PEAK INDEX

PEAK INDEX

UIAA	F	USA	GB	AUS
I	1	5.2	moderate	
II	2	5.3	difficult	11
III	3	5.4	very difficult	12
IV	4	5.5	4a	
V −	5	5.6	4b	13
V	5	5.7	4c	14
V +	5		4c	15
VI −	5	5.8	5a	16
VI	6a	5.9	5a	17
VI+	6a+	5.10a	5b	18
VII −	6b	5.10b	5b	19
VII	6b+	5.10c / 5.10d	5c	20 / 21
VII+	6c	5.11a	5c	22
VIII −	6c+ / 7a	5.11b / 5.11c	6a	23 / 24
VIII	7a+	5.11d	6a	25
VIII+	7b / 7b+	5.12a / 5.12b	6b	26
IX −	7c	5.12c	6b	
IX	7c+	5.12d / 5.13a	6c	27 / 28
IX+	8a	5.13b	6c	29
X −	8a+	5.13c	7a	30 / 31
X	8b / 8b+	5.13d	7a	32
X+	8c	5.14a	7b	33

NOTES

NOTES

Mountain Code

Camp site: Remember that another party will be using the same camp site after you have vacated it. therefore. leave the camp site cleaner than you found it and replace turves and stones.

Limit deforestation - make no open fires and discourage others from doing so on your behalf. Where water is heated by scarse firewood, use as little as possible. Use kerosene or petrol stoves when possible, and be self -sufficient in fuel supplies.

In a safe place burn dry paper and packets; bury other paper and biodegradable material. including food. Carry out all non-biodegradable litter. If you come across other peoples rubbish. remove their rubbish as well.

Keep local water clean and avoid using pollutants such as detergents in streams or springs. If no toilet facilities are availables make sure you are at least 30m away from water sources. and bury or cover wastes.

Plants should be left to flourish in their natural environment - takin cuttings and seedlings is illegal in the Parque Nacional Huascaran. Avoid damaging vegetation. Avoid all unnecessary disturbance to birds and animals.

Follow consevation measures and help your guides and arriros to do so. Minimise erosion by keeping to paths where they exist. Do not allow cooks to throw garbage into streams or rivers.

As a guest respect local traditions, protect local cultures. and maintain local pride.

When taking photographs respect privacy - ask permission and use restraint.

Refrain from giving money or sweets to children as it will encourage begging. A donation to a project. health centre. or school is a more effective way to help.